Hacking Movable Type

Hacking Movable Type

Jay Allen, Brad Choate, Ben Hammersley,
Matthew Haughey, & David Raynes

Wiley Publishing, Inc.

Hacking Movable Type

Published by
Wiley Publishing, Inc.
10475 Crosspoint Boulevard
Indianapolis, IN 46256
www.wiley.com

Published by Wiley Publishing, Inc., Indianapolis, Indiana

Published simultaneously in Canada

ISBN-13: 978-0-7645-7499-3

ISBN-10: 0-7645-7499-X

Manufactured in the United States of America

10 9 8 7 6 5 4 3 2 1

1B/QX/QX/QV/IN

For general information on our other products and services or to obtain technical support, please contact our Customer Care Department within the U.S. at (800) 762-2974, outside the U.S. at (317) 572-3993 or fax (317) 572-4002.

Wiley also publishes its books in a variety of electronic formats. Some content that appears in print may not be available in electronic books.

Library of Congress Cataloging-in-Publication Data

Hacking Movable Type / Jay Allen ... [et al.].
   p. cm.
  Includes index.
  ISBN-13: 978-0-7645-7499-3 (paper/website)
  ISBN-10: 0-7645-7499-X (paper/website)
  1. Movable Type (Computer file) 2. Web sites--Design. 3. Weblogs.
 I. Allen, Jay, 1970-   .
 TK5105.8885.M67H34 2005
 006.7--dc22

                     2005012598

About the Authors

Jay Allen has been hacking Movable Type since before its first public release and has deployed MT on over a billion and a half systems, give or take a few orders of magnitude. He created the first MT plugin, called MT-Search, as well as one of the most necessary plugins, MT-Blacklist. He currently resides in the ever beautiful and weird San Francisco and works at Six Apart as Product Manager for Movable Type. He spends his off hours split almost evenly between spinning true house music, recharging personal electronic devices, and trying to find his keys.

Brad Choate has been hacking Movable Type since it was first released. He is now a Six Apart software engineer where he hacks Movable Type for a living, supporting his incredibly understanding wife and three little hackers.

Ben Hammersley is an English journalist and writer, and has been using Movable Type since version 1. He lives in Florence, Italy, with his beautiful wife and three greyhounds and is currently tending his cigar and dressing gown habit with little success. He invites you to visit.

Matthew Haughey is closing in on ten years of building websites and runs the popular MetaFilter weblog as well as half a dozen smaller weblog projects. He's been tinkering with Movable Type since the very first private alpha that his friends, Ben and Mena Trott, let him test out. He's been hacking away at it ever since.

David Raynes got his first taste of blogs in the first half of 2002, and was running his own by summer's end that same year. Shortly after, his first plugin, MTSearches, was released, and the rest is history. One of his most popular plugins, SubCategories, was even integrated into Movable Type as of version 3.1. David works as a software engineer in Maryland, where he lives with his wife, Jenn, and their four cats (two his and two hers): Hans, Franz, Tim, and Gizmo. Eventually the feud between Tim and Franz will be resolved and there shall be only three.

Credits

Executive Editor
Chris Webb

Development Editors
Marcia Ellett
Sharon Nash

Production Editor
William A. Barton

Copy Editor
Luann Rouff

Production Manager
Tim Tate

Editorial Manager
Mary Beth Wakefield

Vice President & Executive Group Publisher
Richard Swadley

Vice President and Publisher
Joseph B. Wikert

Project Coordinator
Ryan Steffen

Graphics and Production Specialists
Jennifer Heleine
Stephanie D. Jumper
Melanee Prendergast
Amanda Spagnuolo
Mary Gillot Virgin

Quality Control Technicians
Leeann Harney
Jessica Kramer
Carl William Pierce
Dwight Ramsey

Book Designer
Kathie S. Rickard

Proofreading and Indexing
TECHBOOKS Production Services

Foreword

Almost four years ago, my husband, Ben, and I decided to create a weblogging tool for one simple reason: I had my own weblog, dollarshort.org, and I wanted a better blogging tool for myself. As luck would have it, Ben and I were in between jobs (this was 2001 after all and the tech industry wasn't exactly booming) and we had some free time to work on a software project as a hobby.

The more we worked on Movable Type—our ideal blogging tool—the more ambitious Ben and I became in our goals. We not only wanted to create great software for us and our friends—fellow engineers, web designers, and writers—to use, but we wanted to give all sorts of bloggers the power to easily create professional-looking weblogs. The code needed to be modular and extensible, and the design needed to be clean and simple. What we couldn't have imagined is how Movable Type would grow past our own initial ambitions and how it would be shaped into a platform used by thousands of people worldwide.

Fast-forward to the present day as I sit here writing the foreword to *Hacking Movable Type*, the book you now hold in your hands. The fact that this book exists today is a testament not just to Movable Type itself, but also to the community that has helped grow the platform into what it is today.

The authors of this book, Jay Allen, Brad Choate, Ben Hammersley, Matt Haughey, and David Raynes, represent some of the earliest, most passionate, and talented members of the Movable Type community. While Ben and I were responsible for the core Movable Type product for the first couple of years in the life of Six Apart, it is these people who helped spread the word about the power of the platform and helped *us* learn about what the platform could do.

This team of authors has written tutorials, introduced the product to clients, written plugins, and helped shape the product's direction. When Movable Type was first released, the blogging industry didn't exist. Today, because of these authors and because of people like you (people who want to take advantage of Movable Type's potential to take their projects and their clients' projects to the next level), we have great resources such as this book to help expand what blogging can do.

Jay Allen and Brad Choate, two of the *Hacking Movable Type* authors, have been especially pivotal in Movable Type's development: Jay, with his work on MT-Blacklist, and Brad with his substantial plugin development. It is only fitting that because of their dedication to Movable Type and because of their talent, they have since (over the course of this book's development) become members of the Six Apart staff, working on the Movable Type team to improve the platform itself.

The generosity that all of these authors have shown by sharing their ideas and code reflects the values that have grown the Movable Type community over the past few years. That generosity continues with the sample code, documentation, and most important, the ideas that this talented group of authors shares in the pages that follow.

With Movable Type's rise in popularity comes the rise in demand for talented developers, designers, and consultants who really understand the software and weblog integration with an existing website. While this book is great for the early adopters and tinkerers who were the original target audience for Movable Type, it is essential reading for anyone who wishes to earn a living or make a career in providing weblogging solutions in today's business world.

Hacking Movable Type should serve as your guide to what you can accomplish with the software. As you read this book, you'll discover why Movable Type has become the leading weblog publishing platform. We can't wait to see the creativity your contributions bring to the community.

Mena Trott
Co-founder and president of Six Apart

Acknowledgments

All of the authors would like to thank Chris Webb, Sharon Nash, and Marcia Ellett of Wiley for their superhuman patience, indulgence, and skill. Thanks, guys.

Jay Allen: I'd like to thank the following wonderful people and random inanimate things: Ezra Cooper and Anil Dash for helping us when we were helpless, Six Apart for making love in the form of software, my mom for the love, support, and coffee from home, to my Budapesti baratok for the Unicum and the distractions, és végül de nem utolsósorban, a kisbogaramnak es a masodik anyukamnak, Gabi: Köszönöm mindent hogy nekem csináltatok. Mindig foglak szeretni.

Brad Choate: For my family, Georgia, Savannah, Seth, and Arwen.

Ben Hammersley: My part of this book is, as always, thanks for the patience and love of my wife, Anna: Jag älskar dig. Thanks and love, too, to Lucy, Mischa, and Pico for their ambulatory breaks, and Ben and Mena Trott for making their hobby my livelihood. And cheers to my fellow writers, the sort of men-gods that put the Thor into co-author: it's been an honor.

Matthew Haughey: I'd like to thank co-authors Jay Allen and Ben Hammersley for carrying the brunt of the workload on this project. I'd like to thank my wife for going to sleep alone while I stayed up until 2 A.M. every night as a chapter approached deadline. I'd like to thank the folks at Wiley for taking the risk and letting us share our knowledge of MT with the world. And, most of all, I want to thank that wacky duo, Ben and Mena Trott, for taking a little weblog application they wrote for themselves and turning it into an empire.

David Raynes: For both of my parents, who sacrificed so much to give me the education that got me where I am today. For my father, who first introduced me to the wondrous feats that can be performed by typing a few choice magic words into that little box hooked up to our television. And to my lovely wife, who puts up with all the time I spend doing this stuff.

Introduction

Welcome to *Hacking Movable Type*. Inside this book you will find everything you need to know to take an ordinary installation of Movable Type and turn it into something extraordinary.

Movable Type?

Movable Type is the world's most advanced personal publishing application. Designed by Six Apart, originally the husband and wife team of Ben and Mena Trott and now one of the world's most dynamic software houses, Movable Type brings professional-quality content management to the masses. Thousands of users, from webloggers to professional online publications, are using Movable Type to display their content. It's one of the greatest Internet success stories of this century.

Hacking Movable Type?

You might be familiar with Movable Type from the weblogging world. You may well have installed and used it yourself, but did you know that Movable Type is also perfect fodder for hacking on?

Nestled inside that sturdy but unassuming exterior is a framework for an exceptionally powerful publishing system, and one that bristles with the latest interfaces, standards, and Internet thinking.

This book teaches you everything you need to know about the internal features of Movable Type, and how to extend, stretch, push, and pummel the application from something already superpowerful into something almost unbelievable.

What's in This Book?

Luckily, this isn't some Proustian epic requiring you to plow through from beginning to end. It's separated into parts, and you're free to skip around. But here's a taste of what we have in store for you:

- Hacking the Perfect Installation
- Hacking the Database
- XML-RPC API

- Atom API
- Perl API
- Advanced Plugin Writing
- Dynamic Publishing
- Hacking Together Powerful Blog Applications
- Advanced skills

Of course, also included are pages of reference material, recipes for great uses of the Movable Type system, complete rundowns of the internal structure of the application, the databases, and the APIs, and clear and concise instructions on just about every aspect of the system.

Hacking Carefully

We know you're sensible people. Hey, you bought this book, right? So you should know to back up your data. A lot of things we do in here are potentially hazardous to your stuff, not in a horrible, screaming, bloodcurdling sort of way—it's all fixable if you make a false move—but to fix stuff you are going to need backups. Both Jay and Ben's hard drives died during the writing of this book, and the wailing and gnashing of teeth was something to behold. So do us a favor, as we don't want to see that sort of thing again, for the sake of all that is good and proper, **BACK UP YOUR WEBLOGS BEFORE YOU DO ANYTHING.**

Our lawyers would like to point out that we take no responsibility for anything you do. They do this more formally elsewhere.

Companion Website

For links and updates, please visit this book's companion website at `www.wiley.com/compbooks/extremetech`.

Conclusion

Pablo Picasso once said, "I'm always doing things I can't do, it's how I get to do them." And so it is with Movable Type. This is a powerful piece of software, and by reading this book you will be in a position to take full advantage of it. We can't wait to see what you build. Have fun.

Contents at a Glance

Contents

Part II: Hacking the Database   29

Part IV: Hacking with Plugins   143

Chapter 9: The Wonderful World of Plugins 145

Chapter 11: Advanced Plugin Writing 197

Chapter 12: Hacking Dynamic Publishing 215

Part V: Hacking Powerful Blog Applications Together   235

Chapter 13: Photo Blogs 237

Chapter 14: Linklogs 249

Chapter 15: Blogroll. 257

Chapter 16: Events, Reminders, To-Dos 265

Hacking the Perfect Installation

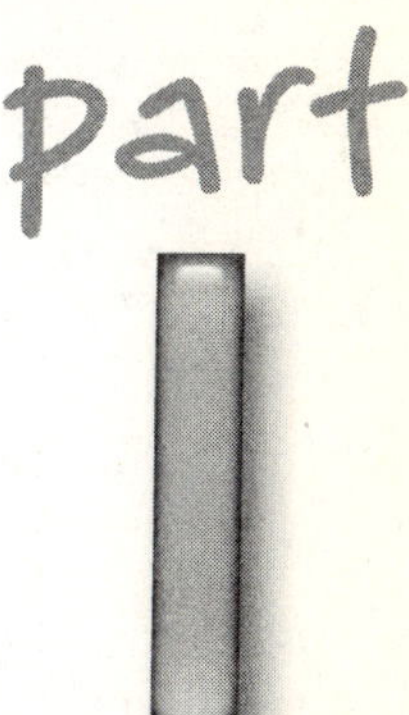

Preparing Your Installation

Stop worrying. You've chosen Movable Type (MT). It's a remarkably stable, easy to prepare and maintain piece of software. Indeed, part of its charm is that straight out of the box, with nothing added to it, and none of the hacks that make up the rest of this book applied, MT pretty much takes care of itself. Nearly three years of heavy use, plus two major code revisions, and the experience of the weblogging world's finest developers have produced a package that can look after itself.

We're not going to go into detail about how you install Movable Type. Frankly, we think you're able to follow instructions, and Six Apart's documentation is very good in this respect. In addition, the publishers of this book have another, *Movable Type Bible, Desktop Edition*, by Rogers Cadenhead, which deals with the nuts and bolts of installation very admirably.

Instead, we're going to jump straight into the more interesting stuff. First up: Site Architecture.

Site Architecture

Weblogs, by their very frequently updated natures, grow very quickly. It is not uncommon to have sites of more than a thousand pages, and many are 10 times that. Add in comments and TrackBacks, images, feeds, and perhaps some audio and video too, and you'll start to find that a server can get a little messy. Furthermore, everything on the site itself has a URL, and it is common practice for readers to play with the URLs to move around. How many times have you looked around someone's blog archives by changing the URL a little to see what you get?

Therefore, you need to plan a site architecture that will both keep things in order and make for sensible and future-proof URLs that encourage exploration.

Much of the following is based more on art than science.

Images

I like to place all of my images in a separate directory, `/images`. This keeps them organized but also available for any interesting scripting projects I might like to do in the future. To do this consistently, you need to remember that MT's image upload interface will need an extra bit of typing, as shown in Figure 1-1.

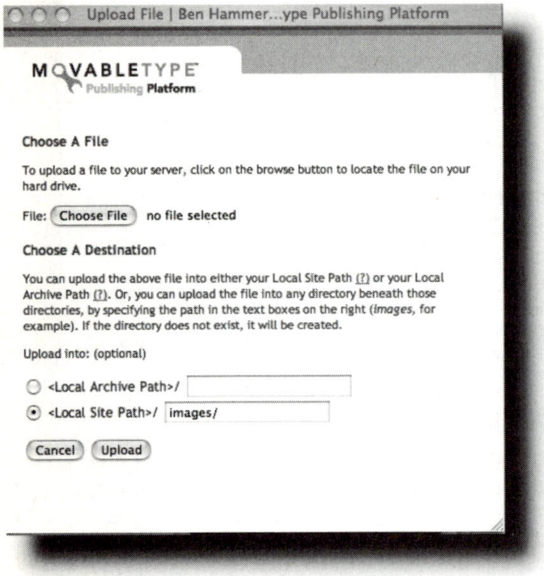

FIGURE 1-1: Using the Upload File dialog box

You will need to do the same in any desktop blogging tool you may be using as well.

Note that you can't move all of the images to this directory. Without an option, MT will automatically place, and replace if it's removed, a file called `nav-commenters.gif` into the root directory of every blog. It's the tiny little person with a speech bubble icon that the default templates use to indicate the commenting link (see Figure 1-2). At the time of writing, you can't stop this file from being replaced.

Archives

With respect to the post archives, things have moved on since versions 1 and 2 of MT. Since 3.0 Movable Type, creating archives occurs in an extremely sensible URL structure (namely, for the individual entry page):

```
Archive_Path/YYYY/MM/DD/Dirified_Entry_Title.html
```

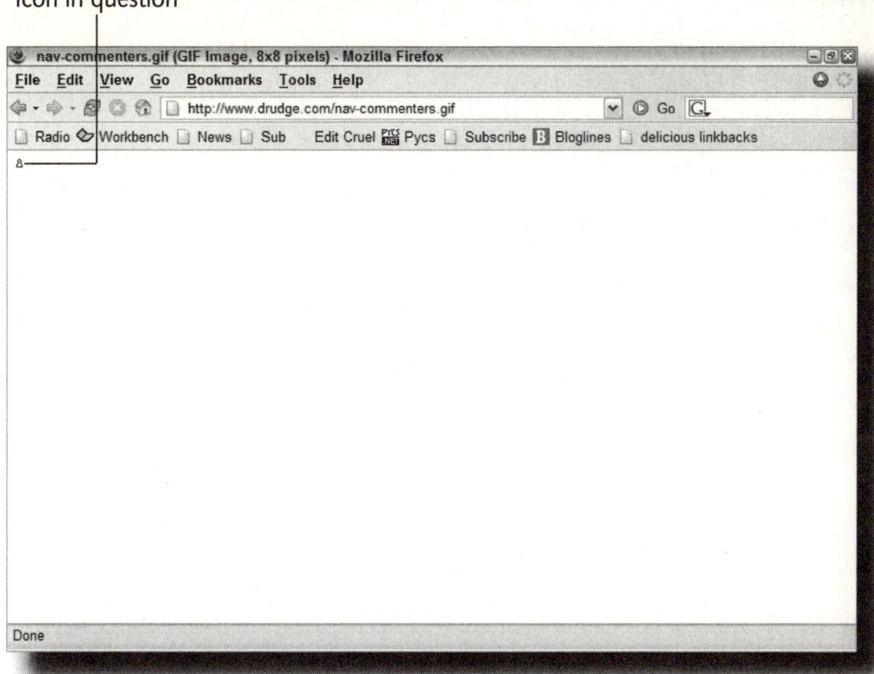

FIGURE 1-2: The Nav-Commenters icon

This is very sensible for two reasons. First, it produces URLs that are independent of the content management system's (CMS) own variables. It might sound strange in a book touting the usefulness of Movable Type, but there's always a possibility that you will change your CMS in the future. Having as neutral a file structure as possible will prove invaluable. Second, the logical structure of the URLs means that people can move around your site from their browser's address bar. Consider the logical positions of all of the types of archive indexes:

- Yearly archives: `Archive_Path/YYYY/index.html`

- Monthly archive: `Archive_Path/YYYY/MM/index.html`

- Complete archive index: `Archive_Path/index.html`

It makes sense to do it like this, as this is exactly how a slightly curious reader will try to look around your site — by deleting bits from the URL and seeing what she finds. There is one exception: currently, the Weekly indexes default to `Archive_Path/week_YYYY_MM_DD.html`, which I do not like. Rather, I would change it to

`Archive_Path/YYYY/MM/DD-DD.html`

by adding the following line in the Archive File Template box in the Archive Files configuration page:

```
<$MTArchiveDate format="%Y/%m/%d"$>-<$MTArchiveDateEnd
format="%d"$>.html
```

All this done, you end up with a filesystem that looks like the one shown in Figure 1-3.

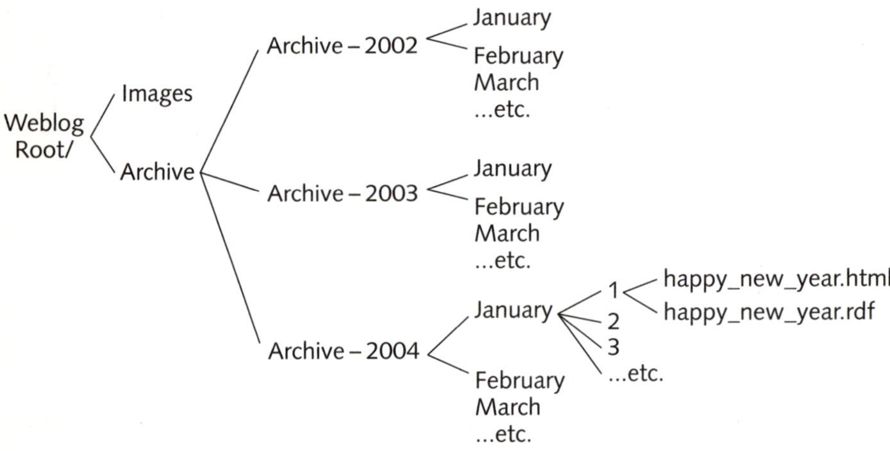

FIGURE 1-3: Exploring the Archive filesystem

Note that the space for the individual archive is taken by two different files: the standard HTML page and an RSS file for the entry and its comments. As new formats appear, they can fit into the architecture very easily in this same manner.

Maintenance and Regular Tasks

As a professionally produced piece of software running on and with provably reliable platforms, MT really doesn't need any regular maintenance. There aren't any temporary files to remove, or automatically generated crud to delete. However, there are some preventive measures you should take.

Since MT3.1, Movable Type has shipped with a plugin pack containing Sebastian Delmont's TypeMover plugin. This plugin enables you to back up your entire weblog data, including preferences and templates. You are very much advised to install and use this regularly.

Sadly, there appears to be no way to automate the downloading of the backups, so you have to do it manually, but it's very straightforward. The same plugin, incidentally, is very useful if you want to build an MT-based site on a local machine and then move it en masse to a public server. I find this makes templates a whole lot snappier to develop.

Streamlining Your Installation

Right out of the box, Movable Type is already pretty fast. With 3.1's introduction of dynamically built pages, performance has increased a great deal. Even so, and especially if you are not using the dynamic build option, there are a few changes you can make from the default. First, look at what you begin with. A clean installation of MT saves the following in the root directory of the blog:

- Main Index
- Archives Index
- RSS 1.0 Index
- RSS 2.0 Index
- Atom Index
- Stylesheet
- RSD file

Despite the loud brayings of the content syndication communities, you really do not need to be producing both RSS and Atom feeds. Personally, I prefer to produce only one, RSS 1.0, and then use external services to convert it to RSS 2.0 or Atom for the people who really care. (Technically speaking, I do it in this order because RSS 1.0 is the most complicated and data-rich format and so downgrades nicely. I couldn't really go from 2.0 to 1.0, especially when you consider the additional information you can place within the feed after you have visited Chapter 3.) Services such as that found at `www.feedburner.com` are good for this. Either way, you can delete all but one of the feeds straight away.

In addition, turn off the rebuilding of the Stylesheet and RSD files. These do not need to be rebuilt unless you change your design or upgrade your installation, respectively.

Posting Frequency

Consider how often you post to your site and adjust the number of day's posts on the front page to suit. If you're posting multiple times a day, this should be set pretty low. If you're posting only once a month, make it high. The risk is that you will have either an enormously large front page, or, should you not post for a while and then have a comment cause a rebuild, a completely empty one. Neither is good — you should pay attention to this if you're going on holiday, for example. I have been caught out with a setup of "Display 10 days' worth of posts," when on day 11 someone left a comment on an old entry. The front page rebuilt and was left empty for a week. In the spider-filled ecosystem of the web, a week's worth of an empty front page can cause terrible malady, not the least of which is a loss of stumble-upon readership.

If you are very committed to a minimalist filesystem, you can delete the RSD file altogether. The file makes the setting up of offline editing tools a few seconds faster, but if you remember the path to your `mt-xmlrpc.cgi` file and your blog ID, you actually don't need it. Mine is history.

Relying on Third-Party Services

Consider moving all web-services-based things out of your templates and into other files pulled in by server side includes. If you are using MT, specifically MT-PerlScript, to pull data from another site while you rebuild your indexes, you will slow the process down considerably. It also helps, in these sorts of scripts or plugins, to use as much caching as possible. A bad day of network congestion or a slow response time from the remote server might even kill your rebuild process. The more recent plugins, such as Tim Appnel's MT-Feed, take this into account, and plugin developers should give serious thought to any potential slowing effects their plugin might have on page rebuilds.

Ping and Comment Time-Outs

This slowing effect is particularly noticeable with comments and TrackBacks. MT installations with slow rebuilds will find that their readers leave the same comment two or three times, believing the first attempt to have failed when the browser timed out. TrackBacks, too, can time out, meaning that the remote server doesn't know it was successful. Automatic trackbacking then tries again the next time the remote site is itself rebuilt. By improving the chances of the rebuilds happening quickly, you will stop these repeated attempts.

For TrackBacks, you can edit mt.cfg to increase the time-out interval to allow other sites to be slow when you TrackBack to them. Simply uncomment the following line:

```
# PingTimeout 20
```

The number is the time, in seconds, with the default being 15. But 20 is better, and 30 just right.

Temp Files

Movable Type produces and saves temporary files to disk during page rebuilds. You can turn this off, which speeds up rebuilds considerably, albeit at the expense of server memory. If you believe your machine is big enough to deal with it (and it most probably is, to be honest), edit mt.cfg and find this line:

```
# NoTempFiles 1
```

Uncomment it, like so:

```
NoTempFiles 1
```

Save the config file again. Obviously, this will have no effect at all on post-version 3.1 dynamically produced pages.

Security

By now, you should have read the install documents and deleted mt-load.cgi and the mt-upgrade scripts and removed the Melody/Nelson identity. For security purposes, you should take a couple of other steps as well.

Installing MT-Blacklist

Next, you must install MT-Blacklist. It comes within the plugin pack included with MT3.1, and its workings are covered elsewhere in this book. MT-Blacklist will keep the vast majority of comment spammers at bay, and it works well to stop multiple copies posted by visitors to flood a site. As I write this chapter, this past week my own site has been hit by over 1,000 attempted comment spams, all of them stopped by MT-Blacklist. It is extremely necessary to install it.

Then, as the installation instructions suggest, but right at the bottom where it tends to be overlooked, you should protect your `mt.cfg` file by adding the following to the `.htaccess` file within the directory `mt.cfg` is found:

```
<Files mt.cfg>
    <Limit GET>
    deny from all
    </Limit>
</Files>
```

This will prevent anyone from looking at your settings from the open web.

SuExec

The most extreme method of securing your installation is to use Apache enabled with SuExec. SuExec enables CGI scripts to run under an individual's user ID, meaning that you don't need to set the folder permissions to 777 as before. By eschewing this, you lock the directories down.

Currently, Apache does not have SuExec enabled by default: You need to enable it yourself or, more likely, ask your system administrator or hosting company to do it for you (this explanation is beyond the scope of this book). The truly interested can look here: `http://httpd.apache.org/docs-2.0/suexec.html`.

Once SuExec is up and running, you need to tell MT to take advantage of it. This means changing `mt.cfg`. Backup your system first, and then scroll through the file for these lines:

```
# DBUmask 0022
# HTMLUmask 0022
# UploadUmask 0022
# DirUmask 0022
```

Uncomment them to the following:

```
DBUmask 0022
HTMLUmask 0022
UploadUmask 0022
DirUmask 0022
```

Then find this section:

```
# HTMLPerms 0777
# UploadPerms 0777
```

Again, uncomment the lines like so:

```
HTMLPerms 0644
UploadPerms 0644
```

These changes will enable MT to work within the secure constrains of SuExec, and you won't have to make your folders world-writable.

Summary

The experience of using a content management system such as Movable Type is a "Eureka!" moment for most web publishers. There's no better way to create new content and edit existing pages than an effective CMS, which makes the old way of editing pages by hand in a text editor seem vastly inferior.

Movable Type removes the need for hand-editing toil on weblogs and other rapidly changing websites. In the hands of a Movable Type hacker, the software can be extended into specialized areas or used to develop new kinds of sites entirely.

Tweaking the Templates

☑ Template modules

☑ Linked template files

☑ MT-TemplatePro plugin

☑ Fast experimental template editing

☑ No-rebuild static content

☑ The static blog

☑ Contextual edit links

☑ Best practices usability changes

Have you ever had to edit one piece of text in many different templates even across several different weblogs and perhaps rebuild each blog along the way? Did you ever wish you could just edit it once and be done with it? Are you a victim of the Rebuild Two-Step?

Have you ever wanted to experiment with your templates (for example, adding some cool widget or making changes to your stylesheet) but couldn't do it on your local computer because it required an element of your live site and you didn't want expose the havoc you may wreak on your visitors?

Have you ever made a change to a template and then wished fervently to have the original template back? Wouldn't version control be a dream?

If you answered yes to any of these questions, you are certainly not alone. In fact, for any web developer using Movable Type in client work, template management is one of the most onerous tasks of the project.

As important as the templates are to Movable Type, the template management interface has remained almost unchanged since the very first beta version of Movable Type was released years ago. Given the need, it is surprising that almost no plugins or applications for dealing with templates have been released — until now, that is (but more about that in a minute).

Luckily, even eschewing the use of plugins, you can do several things to relieve the burden. This chapter leads you through many of the things I do at the very beginning of every client project that uses Movable Type. We'll start with some of the basics and then move into the really cool stuff.

MT Template Management Features

Movable Type may not provide much in the way of power management features for templates, but the two it does provide — template modules and linked template files — are crucial features to making the templates more manageable.

Template Modules

One of the advantages of using a templating system is that it separates content from structure and presentation, at least in theory. The default templates provided with Movable Type stay fairly true to this goal in that most of the nonstructural content is dynamically generated using template tags.

However, if you've customized your templates, you are most likely guilty of putting some static content in there along with the dynamic content (for example, a blogroll, upcoming travel, your e-mail address, a short blurb about you, or even the image source [src] and alternative text for a picture of you). The list goes on. It's okay. We all do it.

If you're developing for commercial clients, this problem is compounded by the mountain of marketing content, navigation elements, and other consistently displayed text, all of which may need to be edited by someone who is potentially nontechnical. Separating static and dynamic content shields your client from complex templates and frees them to easily make edits to the content they really care about.

This separation can be done using *template modules*, which you can find at the bottom of the template management screen. Template modules are separate mini-templates intended for use inside of other Movable Type templates.

Template modules are included in MT templates via the use of the `MTInclude` tag, like so:

```
<$MTInclude module="MODULE_NAME"$>
```

For example, suppose a company called BigCo has its slogan on the main index of its website. Because they have trouble sticking with one slogan, it changes quite often. You would prefer to put this in an easily accessible place where they can edit it at will without having to pore over pages of HTML and MT template tags, which may only confuse them. The solution is to place this content into a template module. Let's call it "home-bigco-slogan" and make the following the content of the template module:

Big Co. does business like it's nobody's business.

Then, in your home page template, you can have something like this:

```
<p id="bigco-slogan">
<$MTInclude module="home-bigco-slogan"$>
</p>
```

Upon rebuild of the home page index template, the contents of the home-bigco-slogan template module will replace the preceding `MTInclude` tag with the following:

```
<p id="bigco-slogan">
Big Co. does business like it's nobody's business.
</p>
```

BigCo is happy and can be as indecisive as they like, but understandably, they are annoyed at having to rebuild their templates each time they make a change in one of the template modules you set up for them. In a second, I'll show you how to set things up so that in some cases, they can skip the rebuild and their changes will be applied immediately.

Real-Time Remote Text Editing

Even if you don't have shell access or don't care to edit your templates in any other way than through the web interface, linked template files are still invaluable for static files (for example, an external stylesheet or JavaScript file) that don't include any MT template tags and don't need to be dynamically generated by the application.

Simply set both the template output file and linked template file to the same file, and any changes (whether through the web interface or the filesystem) are synchronized and immediately effective. Movable Type then becomes a regular real-time remote text editor.

Linked Template Files

Face it, the web interface, with its tiny edit box and none of the cool features of your favorite text editor, is for the birds. It's fine for making one-off edits or very small tweaks to the template, but anything larger and you'll be yearning for more functionality than a simple web browser can provide.

For this reason, Movable Type provides the linked template file functionality found on the individual template editing page. If you provide a server filepath and filename upon saving the template, a file containing the template will be written to the filesystem.

When the file is created, its size and modification time are recorded in the database, allowing for synchronization between the file and the database-cached version of the template. If you make an edit to the file, the changes are recognized and cached in the database and used for rebuilds or viewing the template itself. If you make an edit through the web interface, Movable Type caches the new template in the linked file on the filesystem.

One important thing to note, which may be less than obvious, is that if you make an edit to a linked file while the template is open in your web browser, you will lose all of your changes if you subsequently click the Save button on the editing page. The browser's version, which did not incorporate the most recent edits, is written to the linked file. Rebuilds always take into account the most recent change, whether it is through the web browser or the linked file.

Advanced Template Management

Template modules and linked files are more than enough for many people. In fact, I would venture to guess that nearly three-quarters of MT users have yet to even think about using these two features. But for you, the MT hacker, it's only just the beginning.

MT-TemplatePro Plugin

In laying out the topics I wanted to cover in this chapter, it quickly became obvious to me just how much was lacking in the way of template management, or how difficult it would be to explain all of the shortcuts and tricks that I use along the way to mitigate the effects of these shortcomings on my work. In fact, it seemed more difficult and prone to errors than simply creating a solution to obviate the need for such trickery.

The solution I created is a plugin called MT-TemplatePro, which provides the following functionality:

- Versioning and source control for all templates in the system
- Selective multi-template search-replace and rebuild
- Easy and fast linked file creation and management
- A page with direct links to all of the templates you have permission to edit across all blogs in the system

If you've done any serious Movable Type development in the past, I think you'll find this plugin indispensable. The source and documentation can be found at the companion website to this book: www.hackingmt.com/plugins/templatepro.

If you have any suggestions for additional functionality, please don't hesitate to e-mail me at the address listed in the documentation.

Fast Experimental Template Editing

Often, I want to make an experimental edit to my templates and either I don't feel like replicating everything on my local computer or, for some reason, something in the server environment is necessary to get the full effect of the changes. At the same time, I don't want these changes (a euphemism for potential disasters) to be seen by all of my visitors. Achieving this goal is surprisingly simple, although not entirely obvious to most MT users.

Index templates are easy because they are individually rebuilt. Simply create a new index template and copy the code from the original. Use a different output filename and you now have a nondestructive, untrafficked copy of your index template to edit.

If you are editing any of the other templates, make and save your changes to the template and — instead of rebuilding the template type — find an old, rarely viewed entry in the weblog and resave that entry without editing it.

By doing this, only the indexes and individual, category, and date-based templates containing that one entry will be rebuilt. This is not only much faster than an archive type rebuild, but also far less prone to accidental exposure to your readers.

Building index templates can unnecessarily become a big source of performance problems. When you're done experimenting and have made the changes to the real index template, be sure to either remove the experimental template or turn off its page rebuilds — open the template for editing and uncheck the option Rebuild This Template Automatically When Rebuilding Index Templates.

No-rebuild Static Content

Previously, I explained how to easily separate out your static content using template modules. One of the biggest problems you will encounter, however, is that template modules require a rebuild of whichever templates include their content before the changes will be displayed.

There is no getting around the fact that any content containing MT template tags must go through the rebuilding process. However, if your content is completely static and void of template tags, you can avoid rebuilds altogether through the use of the linked file feature and server-side includes (SSIs) or PHP.

To do this, specify a linked file for the template module containing the static content. I find it best to name these files with an `.inc` file extension and group them together in a directory with other included files, just to make things clear down the line for someone who may be browsing through the filesystem.

Using the previous BigCo slogan example, replace the `MTInclude` tag in the index template with the appropriate include function.

For PHP:

```
<p id="bigco-slogan">
<?php include("/path/to/include/file"); ?>
</p>
```

For SSI:

```
<p id="bigco-slogan">
<!--#include virtual="/path/to/include/file" -->
</p>
```

These solutions require web servers that support server-side includes or PHP. When you make a change to the template module, the linked file is updated, and, because it is dynamically included on page load, the change takes effect immediately and rebuilds. For static content, changes are a thing of the past for BigCo.

The Static Blog

Although template modules and linked files make website management easier, there are times when they fall very short, as in the following examples:

- When granular permissions are necessary (for example, in a company setting where each employee should only have privileges to edit the specific content they are authorized to edit)

- When several blogs (in addition to a regular blog, such as a recent press blog, an upcoming events blog, and so on) are used to compile different parts of the same website, leading to an increase in the overhead of the template management process

- When you want MT to manage an entirely static page as opposed to a static section of a page

- When you would like your static content to be searchable by visitors

To make the site management process easier, we turn to the use of a *static blog*.

A static blog isn't a blog in the traditional sense. It has no entries (per se), date context, archives, or even many templates other than the template modules you add. As you'll see later, however, it is an extremely powerful concept that turns Movable Type into a heavy-duty content management system.

The important thing to understand at this point is that through the use of a static blog, you have a powerful static content manager (or more than one manager, using permissions granted to different groups) at your fingertips.

Cookie-based Deep Contextual Edit Links

Back in the fall of 2001, I introduced MT-Search as the first add-on to Movable Type (I say add-on and not plugin because, at the time, there was no such thing as a plugin architecture). One of its features was an editing link next to each search result, which would only appear if you were logged into the MT installation via a cookie.

Later, David Gagne (`http://davidgagne.net/`) came up with the idea of adding a templatized version of the edit link to the weblog templates so that it would show up contextually next to the entry wherever it appeared. Brenna Koch ("bmk" of Movable Type support boards fame) improved upon that idea by using a bit of PHP and a secret cookie-setting page to make the link apparent only for the user or users who had the cookie set.

While all of these ideas are fantastic, they only deal with entries. Why not have every single piece of content editable directly from the website itself? This is completely possible and something I call "cookie-based deep contextual edit links."

The Cookie Page

If you've extracted all of your static content from your templates, each static element of the interface is now editable. Chances are good that if you were to separate all of the elements into their own templates, there would be quite a lot of them to display. In an ideal world, these links could only be seen by the person authorized to edit that content. Unfortunately, because of the way Movable Type sets its authentication cookie, setting up differential display based on it is very difficult (although not impossible). Fortunately, there is a far easier solution that satisfies the same goal.

To run this solution, you need three things:

- Use of PHP (although there are ways around this requirement)
- A cookie setting page
- A template with static content

To suppress display of the links for your visitors, you can use PHP to display them only if the browser has a cookie set by some arbitrary page on your site. Again, because a login (or MT cookie) would still be required after clicking on the link, it's not important that the page be secret, but it should be one that is unlinked and not visited by a non-author, to minimize confusion for your site visitors. In addition, to keep the potentially large number of edit links from cluttering your own view until you need them, you will want to make the cookie toggleable.

The following code, saved in that nonlinked page on your site, will achieve all of these goals. Change the $domain variable to match your site's domain (minus any subdomains):

```php
<?php

$domain = 'EXAMPLE.COM';

$c_name = 'mteditprivs';
if ($_COOKIE[$c_name]) {
  setcookie($c_name,'0',time()-31536000,'/',$domain,'0');
} else {
  setcookie($c_name,'1',time()+31536000,'/',$domain,'0');
}

if ($_GET['return']) {
        header("Location: ".$_GET['return']);
} elseif ($_COOKIE[$c_name]) {
        print "Cookie is on.";
} else {
        print "Cookie is off.";
}
?>
```

You can access this page directly, in which case the cookie will be toggled appropriately, or you can access it from any page on your site via your browser's toolbar using the following bookmarklet. Replace 'http://example.com/PAGE' with the actual URL to the cookie-setting page:

```
javascript:document.location.href='http://example.com/
PAGE?return='+document.location.href;
```

If you use the bookmarklet, you will be automatically redirected back to the page you were on when you clicked it after the cookie was set.

The Edit Link

Now you will want to put an edit link into each template module (or template in a static blog) you may want to edit:

1. Click on the link to the static blog template or template module containing the content you wish to be able to edit and copy the URL in the address bar into your clipboard.

2. Paste the link within the following code somewhere in that same template. Replace EDIT_URL with the URL copied in the previous step:

   ```php
   <?php
   if ($_COOKIE['mteditprivs']) {
     echo '<a href="EDIT_URL">[edit]</a>';
   }
   ?>
   ```

3. Save, activate the JavaScript cookie, and edit.

Hereafter, by using the cookie-setting page or a bookmarklet to (and back from) it, you will have immediate access to every single piece of static content on your site placed contextually throughout your website without having to navigate through the myriad of MT administration screens.

Blog Template Best Practices

So far, you've learned what you can do to make your template management experience a better one. On the other side of the equation is the user. Over the past few years, Six Apart has done a fabulous job of making usability improvements in their default templates. Of course, being fairly avid readers of weblogs, we have a few of our own to suggest. Following is a list of changes you can make to your templates of any regular weblog that will make your visitors' experience an even better one.

Recent Comments List

Comments are often the most dynamic part of any regular blog. By displaying recent comments on the front page of the site, you can easily improve the user experience for your frequent visitors by pointing them to where the action is.

To include a listing of recent comments, Movable Type provides a global attribute to the MTEntries tag: `recently_commented_on`:

```
<ul>
<MTEntries recently_commented_on="20">
<MTComments lastn="1" sort_order="descend">
<li><a href="<$MTEntryLink$>#c<$MTCommentID$>"><$MTEntryTitle$> -
<$MTCommentAuthor$> (<$MTCommentDate format="%Y.%m.%d"$>)</a></li>
</MTComments>
</MTEntries>
```

The preceding code will print out a listing of metadata for, and links to, the last comment posted in the last 20 recently commented-on entries.

You also could display recent comments in reverse chronological order without regard to grouping them by entry. The following code displays the last 10 comments:

```
<MTComments lastn="10" sort_order="descend">
<MTCommentEntry>
<p><a href="<$MTEntryLink$>"><$MTEntryTitle$></a>
<$MTCommentBody$>
Posted by <$MTCommentAuthorLink spam_protect="1"$></MTCommentEntry>
<$MTCommentAuthorIdentity$> at <$MTCommentDate$><MTCommentEntry> | <a
href="<$MTEntryLink$>#reply">Reply</a><br clear="all">
</MTCommentEntry>
</MTComments>
```

This code incorporates a workaround to a subtle quirk of Movable Type: The `MTCommentDate` tag acts differently inside an `MTCommentEntry` container tag.

When inside an `MTCommentEntry`, `MTCommentDate` displays the date and time of the entry. By putting it outside the container, `MTCommentDate` displays the date and time of the comment, as desired.

Much-improved Comment Listings

There are a few annoyances in the way that Movable Type displays comments, which can be easily solved with a few minor tweaks.

Properly Named Anchors and Links to Them

Named anchors are URL fragments used to point directly to a specific piece of content on a web page. Movable Type creates empty named anchors for each comment:

```
<a id="c<$MTCommentID$>"></a>
```

This way, if a `#cID` (where `ID` is the comment ID) is tacked onto the end of the URL to the individual archive page, the page will be scrolled directly to that comment, effectively creating a permalink to each comment.

Unfortunately, not only is this a syntactically meaningless use of HTML (for those of you who care about such things), but nowhere in the default templates is there even a link provided to these anchors, making them useful only to people who read the HTML source.

To offer proper comment permalinks, you should get rid of the empty anchor and use the `id` attribute on an existing tag (for example, `<div id="c<$MTCommentID$>">`) related to each comment. Then, link some part of the comment to this anchor. The byline date, for example, is a generally accepted place for a permalink:

```
Posted by <$MTCommentAuthor$> at
<a href="#<$MTCommentID$>"><$MTCommentDate$></a>
```

The Faceless Author

Movable Type produces a comment listing with each comment's text listed first, followed by the author byline. If the comment is short and the byline is visible, this is not a problem. However, longer comments create a situation in which you are reading words without knowing the writer's identity.

There are few real-world situations in which you hear what is being said or read what was written before you ever discover the source, and there is no reason to create one on your weblog.

To really enhance personalization of the comment, print out the comment link in parentheses next to the author's name and link it as well.

Suppress the Commenter's E-mail Address

Although MT provides the global `spam_protect` attribute on the `MTCommentAuthorLink`, it is a very weak protection because programmatic obfuscation can always be programmatically decoded by a spammer, especially when the source is completely open and relies on standard encoding techniques or JavaScript.

If you want to make your visitors happy (or keep them from getting very irate), replace the `spam_protect` attribute with the `no_email` attribute to suppress e-mail addresses entirely if no URL is provided.

Redirection Is Lame

Not long ago, Six Apart introduced `CommentAuthorLink` redirects as a defensive weapon against comment spam. By changing the `CommentAuthorLink` to an internal link, which then redirects the user to the actual author's link, the Google PageRank (that is, the spammer's *raison d'être*) for the spammer's link is not increased.

Unfortunately, it has been shown that spammers are completely unfazed by this, as demonstrated by their continued use of scattershot spamming even on blogs where a redirect exists. What's more, there are three major problems with this technique:

- It breaks a well-accepted and relied-upon tenet of usability that you never want to obscure the target of the link in the status bar.

- It breaks the referrer generated by clicking on the link by disassociating it with the page on which the link is found.

- It violates one of the most important rules of web usability in that it completely breaks the Back button.

For all of these reasons, we greatly dissuade you from using this technique; it doesn't help in the fight against spam and hurts in many different ways. It can be turned off with the `no_redirect` attribute to `MTCommentAuthorLink` tag.

Putting It All Together

The original comment listing code looks like this:

```
<MTComments>
<a id="c<$MTCommentID$>"></a>
<$MTCommentBody$>
<p class="posted">Posted by: <$MTCommentAuthorLink spam_protect="1"$>
<MTCommentAuthorIdentity> at <$MTCommentDate$></p>
</MTComments>
```

Incorporating all of the preceding suggestions gives you the following:

```
<div id="c<MTCommentID>">
<p>
  <$MTCommentAuthor$>
  (<a href="<MTCommentURL>"><MTCommentURL></a>)
</p>
<$MTCommentBody$>
<p class="posted">
```

```
Posted on
<a href="#c<MTCommentID>" title="Permalink to this comment">
 <$MTCommentDate format="%x %H:%M TZ"$>
</a>
</p>
</div>
```

If you find the printed comment author link text to be a bit too long for your liking, you can easily modify it with Brad Choate's MT-Perlscript plugin (`http://mt-plugins.org/archives/entry/perlscript.php`) to remove common elements such as the `http://www`. To do so, replace

```
(<a href="<MTCommentURL>"><MTCommentURL></a>)
```

with the following:

```
<MTPerlScript>
my $url = '<MTCommentURL encode_php="q">';
if ($url =~ m#^\w+://#i) {
        (my $stripped_url = $url) =~ s#^http://(www\.)?##;
        $stripped_url =~ s#/$##;
        print ' (<a href="'.$url.'">'.$stripped_url.'</a>)';
} elsif ($url =~ m#\w+#) {
        (my $stripped_url = $url) =~ s#^(www\.)?##;
        $stripped_url =~ s#/$##;
        print ' (<a href="http://'.$url.'">'.$stripped_url.'</a>)';
}else {
        print '';
}
</MTPerlScript>
```

Integrating Comments and Trackbacks

Trackbacks are a Six Apart innovation that enables remote notification of and linking back to posts that refer to a particular trackback-enabled entry or category on any site. They are, indeed, a form of remote comments.

The default templates and MT functionality dictate that these two types of comments be two separate lists. The biggest problem with this requirement is that it destroys the chronology of submissions and tends to treat trackbacks (and the people who link to your entries) as the unwanted cousins at the family reunion.

Luckily, there is a fabulous plugin called SimpleComments (`http://sixapart.com/pronet/plugins/plugin/simplecomments.html`) that strives to reconcile this disparity. With SimpleComments, you can list comments and trackbacks together in the exact order in which they were sent and received; and aside from any stylistic differences you choose to make to differentiate the two, all of your visitors' submissions will be treated equally.

Fixing Up Your Syndication Feeds

The syndication feed templates supplied with Movable Type are perfectly serviceable, but they don't take full advantage of MT's capabilities. We can certainly improve them. First up: the RSS 1.0 feed.

RSS 1.0

RSS 1.0 is, by design, a very rich vocabulary for describing your content. Far too rich, indeed, for the average RSS application. Much of the data we're about to provide will not be seen by your average RSS consumer. However, by providing the data anyway, you enable yourself and others to write applications that do tap into this data.

To start, for a comparison, here's the current template (as of 3.15, RSS 1.0):

```
<?xml version="1.0" encoding="<$MTPublishCharset$>"?>

<rdf:RDF
xmlns:rdf="http://www.w3.org/1999/02/22-rdf-syntax-ns#"
xmlns:dc="http://purl.org/dc/elements/1.1/"
xmlns:sy="http://purl.org/rss/1.0/modules/syndication/"
xmlns:admin="http://webns.net/mvcb/"
xmlns:cc="http://web.resource.org/cc/"
xmlns="http://purl.org/rss/1.0/">

<channel rdf:about="<$MTBlogURL$>">
<title><$MTBlogName encode_xml="1"$></title>
<link><$MTBlogURL$></link>
<description><$MTBlogDescription encode_xml="1"$></description>
<dc:creator></dc:creator>
<dc:date><MTEntries lastn="1"><$MTEntryDate format="%Y-%m-
%dT%H:%M:%S"
language="en"$><$MTBlogTimezone$></MTEntries></dc:date>
<admin:generatorAgent
rdf:resource="http://www.movabletype.org/?v=<$MTVersion$>" />
<MTBlogIfCCLicense>
<cc:license rdf:resource="<$MTBlogCCLicenseURL$>" />
</MTBlogIfCCLicense>

<items>
<rdf:Seq><MTEntries lastn="15">
<rdf:li rdf:resource="<$MTEntryPermalink encode_xml="1"$>" />
</MTEntries></rdf:Seq>
</items>

</channel>

<MTEntries lastn="15">
<item rdf:about="<$MTEntryPermalink encode_xml="1"$>">
<title><$MTEntryTitle encode_xml="1"$></title>
<link><$MTEntryPermalink encode_xml="1"$></link>
<description><$MTEntryBody encode_xml="1"$></description>
```

```
<dc:subject><$MTEntryCategory encode_xml="1"$></dc:subject>
<dc:creator><$MTEntryAuthor encode_xml="1"$></dc:creator>
<dc:date><$MTEntryDate format="%Y-%m-%dT%H:%M:%S"
language="en"$><$MTBlogTimezone$></dc:date>
</item>
</MTEntries>

</rdf:RDF>
```

We can improve on this. Starting with the `<channel>` information, a considerable amount of information is provided here, and there is really only one element left to add in, the `<admin:errorReportsTo>`.

This element holds your e-mail address, enabling anyone who might be using your feed finds to contact you. With my own e-mail address, I add this line to the template:

```
<admin:errorReportsTo
rdf:resource="mailto:ben@benhammersley.com"/>
```

Be warned, however, that many spambots are harvesting e-mail addresses from RSS feeds. Personally, I've given up trying to protect my e-mail address online, and instead rely on spam filtering. Your mileage, as they say, might vary regarding this.

Moving on, we get to the `<item>` sections. With weblogs, each `<item>` refers to an individual entry, and there is a lot we can say about these. We're already listing who wrote it, when, and on which subject, so no need to worry about that. However, we can add more. Comments, for example, can be listed according to who has contributed to the posting.

In this way, aggregators that recognize this field, such as NewsMonster, can display a list of commentators, and perhaps provide aggregation based on items for which your friends have left comments.

Of course, you might turn off commenting for some entries, so we must wrap the entire section of the template in an `<MTEntryIfAllowComments>` tag:

```
<MTEntryIfAllowComments>
  <annotate:reference rdf:resource="<$MTEntryPermalink
encode_xml="1"$>" />
  <MTComments>
    <dc:contributor>
      <foaf:person foaf:name="<MTCommentAuthor encode_xml="1">">
        <foaf:homepage rdf:resource="<MTCommentURL
encode_xml="1">" />
        <foaf:email rdf:resource="<$MTCommentEmail
encode_xml="1"$>" />
      </foaf:person>
    </dc:contributor>
  </MTComments>
</MTEntryIfAllowComments>
```

You'll notice that we're providing details of the commentator inside of Friend of a Friend (FOAF) elements. FOAF is a Resource Description Framework (RDF) vocabulary that gives us a lot of scope for describing people. For more on that, visit the project's home page at `www.foaf-project.org`. There's also a lot to be found in a search of Google; it's a rapidly developing field, and new tutorials are out almost weekly.

Trackbacks are also good to include, as they list sites that are related (albeit sometimes loosely). As trackbacking goes both ways, this is a great bit of metadata to include in one's feed. We can add the following to show the pings sent out by the entry itself:

```
<MTPingsSent>
  <trackback:about rdf:resource="<$MTPingsSentURL
encode_xml="1"$>"/>
</MTPingsSent>
```

The following template snippet deals with which pings have been received by the entry in question, detailed with the `<dcterms:isReferencedBy>` element, checking first to determine whether trackbacking that entry has been allowed, and if so, detailing the URL to ping to trackback to that entry as well:

```
<MTEntryIfAllowPings>
  <trackback:ping rdf:resource="<MTEntryTrackbackLink
encode_xml="1">"/>
  <MTPings>
    <dcterms:isReferencedBy rdf:resource="<$MTPingURL
encode_xml="1"$>" />
  </MTPings>
</MTEntryIfAllowPings>
```

All of the connections to the rest of the web have been detailed. Now, about the content: The `<content:encoded>` element is increasingly recognized and used by many to display their entire entry with the feeds. I like doing this myself, so add this line to the `<item>` section:

```
<content:encoded>
<$MTEntryBody encode_xml="1"$>
<$MTEntryMore encode_xml="1"$>
</content:encoded>
```

Here's the full template in action:

```
<?xml version="1.0" encoding="<$MTPublishCharset$>"?>

<rdf:RDF
  xmlns:rdf="http://www.w3.org/1999/02/22-rdf-syntax-ns#"
  xmlns:dc="http://purl.org/dc/elements/1.1/"
  xmlns:sy="http://purl.org/rss/1.0/modules/syndication/"
  xmlns="http://purl.org/rss/1.0/"
  xmlns:admin="http://webns.net/mvcb/"
  xmlns:annotate="http://purl.org/rss/1.0/modules/annotate/"
  xmlns:dcterms="http://purl.org/dc/terms/"
  xmlns:cc="http://web.resource.org/cc/"
  xmlns:content="http://purl.org/rss/1.0/modules/content/"
  xmlns:foaf="http://xmlns.com/foaf/0.1/"
  xmlns:trackback="http://madskills.com/public/xml/rss/module/
trackback/"
  >
```

```
  <channel rdf:about="<$MTBlogURL$>">
    <title><$MTBlogName encode_xml="1"$></title>
    <link><$MTBlogURL$></link>
    <description><$MTBlogDescription
encode_xml="1"$></description>
    <dc:language>en-us</dc:language>
    <dc:creator>Your Name Here</dc:creator>
    <dc:date><MTEntries lastn="1"><$MTEntryDate format="%Y-%m-
%dT%H:%M:%S"
      language="en"$><$MTBlogTimezone$></MTEntries></dc:date>
    <admin:generatorAgent
       rdf:resource="http://www.movabletype.org/?v=<$MTVersion$>"
/>
    <admin:errorReportsTo rdf:resource="mailto:your email here"/>

    <MTBlogIfCCLicense>
      <cc:license rdf:resource="<$MTBlogCCLicenseURL$>" />
    </MTBlogIfCCLicense>

    <items>
      <rdf:Seq><MTEntries lastn="15">
        <rdf:li rdf:resource="<$MTEntryPermalink encode_xml="1"$>"
/>
      </MTEntries></rdf:Seq>
    </items>

  </channel>

  <MTEntries lastn="15">
    <item rdf:about="<$MTEntryPermalink encode_xml="1"$>">
    <title><$MTEntryTitle encode_xml="1"$></title>
    <link><$MTEntryPermalink encode_xml="1"$></link>
    <description><$MTEntryExcerpt encode_xml="1"$></description>
    <dc:subject><$MTEntryCategory encode_xml="1"$></dc:subject>
    <dc:creator><$MTEntryAuthor encode_xml="1"$></dc:creator>
    <dc:date><$MTEntryDate format="%Y-%m-%dT%H:%M:%S"
      language="en"$><$MTBlogTimezone$></dc:date>
    <content:encoded><$MTEntryBody encode_xml="1"$><$MTEntryMore
      encode_xml="1"$></content:encoded>

    <MTEntryIfAllowComments>
      <annotate:reference rdf:resource="<$MTEntryPermalink
encode_xml="1"$>" />
      <MTComments>
        <dc:contributor>
          <foaf:person foaf:name="<MTCommentAuthor
encode_xml="1">">
            <foaf:homepage rdf:resource="<MTCommentURL
encode_xml="1">" />
            <foaf:email rdf:resource="<$MTCommentEmail
encode_xml="1"$>" />
          </foaf:person>
```

```
           </dc:contributor>
         </MTComments>
       </MTEntryIfAllowComments>

       <MTPingsSent>
         <trackback:about rdf:resource="<$MTPingsSentURL
encode_xml="1"$>"/>
       </MTPingsSent>

       <MTEntryIfAllowPings>
         <trackback:ping rdf:resource="<MTEntryTrackbackLink
encode_xml="1">"/>
         <MTPings>
           <dcterms:isReferencedBy rdf:resource="<$MTPingURL
encode_xml="1"$>" />
         </MTPings>
         </MTEntryIfAllowPings>
       </item>
     </MTEntries>
</rdf:RDF>
```

Note Remember: If your site is not in English, you need to change the `<dc:language>` tag at the top of the feed.

RSS 2.0

The RSS 2.0 template is much simpler than the RSS 1.0 template just examined. It currently looks like this:

```
<?xml version="1.0" encoding="<$MTPublishCharset$>"?>
<rss version="2.0">
<channel>
<title><$MTBlogName remove_html="1" encode_xml="1"$></title>
<link><$MTBlogURL$></link>
<description><$MTBlogDescription remove_html="1"
encode_xml="1"$></description>
<copyright>Copyright <$MTDate format="%Y"$></copyright>
<lastBuildDate><MTEntries lastn="1"><$MTEntryDate
format_name="rfc822"$></MTEntries></lastBuildDate>
<generator>http://www.movabletype.org/?v=<$MTVersion$></generator>
<docs>http://blogs.law.harvard.edu/tech/rss</docs>

<MTEntries lastn="15">
<item>
<title><$MTEntryTitle remove_html="1" encode_xml="1"$></title>
<description><$MTEntryBody encode_xml="1"$></description>
<link><$MTEntryPermalink encode_xml="1"$></link>
<guid><$MTEntryPermalink encode_xml="1"$></guid>
<category><$MTEntryCategory remove_html="1"
encode_xml="1"$></category>
<pubDate><$MTEntryDate format_name="rfc822"$></pubDate>
```

```
</item>
</MTEntries>

</channel>
</rss>
```

As before, we can add the e-mail address to contact in case of technical trouble. In RSS 2.0, this is done with the `<webMaster>` element, like so:

```
<webMaster>ben@benhammersley.com</webMaster>
```

Use your own e-mail address in place of mine, of course.

RSS 2.0 also enables you to place the author's name and e-mail address within the `<item>` section. This is done in the format "example@example.com (Joe Example)," so we add this line:

```
<author><MTEntryAuthorEmail> (<MTEntryAuthor>)</author>
```

That is really as far as we can go with RSS 2.0. Therefore, to sum up, here's the whole template again:

```
<?xml version="1.0" encoding="<$MTPublishCharset$>"?>
<rss version="2.0">
<channel>
<title><$MTBlogName remove_html="1" encode_xml="1"$></title>
<link><$MTBlogURL$></link>
<description><$MTBlogDescription remove_html="1"
encode_xml="1"$></description>
<language>en-us</language>
<copyright>Copyright <$MTDate format="%Y"$></copyright>
<lastBuildDate><MTEntries lastn="1"><$MTEntryDate
format_name="rfc822"$></MTEntries></lastBuildDate>
<pubDate><$MTDate format_name="rfc822"$></pubDate>
<generator>http://www.movabletype.org/?v=<$MTVersion$></generator>
<webMaster>ben@benhammersley.com</webMaster>
<docs>http://blogs.law.harvard.edu/tech/rss</docs>

<MTEntries lastn="15">
<item>
<title><$MTEntryTitle remove_html="1" encode_xml="1"$></title>
<description><$MTEntryExcerpt encode_xml="1"$></description>
<link><$MTEntryPermalink encode_xml="1"$></link>
<guid><$MTEntryPermalink encode_xml="1"$></guid>
<category><$MTEntryCategory remove_html="1"
encode_xml="1"$></category>
<pubDate><$MTEntryDate format_name="rfc822"$></pubDate>
<author><MTEntryAuthorEmail> (<MTEntryAuthor>)</author>
</item>
</MTEntries>

</channel>
</rss>
```

Summary

Though Movable Type is ostensibly a weblog publishing tool, the software could just as easily be described as a content management system that can be used on any dynamic web site, especially one that must be updated frequently over time.

The software's template-driven publishing system, in the hands of a hacker, can deliver the content of online magazines, photo albums, marketing presentations, or any other kind of site.

As you gain confidence in your ability to edit templates, you'll find more ways to put Movable Type to work.

The software provides support for dozens of template tags and can be supplemented by new tags implemented as software plugins. These tags integrate completely with the template publishing system, appearing to users as if they were a built-in part of the software.

By learning the ins and outs of Movable Type's tags and extending them with plugin tags, you can take a lot of the sweat out of site maintenance and provide more features to your visitors.

Hacking the Database

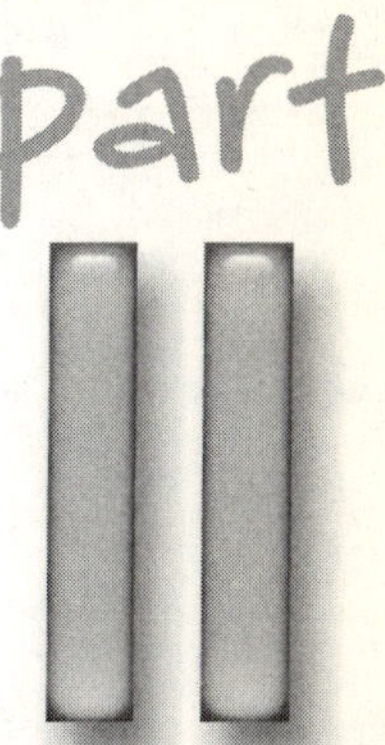

MT and Database Storage

In the mid-1990s, I did UNIX System Administration for the Internet division of a monstrously large telecom company. My team managed a farm of over 40 immensely powerful Sun servers whose *raison d'être* was the presentation of a major high-traffic search portal.

The site contained thousands of articles, reviews, pictures, maps, business listings, and anything else you can think of, including advertising proudly displayed alongside of it. The content we served was in constant motion, going up and coming down every single day.

A colossus of a website such as this required a robust and sophisticated program to manage it all. Ours provided us with workflow process control, audit trails, version control, timed publishing and expiration, ad management, and about a billion other features that make geeks drool and accountants weep.

This software was known as a *content management system (CMS)*.

Our day-to-day system administration chores were numerous and often intense. When we weren't forming a bucket brigade to put out major fires (metaphorically speaking, of course), we were constantly fine-tuning these servers, upgrading software and hardware, and making security enhancements to the system.

One problem we constantly faced was not knowing what was done when and by whom. With a large team of people maintaining such a complex system, it was crucial that we worked to create a sort of hive brain, whereby each member of the team had the same knowledge of the system's state as every other member.

To that end, I created a small Perl program called *slogger* (short for system logger) that enabled members of the team to quickly record any activities and changes they made to the system. The program automatically recorded the time and date of the submission as well as the UNIX user ID of the submitter, but it did little else.

Slogger, while infinitely more primitive than the software that ran the site, was a content management system as well.

Database-driven Web Publishing

As the previous story illustrates, content management systems cover a broad spectrum of complexity, but they share one basic, common denominator: the database.

All content management systems have a critical reliance on information storage and retrieval. At the heart of every CMS is a database. Without the database, there is no content. Without content, a content management system is nothing.

With our portal CMS, all of the content and every single configuration setting was stored in the biggest and baddest multi-processor-scorching Oracle database the world had seen. Slogger, conversely, was powered by single, simple text file. Both of these, when structured in a predictable way, made programmatic data storage and retrieval by a CMS possible.

Movable Type, of course, is no different. Each piece of configurable data or user-added content is stored in a database. Every time you click a link or a button in the administrative interface, the database is consulted regarding what data to display as well as whether you have the appropriate permissions for the action you are attempting to perform.

In essence, the database is the fuel that makes the Movable Type CMS burn brightly.

The Power of the Database

The big question is, between the web interface and several application programming interfaces (API) you can use to interact with the MT system, do you really need to know about the database? The simple answer, of course, is that you don't — as long as you don't want to do anything interesting and you never have any problems.

By virtue of the fact that you are reading this book, I think it's safe to assume that you do want to do interesting things. This is good. Understanding the underlying data structure and the ways to access that data opens up a whole new world of possibilities. With just a few standard Structured Query Language (SQL) statements, you can do everything to or with your data that Movable Type can.

Have you ever wanted to do the following?

- Perform a global search-and-replace across all of your blogs' entries and/or templates

- Edit a trackback to remove validation-destroying characters

- Include MT-related information on non-MT published pages

- Clone your MT installation or migrate it from one server to another

- Merge two blogs or move entries (and associated comments/trackbacks) from one blog to another

The possibilities of what you can do are really only limited by your imagination.

As far as problems are concerned, as much as we like to stick our heads in the sand, cross our fingers, and shake chicken bones to keep them away, problems always happen. The difference between the big ones and the small ones is often a matter of preparedness, to which understanding the database is key.

Following are some common problems that can be cured with a little DB magic:

- Making changes *en masse* to anything (setting entries to draft, changing author, etc.)
- Moving stray comments to their rightful entries
- Recovering a forgotten password with no author e-mail or hint
- Cleaning up thousands of comments after an abusive user floods the site with junk messages
- Major, catastrophic data loss

Do I have your attention? Perhaps I've piqued your interest? Well, good! We'll get to many of these issues in Chapter 5.

Moreover, in this and the following two chapters, you will learn everything there is to know about the Movable Type database. With that knowledge, not only will you better understand what is happening under the hood, you'll also learn how to get in there and fix it when things go wrong.

Database Support in MT

Movable Type supports the following four different types of databases:

- BerkeleyDB
- MySQL
- SQLite
- PostgreSQL

BerkeleyDB is the one database system supported since the first version of Movable Type. Ironically, with the MT 3.0 release, it became the only one that Six Apart is actively dissuading users from adopting due to performance and reliability issues. For our purposes, BerkeleyDB is of no use because it is nearly impossible to access the stored data directly. In short, if you're using BerkeleyDB, rip out this entire section of the book and move on.

The other three systems are all fabulous and free database management systems, and each has its own special characteristics, which attract a legion of rabid devotees. PostgreSQL is mostly adored by the super-hardcore techie crowd for its sophisticated feature set, standard SQL support, and GPL license. SQLite is championed by those who are wowed by its compact size and memory imprint. MySQL is loved for its simplicity, stability, and great tool set.

Putting the religious wars aside, in this book I focus on MySQL when I present database-specific information, such as SQL statements or connection details. The rationale is two-fold:

- MySQL has a far larger install base both in general and among MT users because its lower support costs, native multi-threaded design, and fine-grained permission model make it the best choice in a shared server environment common to most web-hosting companies.

- If you are using PostgreSQL or SQLite, you most likely already know how to connect to the database and are intimately familiar with SQL. For the reason mentioned previously, the same is not generally true for MySQL users.

If you are using PostgreSQL or SQLite and are unfamiliar with SQL, this section of the book will still provide you with a great deal of important nonvendor-specific information about the MT database. For more information about comparable SQL statements and connection details for your platform, you can refer to this book's companion websites at `www.wiley.com/compbooks/allen` and `hackingmt.com`.

You can download MySQL from `www.mysql.com`, PostgreSQL from `www.postgresql.org`, SQLite from `www.sqlite.org`, and BerkeleyDB from Sleepycat Software at `www.sleepycat.com`.

Accessing the Database

You can access your MySQL database either through the command line (if you have shell access) or via a Web interface that either you or your web-hosting company has installed.

Command-line Access

Log into your shell account and type the following:

```
mysql -u USERNAME -h HOST -p DATABASE
```

At the same time, replace USERNAME, HOST and DATABASE with the MT configuration variables found in `mt.cfg` (DBUser, DBHost and Database). If DBHost is commented out in `mt.cfg` or is set to localhost, you can simply omit it like this:

```
mysql -u USERNAME -p DATABASE
```

You will be prompted for your password, which you can find in `mt-db-pass.cgi`. If you have been granted command-line access to MySQL, you should see something like this:

```
Reading table information for completion of table and column names
You can turn off this feature to get a quicker startup with -A

Welcome to the MySQL monitor.  Commands end with ; or \g.
Your MySQL connection id is 12152 to server version: 3.23.44
```

```
Type 'help;' or '\h' for help. Type '\c' to clear the buffer.
mysql>
```

At that point, you are ready to go. While we will use this more in the coming chapters, here are a couple of quick SQL commands just to get you started. Note that each ends with a semicolon:

- `show tables;` — View all of the available tables in a database.

- `desc TABLENAME;` — View the definition for table `TABLENAME`.

- `select * from TABLENAME;` — Display all of the rows from the table `TABLENAME`.

Web Interface Access

Although many packages are available for web-based management of a MySQL database, `phpMyAdmin` (`www.phpmyadmin.net`) is the most widely installed and sophisticated interface that I have found. Because of its powerful feature set and the fact that it can be installed in an unprivileged user's account in under five minutes, it is the package that I most strongly recommend.

Although the documentation is excellent, it is also quite extensive, so here is the five-minute quick-start guide to default installation and configuration:

1. Download the latest stable build (currently version 2.6.1) from `www.phpmyadmin.net` to your computer.

2. Unpack the archive using your favorite decompression utility, just as you did with Movable Type.

3. Change the name of the uncompressed folder to `phpmyadmin` (or anything you prefer to the current name) and upload the entire package to the desired location within the web-accessible document root of your web server (for example, in the same directory as your main index file).

4. Inside of the `phpmyadmin` folder on your computer, find and open the file `config.inc.php` in a basic text editor.

5. Find the following line:

   ```
   $cfg['PmaAbsoluteUri'] = '';
   ```

   Enter the URL to the `phpmyadmin` directory, ending in a slash (/). If you followed the previous suggestions, this would be as follows:

   ```
   $cfg['PmaAbsoluteUri'] = 'http://YOURDOMAIN.COM/phpmyadmin/';
   ```

6. Find the first instance of the following three lines:

   ```
   $cfg['Servers'][$i]['host']         = 'localhost';
   $cfg['Servers'][$i]['user']         = 'root';
   $cfg['Servers'][$i]['password']     = ''
   ```

Modify these lines to reflect your database configuration found in `mt.cfg` (DBHost and DBUser) and `mt-db-pass.cgi`. Don't change the host setting unless you also had to do so in your `mt.cfg`.

7. Re-upload your modified `config.inc.php` to the `phpmyadmin` directory and load the URL from step 5 in your web browser.

If you followed the previous instructions carefully, you should be looking at the `phpMyAdmin` welcome screen. On the left, you can find a drop-down listing of any databases in your installation.

Select your MT database and familiarize yourself with the interface. Most of this section's exercises are done using the SQL functionality accessible from the SQL tab on top, although the Query functionality on the main database page and the Browse and Search features from the table view pages are also enlightening and extremely useful.

The `phpMyAdmin` directory you just installed is unprotected, and anyone can access it and do anything they like to your data. It is vitally important that you at least provide `.htaccess` protection on the directory even if you do not employ stronger access controls provided by the program. See the `phpMyAdmin` documentation for these and other configuration details.

Database Backups

Now that you have direct access to the database, the first thing you should do is back it up. In fact, back it up now, and before you ever do anything to it. In addition, back it up regularly, maybe even twice regularly, which I think is called bi-regularly or semi-regularly. . .

Seriously, my dentist used to tell me that I should only floss the teeth I want to keep. I am telling you that you should only back up the data you want to keep. I personally back up my entire MT database every single day, and it is downloaded to my computer every single night. That way, if something catastrophic happens, I haven't lost much.

The following sections describe the two ways to back up and restore your data.

Backing Up via the Command Line

To back up from the command line, log into your shell account and type the following at the prompt, replacing USERNAME and DATABASE as described previously:

```
mysqldump -a -u USERNAME -p DATABASE > FILENAME.mysql
Enter password:
#
```

The resulting file, `FILENAME.mysql`, is a full backup with which you can fully restore your database in case of problems.

Restoring via the Command Line

Restoring from `FILENAME.mysql` is a three-step process:

1. Drop the database:

```
# mysqladmin -u USERNAME -p drop DATABASE
Enter password:
Dropping the database is potentially a very bad thing to do.
Any data stored in the database will be destroyed.

Do you really want to drop the 'DATABASE' database [y/N] y
Database "DATABASE" dropped
#
```

2. Re-create the database:

```
#   mysqladmin -u USERNAME -p create DATABASE
Enter password:
#
```

3. Import the backup data:.

```
# mysql -u USERNAME -p DATABASE < FILENAME.mysql
Enter password:
#
```

Backing Up via phpMyAdmin

As is often the case, backing a database up via `phpMyAdmin` is even easier than doing it manually (after you've done it once, that is). From the main database page, click Export in the top button bar. Set up the options as follows:

Export Section

This section specifies from which tables data should be exported and the format of the file itself. You should select all tables and choose SQL as the data type.

SQL Section

This section gives you various SQL syntax options that you can choose for your export. You should check both the Structure and Data checkboxes.

Structure

Check the following SQL structure options:

- Add drop table

- Add `AUTO_INCREMENT` value

- Enclose table and fieldnames with backquotes

Data

Do not check any of the SQL insert syntax options (for example, Complete, Extended, or Delayed) but make sure that the export type is set to Insert.

Save as File Section

This section enables you to choose options about the exported file itself. If you want to save your export to a file (always helpful when you want to actually back up your data), check the Save as File option.

In Filename Template, you can set the name of the file to be saved to your desktop. The default is `__DB__`, which yields the database name plus the `.sql` file extension. This is fine for a one time backup, but I tend to prefer `%Y%m%d%H%M%S-__DB__`, which yields a time-stamped file-name (for example, `20040510120000-mt.sql`).

By default, the export will be downloaded in a plaintext file format. If, however, your exports are as big as mine (about 6MB), you may want to choose some form of compression to shorten your download and save on bandwidth. Note that due to a bug in the software at the time of writing, if you choose a compression format, the `.gz` and `.zip` extensions may not be added on, so you may want to add them yourself after the download is complete.

Go

Once you click the Go button, the download of your export file will proceed and `phpMyAdmin` will remember your settings for the next time.

Restoring via phpMyAdmin

To restore from a backup, click the SQL tab in the top menu bar. You will see a button labeled Choose File. Click it and select the file from your computer in the resulting dialog box. Leave the Compression option at Autodetect unless you experience problems. Click Go and your database will be restored. It just keeps getting simpler, doesn't it?

Summary

Movable Type integrates seamlessly with four database programs, the simpler, file-based programs BerkeleyDB and SQLite, and the more sophisticated relational databases MySQL and PostgreSQL. Because all four are either open source or public domain, the only costs to pay are in the time spent installing the programs and mastering their use.

Because Perl modules function as drivers, providing an interface between the MT content management system and a database, an MT user need not know anything about how the two programs interact.

This chapter just begins to demonstrate how you can abandon the know-nothing approach, take advantage of database knowledge, and extend the capabilities of an MT-driven website. You'll learn more in the next two chapters, "Tables in the MT Database" and "Absolutely Necessary Database Tricks."

Tables in the MT Database

I f you have ever done software development against a poorly structured database or seen one, you know how difficult life can be. Tables and/or columns named `'Cross Reference'`, `PendingUser-datas`, `days_in_advance_for_notifies`, `XX_KE_CMTR`, `pfield17`, and the ubiquitous `id` are enough to turn a relatively sane and stable individual into — well — neither.

Luckily, despite the growth of Movable Type (and its database) over the years, it is *not* one of those types.

As you may know, Movable Type is written in object-oriented (OO) Perl, which simply means that it is based on a collection of highly encapsulated and modular object classes (for example, blogs, authors, entries, comments, and templates) whose member objects have common attributes and interact with each other through each of their class methods.

Using a generic `Object` class (which is covered in Chapter 8) and Perl's DBI class, each major system object and its attributes are mapped directly into the database in the form of tables, fields, and records. That is, each major system class is a table, its attributes are columns in that table, and each instance of the class is a record in that table.

You can find a listing of each major system class and the table in which its objects are stored in Table 4-1. If you are unfamiliar with object-oriented concepts, see the sidebar later in this section entitled "A Quick Primer on MT and OO."

in this chapter

☑ The object-oriented MT database

☑ The naming scheme

☑ Full descriptions of each table in the MT database

Table 4-1 MT Classes Stored in the Database

Table	Class
mt_author	All authors and registered commenters in the MT installation
mt_blog	Blogs listed in the main menu of the admin interface
mt_category	All categories for all blogs in the installation
mt_comment	All comments submitted on all entries for all blogs in the installation

Continued

Table 4-1 (continued)

Table	Class
mt_entry	All entries for all blogs in the installation
mt_ipbanlist	All IP addresses banned across the installation
mt_log	The items in the Activity log
mt_notification	All e-mail addresses to be sent notifications for each blog
mt_permission	A mapping of author and commenter permissions for each blog
mt_placement	A mapping of the category assignments for each entry
mt_plugindata	Storage of configuration data for plugins that require persistence
mt_session	Active TypeKey sessions and caching of remote data
mt_tbping	Data of incoming TrackBack pings
mt_template	Templates for all blogs in the installation
mt_templatemap	A mapping of templates, blogs, and archiving types
mt_trackback	Information about pingable entries or categories in the system

A Quick Primer on MT and OO

If your eyes began to glaze over or perhaps beads of sweat formed on your brow when you read the words "object-oriented," I have good news for you: You don't really need to know anything about object-oriented programming to understand this chapter. That said, if you understand a few key concepts, the structure of the database will be clearer to you sooner rather than later.

The Movable Type system is made up of lots of "things." We can categorize these things into different classes. For example, some common things that can be grouped together include blogs, entries, authors, comments, and TrackBack pings. Each of these things is called an *object class*.

An object class has a set of *attributes* that are common to each member of that class. Every author has a login ID, a password, a nickname, and a password recovery hint, just to name a few. These are *class attributes*.

When you create a new author, you are creating an instance of the author class (that is, an author object), which inherits the attributes of that author class. This particular author object has a login ID, a password, a nickname, and a password recovery hint that are set at the time of creation. These things are attributes of the new author object.

All of these things are stored in the database in a regular and predictable way. There is a table for each class, a column in each table for each class attribute, and a record in the class's table for each instance of the class. For example, an author table contains records of authors containing values for name, password, author hint, and so on.

The object-oriented data storage model combined with a very consistent and predictable naming scheme for each table and column makes the Movable Type database as easy to understand as the underlying object-oriented code itself.

This chapter is a guided tour of every nook and cranny of the Movable Type database. You'll soon learn how all of your data is stored, and, in doing so, unlock all of the mysteries of this marvelous publishing platform.

What's in a Name?

A handful of easy-to-remember and fairly steadfast rules were adhered to in the design of the MT database. These rules make it easy to remember what tables and columns are called, which is important because there are over 15 tables and 190 columns.

Lowercase Only

All table and column names in the MT database have only lowercase letters. For example, Author becomes author, TrackBack becomes trackback, and so on.

Table Names

As you saw in Table 8-1, the name of a table is simply the name of the object prefixed with "mt_". Therefore, the table for the Author object is mt_author. The comment objects are stored in mt_comment. If the object name is two or more words, you drop the spaces. IP Ban List becomes mt_ipbanlist, and the Template map table is mt_templatemap.

Singular in Number

Although a table holds many things of one type, each record is still a single entity. Hence, all tables are named in the singular.

Column Names

The name of each column in a table is prefixed with the name of the table object. For example, in the mt_entry table, you will find an entry_id. The password of an author would be held in a table named mt_author in a column named author_password. Naming columns in this fashion removes all ambiguity (whether in SQL statements or documentation) regarding the table to which a column belongs. You know that entry_allow_comments is in the mt_entry table and template_text is in the mt_template table.

Underscores for Spaces

Although we eliminated the space between multiword object names for naming tables, looking at column names such as blog_manualapprovecommenters and blog_oldstylearchivelinks would get rather old quickly. Hence, for these we use underscores in places where there would naturally be a space. The extra keystrokes really make a difference: blog_manual_approve_commenters and blog_old_style_archive_links.

A Primary Key Is an "id"

Each table has a column by which a particular record can be uniquely identified. In the database world, this is called a *primary key*.

In the MT database, the primary key is always labeled "id" but follows the normal rules for column naming, as previously described. For example, the primary key for the mt_entry table is entry_id and in the mt_tbping table, tbping_id.

A Foreign Key Is Also a Primary Key

We now know that a comment record in mt_comment has a primary key called comment_id and that this column uniquely identifies the mt_comment record, but all comments are linked to an entry. To uniquely identify the entry to which a comment is linked, store the entry's primary key (entry_id) in the mt_comment record in a column called comment_entry_id.

A primary key from one table stored in another table to link the two records together is called a *foreign key*. In the MT database, a foreign key is named by appending the object name of the table onto the column name from the original table. A blog_id stored in the mt_template table is called template_blog_id. An author_id linked to a set of permissions in the mt_permission table would be a permission_author_id.

Things We Will Skip

Although in general these naming conventions make the database easy to understand, there are a handful of fields whose purpose may not be entirely obvious. Furthermore, many fields contain complex or enumerated options as data. This chapter covers all of these topics in detail.

However, due to the large number of tables and columns in the database, it would be impossible (or at least dreadfully boring) to go over each one in detail. The following list outlines what I will be skipping for most tables:

- **Primary keys** — While the primary key is perhaps the most important field in each table, it is also the most predictable. With the exception of mt_session, every primary key is simply an auto-incrementing integer that is unique within its table. I will, however, cover the deviant nature of session_id in the mt_session section.

- **Foreign keys** — Because foreign keys are simply primary keys from another table, I will not cover them unless the relationship between the two objects is not obvious. The exception to this is that the blog_id is a foreign key in almost every table, even if it is made redundant by another foreign key. The reason for its inclusion is usually for faster indexing and lookups and I will refrain from repeating that for every table.

- **Created and modified fields** — All fields ending in _created_on are date fields that indicate the date of record creation. They are in the format of YYYY-mm-dd HH:MM:SS — for example, 2004-04-23 17:55:01.

All fields ending in `_modified_on` are timestamp fields, which automatically record the time of any change to the record. Time in these fields is measured in Unix epoch time, or number of seconds since disco was first unleashed upon the world.

Many tables also have `_created_by` and `_modified_by` fields. These fields are currently unused (except for `author_created_by`) and therefore NULL in value. In a future version of MT, they may be used for tracking changes to the database for the purposes of an audit trail. For now, we will skip them.

MT Database Description

This chapter is intended to be a reference for all of your database hacking needs. Because of the length and amount of information contained herein, it is not recommended for light reading or if you need to operate a motor vehicle.

For each table, I will provide a short description of its purpose, followed by the table definition and a description of the important fields or those storing more complex values.

mt_author

If you've done any MT hacking in the past, you are probably very familiar with this table, as it holds the identification and authentication (login) data for all registered authors in the system. MT 3.0 expands the scope of this table by also including all TypeKey-authenticated commenters who leave a comment on your site. This was done in order to facilitate management of identity for the purposes of giving you more granular control over who can comment on your site and how (for example, moderated comments). By storing the details of authenticated commenters, MT remembers who you have accepted as an unrestricted commenter, whose comments must first be moderated, and whose comments are not welcome on your site.

However, because the functionality available to commenters is extremely limited in comparison to authors for whom the table was originally made, most of the fields are not applicable and remain NULL in value for their records. In the descriptions that follow, I will point out which fields do indeed contain data for commenters.

Table 4-2 defines mt_author.

Table 4-2   mt_author Definition

```
author_id int(11) NOT NULL auto_increment
```

```
author_name varchar(50) NOT NULL default ''
```

```
author_type tinyint(4) NOT NULL default '0'
```

```
author_nickname varchar(50) default NULL
```

Continued

<table>
<tr><td colspan="2">Table 4-2 (continued)</td></tr>
<tr><td colspan="2"><code>author_password varchar(60) NOT NULL default ''</code></td></tr>
<tr><td colspan="2"><code>author_email varchar(75) NOT NULL default ''</code></td></tr>
<tr><td colspan="2"><code>author_url varchar(255) default NULL</code></td></tr>
<tr><td colspan="2"><code>author_can_create_blog tinyint(4) default NULL</code></td></tr>
<tr><td colspan="2"><code>author_can_view_log tinyint(4) default NULL</code></td></tr>
<tr><td colspan="2"><code>author_hint varchar(75) default NULL</code></td></tr>
<tr><td colspan="2"><code>author_created_by int(11) default NULL</code></td></tr>
<tr><td colspan="2"><code>author_public_key text</code></td></tr>
<tr><td colspan="2"><code>author_preferred_language varchar(50) default NULL</code></td></tr>
<tr><td colspan="2"><code>author_remote_auth_username varchar(50) default NULL</code></td></tr>
<tr><td colspan="2"><code>author_remote_auth_token varchar(50) default NULL</code></td></tr>
<tr><td colspan="2">PRIMARY KEY: <code>author_id</code></td></tr>
<tr><td colspan="2">UNIQUE KEY: <code>author_name (author_name, author_type)</code></td></tr>
<tr><td colspan="2">INDEX: <code>author_email</code></td></tr>
</table>

author_name

This field holds the MT username for authors or the TypeKey username for commenters. This field is required but it is not, by itself, unique.

author_type

This field distinguishes between a regular author and a commenter with values of 1 and 2, respectively. This field and the preceding author_name field combine to form a unique key, which simply means that there cannot be two author records of the same author_type that have the same author_name.

Note that author records (type 1) and commenter records (type 2) in the mt_author table give users completely different and mutually exclusive capabilities. If a user is both an author and an authenticated commenter, that user will be represented by two distinct records, one for each role. This means that on a blog that requires TypeKey authentication, even a blog author can be banned from commenting. If you needed further proof that you should be nice to (or wary of) your co-authors, this is it.

author_nickname

For authors, this field is optional and is set from the author's profile page. For commenters, this field is set to the display name in the user's TypeKey profile at the time of authentication.

If a user changes her TypeKey nickname, her record in the mt_author table will be updated to reflect the new information. It does not mean, however, that previous comments will reflect that change, because the nickname displayed with the comment is permanently stored with the comment record in the mt_comment table.

author_password

This field holds the author's password, encrypted with Perl's `crypt` function using a random salt value. For commenters, this field is always "(none)," as commenters are not authorized to log in.

author_email

For authors, this field contains the e-mail address set in the author's profile. For commenters, this field will normally contain the e-mail address listed in the user's TypeKey profile, although if the weblog configuration does not require revelation of the e-mail address to the weblog authors and the commenter declines to reveal it, it will be encrypted.

Like author_nickname, this field is updated after each TypeKey login for registered commenters.

author_can_create_blog and author_can_view_log

These fields are Boolean flags indicating whether the author is permitted to create blogs or view the system activity log, respectively. For commenters, they are always NULL.

author_created_by

This field contains the author_id of the author who created the author and hence the record. This field is NULL for the initial author created by `mt-load.cgi` as well as for commenters.

author_public_key

This field is currently unused, but in a future version of MT it will hold the author's ASCII-armored public key, with which the system can authenticate incoming e-mail messages from authors for the purpose of remote posting, editing, and configuration.

author_preferred_language

Movable Type can be localized in many different languages through the use of language packs downloadable from movabletype.org. This field holds the author's preferred language, and the interface uses the images and text mappings found in the appropriate language pack. If the value of this field is NULL or if the language pack for the preferred language is removed, the application defaults to American English. This value is NULL for commenters.

author_remote_auth_username and author_remote_auth_token

These fields are currently unused. In the future, they will enable remote TypeKey services.

mt_blog

This table contains all of the configuration data for each weblog in the system. Each of the table's 48 fields precisely match a well-explained option on the weblog configuration screens.

For the sake of brevity, only a few of the more interesting fields are covered in the following sections.

Table 4-3 defines mt_blog.

Table 4-3   mt_blog Definition

```
blog_id int(11) NOT NULL auto_increment
blog_name varchar(255) NOT NULL default ''
blog_description text
blog_site_path varchar(255) default NULL
blog_site_url varchar(255) default NULL
blog_archive_path varchar(255) default NULL
blog_archive_url varchar(255) default NULL
blog_archive_type varchar(255) default NULL
blog_archive_type_preferred varchar(25) default NULL
blog_days_on_index smallint(6) default NULL
blog_language varchar(5) default NULL
blog_file_extension varchar(10) default NULL
blog_email_new_comments tinyint(4) default NULL
blog_email_new_pings tinyint(4) default NULL
blog_allow_comment_html tinyint(4) default NULL
blog_autolink_urls tinyint(4) default NULL
blog_sort_order_posts varchar(8) default NULL
blog_sort_order_comments varchar(8) default NULL
blog_allow_comments_default tinyint(4) default NULL
blog_allow_pings_default tinyint(4) default NULL
blog_server_offset float default NULL
blog_convert_paras varchar(30) default NULL
blog_convert_paras_comments varchar(30) default NULL
blog_status_default tinyint(4) default NULL
blog_allow_anon_comments tinyint(4) default NULL
blog_allow_reg_comments tinyint(4) default NULL
blog_allow_unreg_comments tinyint(4) default NULL
```

```
blog_moderate_unreg_comments tinyint(4) default NULL

blog_require_comment_emails tinyint(4) default NULL

blog_manual_approve_commenters tinyint(4) default NULL

blog_words_in_excerpt smallint(6) default NULL

blog_ping_weblogs tinyint(4) default NULL

blog_ping_blogs tinyint(4) default NULL

blog_ping_others text

blog_mt_update_key varchar(30) default NULL

blog_autodiscover_links tinyint(4) default NULL

blog_welcome_msg text

blog_old_style_archive_links tinyint(4) default NULL

blog_archive_tmpl_monthly varchar(255) default NULL

blog_archive_tmpl_weekly varchar(255) default NULL

blog_archive_tmpl_daily varchar(255) default NULL

blog_archive_tmpl_individual varchar(255) default NULL

blog_archive_tmpl_category varchar(255) default NULL

blog_google_api_key varchar(32) default NULL

blog_sanitize_spec varchar(255) default NULL

blog_cc_license varchar(255) default NULL

blog_is_dynamic tinyint(4) default NULL

blog_remote_auth_token varchar(50) default NULL
```

PRIMARY KEY: blog_id

INDEX: blog_name (blog_name)

blog_archive_type

This field, set via Weblog Config ➪ Archiving, is a comma-separated list of all archive types used for the blog in question. The archive type options (case-sensitive) are Individual, Daily, Weekly, Monthly, and Category.

blog_allow_comment_html

This Boolean flag specifies whether HTML should be stripped from comments when they are displayed or when a page containing comments is built. Regardless of value, MT always stores the comment as it was input into the system by the commenter. If HTML is allowed in comments, it will be sanitized according to the blog_sanitize_spec or that listed in the mt.cfg file.

blog_allow_comments_default

This field holds the default value for the comments setting on new entries (see entry_allow_comments for further description).

blog_allow_pings_default

This field holds the default Boolean value for "Allow Incoming Pings" on new entries (also see entry_allow_pings).

blog_convert_paras and blog_convert_paras_comments

These two fields, misnamed for historical reasons, hold the blog's default value for text formatting of new entries and comments, respectively.

Possible values for these fields include the following:

- "0" for no conversion

- "__default__" for the default Movable Type paragraph conversion

- The unique identifier provided by any text formatting plugins via the MT ⇨ add_text_filter() function discussed in Chapter 10

Multiple comma-separated values are allowed and the filters will be applied in the order of appearance. However, in the current interface, there is no way to select multiple filters, so you will rarely ever see multiple values in these fields. (Also see entry_convert_breaks for more information.)

blog_status_default

This field holds the default status value for the new entries. (See entry_status for possible values.)

blog_allow_anon_comments, blog_allow_unreg_comments, and blog_allow_reg_comments

These three Boolean fields make up a trinary option that dictates the level of commenter anonymity allowed for the blog.

The possible combinations and meanings of those combinations are described in Table 4-4. Note that a true value (1) for allow_unreg_comments effectively overrides allow_anon_comments.

Table 4-4 Comment Identity Configuration Setting

Type	allow_anon	allow_unreg	Commenters Allowed
Anonymous	1	1	All
Not anonymous	0	1	Non-anonymous and registered
Registered	0	0	Registered

blog_moderate_unreg_comments

This Boolean flag dictates whether comments from unregistered commenters should be approved before being displayed on the blog.

blog_require_comment_emails

This Boolean flag dictates whether an e-mail address is required from registered commenters. If this flag is set to 0, the e-mail address will be returned from the TypeKey login but will be encrypted.

blog_manual_approve_commenters

This Boolean flag determines whether registered commenters should be approved before their comments will be displayed. Note that this is different from blog_moderate_unreg_comments, which forces approval of the comments and not the commenter because the true identity of an unregistered commenter is not known.

blog_archive_tmpl_*

These five columns with names that begin with blog_archive_tmpl are no longer used but remain for backward compatibility.

blog_is_dynamic

This Boolean field indicates whether a blog should be dynamically rendered with `mt-view.cgi` or be statically published.

blog_remote_auth_token

This is the blog's TypeKey authorization token. This token enables the TypeKey moderation and registration features for the blog's comments.

mt_category

The mt_category table contains information on every category in all blogs across the installation. Categories may have the same label, but must be unique within the same blog. Hence, category_blog_id and category_label combine to form a unique binary key.

Table 4-5 defines mt_category.

Table 4-5   mt_category Definition
`category_id int(11) NOT NULL auto_increment`
`category_blog_id int(11) NOT NULL default '0'`
`category_allow_pings tinyint(4) default NULL`
`category_label varchar(100) NOT NULL default ''`
`category_description text`

Continued

Table 4-5 (continued)

`category_author_id int(11) default NULL`

`category_ping_urls text`

PRIMARY KEY: `category_id`

UNIQUE KEY: `category_blog_id(category_blog_id,category_label)`

---

category_allow_pings

This Boolean value determines whether a category can receive pings or not. When pings are enabled for a category, a record is created in mt_trackback and the inverse of this value is cached in trackback_is_disabled.

category_author_id

This field holds the primary key of the author who created the category. It currently has no purpose within the program.

category_ping_urls

This is a carriage-return-separated list of TrackBack URLs to ping when an entry is saved with the category of record assigned to it.

mt_comment

This table holds information about comments submitted to any entry in any blog of the installation.

Table 4-6 defines mt_comment.

Table 4-6   mt_comment Definition

`comment_id int(11) NOT NULL auto_increment`

`comment_blog_id int(11) NOT NULL default '0'`

`comment_entry_id int(11) NOT NULL default '0'`

`comment_ip varchar(16) default NULL`

`comment_author varchar(100) default NULL`

`comment_email varchar(75) default NULL`

`comment_url varchar(255) default NULL`

`comment_commenter_id int(11) default NULL`

```
comment_visible tinyint(4) default NULL
comment_text text
comment_created_on datetime NOT NULL default '0000-00-00 00:00:00'
comment_modified_on timestamp(14) NOT NULL
comment_created_by int(11) default NULL
comment_modified_by int(11) default NULL
PRIMARY KEY: comment_id
INDEXES: comment_created_on, comment_entry_id, comment_blog_id
```

comment_ip

This field contains the IP address of the commenter.

comment_author

This field contains either the commenter's name as input into the comment submission form or, in the case of authenticated commenters, the nickname specified on the user's TypeKey profile page. If anonymous comments are allowed, this field can be NULL.

comment_email

Gone are the days when this was a simple text input field. In MT 3.0, the contents of this field are as follows:

1. If the blog requires an e-mail address from the commenter, the e-mail address will be the value stored.

2. If the blog does not require e-mail from TypeKey-authenticated commenters, this field will be the encrypted e-mail address of any TypeKey-authenticated commenter.

3. If the blog allows unregistered, anonymous commenters, the e-mail field may be left blank and hence NULL.

In the first two cases, if the commenter is a TypeKey-authenticated commenter, the comment_email field will be assigned the value of the author_email field after the TypeKey login.

One important thing to note is that if you later change the blog's e-mail address requirements, the effect is not retroactive. You cannot make previous comments with no e-mails disappear just by turning on the requirement in the Weblog Config, nor will past comments from TypeKey-authenticated commenters be encrypted.

comment_url and comment_text

These fields contain the input from the comment form. The comment_url field may be NULL.

comment_commenter_id

For a comment by a registered commenter, this field contains their author_id. In all other cases, it is NULL.

Note that, for purposes of clarity, this column represents a deviation from the MT database naming scheme. Normally, this would be comment_author_id because it is a foreign key from the mt_author table.

comment_visible

This Boolean value determines whether a comment should be shown upon rebuild or whether it is still pending moderation.

mt_entry

This table holds information related to every entry posted to any blog in the installation.

Table 4-7 defines mt_entry.

Table 4-7   mt_entry Definition

entry_id int(11) NOT NULL auto_increment
entry_blog_id int(11) NOT NULL default '0'
entry_status tinyint(4) NOT NULL default '0'
entry_author_id int(11) NOT NULL default '0'
entry_allow_comments tinyint(4) default NULL
entry_allow_pings tinyint(4) default NULL
entry_convert_breaks varchar(30) default NULL
entry_category_id int(11) default NULL
entry_title varchar(255) default NULL
entry_excerpt text
entry_text text
entry_text_more text
entry_to_ping_urls text
entry_pinged_urls text
entry_keywords text
entry_tangent_cache text
entry_created_on datetime NOT NULL default '0000-00-00 00:00:00'
entry_modified_on timestamp(14) NOT NULL
entry_created_by int(11) default NULL

`entry_modified_by int(11) default NULL`
`entry_basename varchar(50) default NULL`
PRIMARY KEY: `entry_id`
INDEXES: `entry_blog_id`, `entry_status`, `entry_author_id`, `entry_created_on`

entry_status

This field indicates whether an entry should be published upon rebuild. Draft and Publish are represented by values of 1 and 2, respectively, in this field. Throughout the MT source code, these values are represented by the constants HOLD and RELEASE. (Also see blog_status_default.)

entry_allow_comments

This value indicates whether comments are disallowed, open, or closed for an entry, with values of 0, 1, and 2, respectively. (Also see blog_allow_comments_default.)

entry_allow_pings

This Boolean value determines whether an entry can receive pings or not. When pings are enabled for an entry, a record is created in mt_trackback and the inverse of this value is cached in trackback_is_disabled. (Also see blog_allow_pings_default.)

entry_convert_breaks

This field holds the text formatting preference for the entry. (See blog_convert_paras for more information.)

entry_category_id

This field is unused and exists only for backward compatibility of upgrades from older versions of Movable Type.

entry_title, entry_text, entry_text_more, entry_excerpt, and entry_keywords

These fields hold the content for the four major text input sections of the entry editing screen. If entry_excerpt is NULL or empty, the excerpt is dynamically created from the entry_text when needed.

entry_to_ping_urls

This field contains a list of all URLs to ping the next time the entry is saved. Although usually a non-NULL value for this field indicates that the entry has not yet been published, failed pings from published entries will also remain stored here until successfully sent.

entry_pinged_urls

This field contains a list of all pings sent at some point during the saving of an entry. If a URL is pinged more than once, duplicates can exist in this field.

entry_tangent_cache

The tangent_cache is a field created for use with the Tangent plugin, which connects web entries from different sites together. Weblog entries are sent to Tangent, receive links from other sites based on the content of the entries, and are presented. See www.tangent.cx for more information.

entry_basename

This field holds the default basename for the entry's individual archive file. In most cases, it is a version of the real or derived entry title, which alters the title to make it suitable for use as a directory name by removing HTML tags, making characters lowercase, stripping non-alphanumeric characters other than underscore (_), and replacing spaces with underscores. The result will be truncated to 15 characters.

The basename is used to avoid the creation of conflicting individual archive filenames for identically titled entries in a given blog. If there is a matching basename on another entry in the same blog, an incremented counter value is appended with an underscore (for example, my_post, my_post_1, my_post_2, and so on).

The entry_basename is ignored if an Archive File template is specified for the individual archive under Weblog Config ➪ Archive Files.

mt_ipbanlist

mt_ipbanlist holds the records for each IP address a user has banned for incoming comments or TrackBacks. Each record contains blog_id, so the settings are on a per-blog basis.

Despite the fact that this field is evaluated as a regular expression, making it possible to ban ranges of IP addresses, this functionality is rarely effective for dismissing unwanted commenters due to the proliferation of dynamic IP addressing for dialup and DSL users. TrackBacks, on the other hand, tend to come from servers with fixed IP addresses and can be easily isolated. Table 4-8 defines mt_ipbanlist.

Table 4-8   mt_ipbanlist Definition

ipbanlist_id int(11) NOT NULL auto_increment
ipbanlist_blog_id int(11) NOT NULL default '0'
ipbanlist_ip varchar(15) NOT NULL default ''
ipbanlist_created_on datetime NOT NULL default '0000-00-00 00:00:00'
ipbanlist_modified_on timestamp(14) NOT NULL
ipbanlist_created_by int(11) default NULL
ipbanlist_modified_by int(11) default NULL
PRIMARY KEY: ipbanlist_id
INDEXES: ipbanlist_blog_id, ipbanlist_ip

mt_log

The mt_log table holds information about each entry in the system-wide activity log accessible from the main menu of the administrative interface. Table 4-9 defines mt_log.

Table 4-9   mt_log Definition

log_id int(11) NOT NULL auto_increment
log_message varchar(255) default NULL
log_ip varchar(16) default NULL
log_created_on datetime NOT NULL default '0000-00-00 00:00:00'
log_modified_on timestamp(14) NOT NULL
log_created_by int(11) default NULL
log_modified_by int(11) default NULL
PRIMARY KEY: log_id
INDEX: log_created_on (log_created_on)

If a log item is created in response to a user's action, the log_ip field contains that user's IP address. The field can be NULL if it's not applicable. For example, if MT-Rebuild, a plugin that is run via cron, were to put an entry in the activity log, log_ip would be NULL.

mt_notification

Table 4-10 defines mt_notification.

Table 4-10   mt_notification Definition

notification_id int(11) NOT NULL auto_increment
notification_blog_id int(11) NOT NULL default '0'
notification_name varchar(50) default NULL
notification_email varchar(75) default NULL
notification_url varchar(255) default NULL
notification_created_on datetime NOT NULL default '0000-00-00 00:00:00'
notification_modified_on timestamp(14) NOT NULL
notification_created_by int(11) default NULL

Continued

Table 4-10 *(continued)*

notification_modified_by int(11) default NULL
PRIMARY KEY: notification_id
INDEX: notification_blog_id (notification_blog_id)

---

mt_permission

The main purpose of this table is to store author permissions for each blog. For instance, one record may give an author permission to do anything to a particular blog, while another record may restrict that author to simply being able to comment on a second blog. For each author/ blog combination, a record will be stored in mt_permission detailing this permission level.

This table also holds display preferences for the entry editing screen for each author.

Table 4-11 defines mt_permission.

Table 4-11   mt_permission Definition

permission_id int(11) NOT NULL auto_increment
permission_author_id int(11) NOT NULL default '0'
permission_blog_id int(11) NOT NULL default '0'
permission_role_mask smallint(6) default NULL
permission_entry_prefs varchar(255) default NULL
PRIMARY KEY: permission_id
UNIQUE KEY: permission_blog_id (permission_blog_id,permission_author_id)

permission_author_id and permission_blog_id

These foreign keys uniquely identify the author and blog for which the permissions detailed in permission_role_mask will be applied.

permission_role_mask

This integer value determines what permissions an author or commenter has for a particular blog. User permissions and calculation of the permission_role_mask are discussed in Chapter 8, "Perl API."

permission_entry_prefs

This field holds an author's layout preferences for the entry editing screen on a particular blog. The format for this field is as follows:

```
FIELDS|POSITION
```

POSITION is the position of the Save/Preview/Delete Entry button bar and can be either Top or Bottom. FIELDS indicates the type of layout or user interface (UI) elements to be included. Acceptable values are Basic, Advanced, or a comma-separated listing of the following:

- category
- extended
- excerpt
- keywords
- allow_comments
- convert_breaks
- allow_pings
- authored_on
- ping_urls

mt_placement

The mt_placement table holds information about the relationships between each entry and any categories to which it may be assigned. In the MT system, an entry can have any number of categories (or *placements*) but only one can be the primary category.

Each record in mt_placement is an entry-category assignment and consists of a primary key, three foreign keys (entry_id, category_id, and blog_id), and one Boolean field to designate the primary category for the entry. Table 4-12 defines mt_placement.

Table 4-12   mt_placement Definition

placement_id int(11) NOT NULL auto_increment
placement_entry_id int(11) NOT NULL default '0'
placement_blog_id int(11) NOT NULL default '0'
placement_category_id int(11) NOT NULL default '0'
placement_is_primary tinyint(4) NOT NULL default '0'
PRIMARY KEY: placement_id
INDEXES: placement_entry_id, placement_category_id, placement_is_primary

mt_plugindata

Most plugins are fairly simple in that they take raw data as an input and simply return it in some consistently processed way. They need no further instructions and they don't need to know what happened the last time they did their work.

Other plugins, however, require detailed configuration or "persistent memory" from one call to the next in order to operate (for example, MT-Blacklist and the subcategories plugin) For these plugins, mt_plugindata offers structured, protected persistent storage that is easily accessible through the Plugin API.

Table 4-13 defines mt_plugindata.

Table 4-13   mt_plugindata Definition
`plugindata_id int(11)` NOT NULL `auto_increment`
`plugindata_plugin varchar(50)` NOT NULL default `''`
`plugindata_key varchar(255)` NOT NULL default `''`
`plugindata_data mediumtext`
PRIMARY KEY: `plugindata_id`
INDEXES: `plugindata_plugin, plugindata_key`

plugindata_plugin

This field holds a name that uniquely identifies the plugin storing the data. This field creates a namespace for the plugin in the mt_plugindata table so that there is no clash between similarly named plugindata_keys.

plugindata_key

This field provides the name or label of the data being stored. This is like the key in an associative array. This field and the preceding plugindata_plugin field combine to form a unique binary key.

plugindata_data

This field contains the serialized data structure stored by the plugin function. Because of its binary format, this field is not directly editable.

mt_session

Three components of the Movable Type system have limited life spans. During these life spans, otherwise known as *sessions*, information about these elements is stored in the mt_session table.

The three nonpersistent elements are as follows:

- Commenter authentication state and related information
- A cache of the TypeKey public DSA encryption key
- A cache of the news box on the main MT administration page for Movable Type news

Table 4-14 briefly lists the contents for each field.

Table 4-14 mt_session Definition

`session_id varchar(80) NOT NULL default ''`
`session_data text`
`session_email varchar(255) default NULL`
`session_name varchar(255) default NULL`
`session_start int(11) NOT NULL default '0'`
`session_kind char(2) default NULL`
PRIMARY KEY: `session_id`
INDEXES: `session_start`

session_id

The session_id field contains the following:

- For commenter sessions, the sig string returned from TypeKey authentication. This string is also stored in the tk_commenter cookie.
- For the public key cache, a timestamp plus eight random characters.
- For the news box cache, it is an empty (but non_NULL) string.

session_data

The session_data field contains the following:

- For commenter sessions, this field is `NULL`.
- For the public key cache, this field holds the TypeKey public DSA key.
- For the news box cache, this holds the cached news items.

session_email

The session_email field contains the following:

- For commenter sessions, this is the e-mail returned from the TypeKey login. It may be encrypted depending on the setting in blog_require_comment_email.
- For the public key cache and new box cache, this field is NULL.

session_name

The session_name field contains the following:

- For commenter sessions, it is the TypeKey login ID also stored in author_name.
- For the public key cache and news box cache, this field has a NULL value.

session_start

For all sessions, session_start is the "created on" timestamp in UNIX epoch time.

session_kind

The session_kind field contains the following:

- SI for commenter sessions
- KY for the public key cache
- NW for the news box cache

mt_tbping

This table holds information about incoming TrackBack pings. Records in mt_tbping are not directly associated with the object of the ping, but instead with a record in mt_trackback. (See mt_trackback for more details.)

Table 4-15 defines mt_tbping.

Table 4-15   mt_tbping Definition

tbping_id int(11) NOT NULL auto_increment
tbping_blog_id int(11) NOT NULL default '0'
tbping_tb_id int(11) NOT NULL default '0'
tbping_title varchar(255) default NULL
tbping_excerpt text
tbping_source_url varchar(255) default NULL

tbping_ip varchar(15) NOT NULL default ''
tbping_blog_name varchar(255) default NULL
tbping_created_on datetime NOT NULL default '0000-00-00 00:00:00'
tbping_modified_on timestamp(14) NOT NULL
tbping_created_by int(11) default NULL
tbping_modified_by int(11) default NULL
PRIMARY KEY: tbping_id
INDEXES: tbping_blog_id, tbping_tb_id, tbping_ip, tbping_created_on

tbping_tb_id

This field contains the ID of the mt_trackback record for the pinged item.

tbping_title

This field contains the title of the source entry from which a TrackBack item was pinged. If the ping was sent with no title, either the first five words of the excerpt or the entry's entire URL is used, in that order of preference.

tbping_excerpt

This contains the excerpt of the entry from which a TrackBack item was pinged. If the excerpt is longer than 255 characters, it is trimmed to 252 and ellipses (...) are added to the end.

tbping_ip

This field contains the IP address of the source of the ping.

tbping_blog_name

This field contains the name of the blog from which the ping was sent.

mt_template

The mt_template table holds information about templates and their related input and output files. It is the source of the Template listing screen in the MT administrative interface for each blog.

Table 4-16 defines mt_template.

Table 4-16   mt_template Definition

template_id int(11) NOT NULL auto_increment
template_blog_id int(11) NOT NULL default '0'

Continued

Table 4-16 *(continued)*

```
template_name varchar(50) NOT NULL default ''
```

```
template_type varchar(25) NOT NULL default ''
```

```
template_outfile varchar(255) default NULL
```

```
template_rebuild_me tinyint(4) default '1'
```

```
template_text text
```

```
template_linked_file varchar(255) default NULL
```

```
template_linked_file_mtime varchar(10) default NULL
```

```
template_linked_file_size mediumint(9) default NULL
```

PRIMARY KEY: `template_id`

UNIQUE KEY: `template_blog_id (template_blog_id,template_name)`

INDEXES: `template_type`

template_type

This field indicates what type of template the record is storing. Functionally, there are 10 different types of templates in the MT system, each having its own special purpose and set of allowed and relevant tags.

The following is a list of the possible values of this field, followed by a short description of its purpose:

- index — Used for generating one single page
- archive — Used for generating date-based archives (Daily, Weekly, Monthly)
- category — Used for generating category archives
- individual — Used for generating individual (per-entry) archives
- custom — Custom template modules for inclusion in other templates
- comment_preview — Template for dynamic comment preview page
- comment_pending — Template for dynamic comment moderated page
- comment_error — Template for error display page for invalid comments
- popup_image — Popup page for displaying uploaded images
- comments — Comment listing page
- pings — TrackBack ping listing page

In a default MT 3.0 installation, you will have seven index templates and one of each of the other types except for custom.

template_outfile

The template_outfile field holds the path to the file where the final static output produced from an index template will be stored. This field is only relevant (non-NULL) for Index templates. Comment, Trackback, and file upload templates are used by the application to dynamically generate pages, and the output files for the other archiving types (archive, category, individual, and so on) are specified in templatemap_file_template because they generate more than one file upon rebuild.

Like all filepaths stored in the MT database, this field can be either an absolute path or relative to the Local Site Path setting under Weblog Config ➪ Core Setup.

template_rebuild_me

This Boolean field determines whether or not the template should be included when all templates or templates of its type are rebuilt. Like template_outfile, this field is only relevant to index files.

Note that for purposes of backward compatibility with older versions of MT, a NULL value in this field is assumed to have a true value, meaning that an index template must have an explicitly set value of 0 to be excluded from rebuilding.

template_linked_file

This field holds the filepath for the file optionally linked to the template.

Like all filepaths stored in the MT database, this field can be either an absolute path or relative to the Local Site Path setting under Weblog Config ➪ Core Setup.

template_linked_file_mtime and template_linked_file_size

These two fields hold the last-known modification time and size of the linked file and indicate whether the content stored in template_text is current for the purposes of rebuilding. Upon check, if either of these file attributes differs from the stored values, the linked file's contents, modification time (mtime), and size are recached in the database.

The modification time is measured in seconds since the UNIX epoch (1970). The file size is measured in bytes.

mt_templatemap

When you create a new archive under Weblog Config ➪ Archiving, a templatemap record is created. Each record represents an association between a blog, a template, and an archive type.

This little understood and underutilized feature enables you, for example, to create an individual entry RSS feed containing comments and TrackBacks, in addition to your regular individual archives.

Table 4-17 defines mt_templatemap.

<table>
<tr><td colspan="2">Table 4-17   mt_templatemap Definition</td></tr>
<tr><td colspan="2"><code>templatemap_id int(11) NOT NULL auto_increment</code></td></tr>
<tr><td colspan="2"><code>templatemap_blog_id int(11) NOT NULL default '0'</code></td></tr>
<tr><td colspan="2"><code>templatemap_template_id int(11) NOT NULL default '0'</code></td></tr>
<tr><td colspan="2"><code>templatemap_archive_type varchar(25) NOT NULL default ''</code></td></tr>
<tr><td colspan="2"><code>templatemap_file_template varchar(255) default NULL</code></td></tr>
<tr><td colspan="2"><code>templatemap_is_preferred tinyint(4) NOT NULL default '0'</code></td></tr>
<tr><td colspan="2">PRIMARY KEY: <code>templatemap_id</code></td></tr>
<tr><td colspan="2">INDEXES: <code>templatemap_blog_id, templatemap_template_id, templatemap_archive_type, templatemap_is_preferred</code></td></tr>
</table>

templatemap_archive_type

This value provides MT with the necessary context to compile the tags contained within the template. The valid archive types are as follows:

- Individual
- Daily
- Weekly
- Monthly
- Category

templatemap_file_template

In producing the archive set, MT needs to know where the files are to be stored. This path and filename schema is created using regular MT template tags as variables and stored in this field. In the MT interface, you will see this schema referred to as an "Archive File Template," which, unfortunately, is most confusing for novice users for obvious reasons.

If, for example, you wanted to store your individual entries by category, you would create and put the following in your Individual Archive File Template:

```
<$MTEntryCategory dirify="1"$>/<$MTEntryTitle dirify="1"$>
```

templatemap_is_preferred

This Boolean field determines whether the given templatemap should be used as the preferred archive in constructing links to the archive for the `<$MTEntryPermalink$>`, `<$MTEntryLink$>`, `<$MTArchiveLink$>`, and `<$MTCategoryArchiveLink$>` tags.

In the previous individual entry RSS feed example, you would probably want to set your normal Individual archives as your preferred archive of the two so that `<$MTEntryPermalink$>` doesn't point to an XML file.

mt_trackback

mt_trackback holds information about each entry or category in the MT install that can be pinged or was pingable at some point in the past. It does not contain any information about incoming pings, as that information is held in the mt_tbping table.

Table 4-18 defines mt_trackback.

Table 4-18   mt_trackback Definition

```
trackback_id int(11) NOT NULL auto_increment

trackback_blog_id int(11) NOT NULL default '0'

trackback_title varchar(255) default NULL

trackback_description text

trackback_rss_file varchar(255) default NULL

trackback_url varchar(255) default NULL

trackback_entry_id int(11) NOT NULL default '0'

trackback_category_id int(11) NOT NULL default '0'

trackback_passphrase varchar(30) default NULL

trackback_is_disabled tinyint(4) default '0'

trackback_created_on datetime NOT NULL default '0000-00-00 00:00:00'

trackback_modified_on timestamp(14) NOT NULL

trackback_created_by int(11) default NULL

trackback_modified_by int(11) default NULL
```

PRIMARY KEY: `trackback_id`

INDEXES: `trackback_blog_id, trackback_entry_id, trackback_category_id, trackback_created_on`

trackback_title, trackback_description, and trackback_url

These fields cache information about the TrackBack item either found in other tables or normally processed through other means. For entries, they contain the title, excerpt, and URL to the archived entry in the preferred archive. For categories, they contain the category label, description, and URL to the category archive.

They are cached so that if an RSS file is generated for each TrackBack item (see GenerateTrackbackRSS in the mt.cfg or the TrackBack section of the Movable Type manual), it can be compiled quickly so that the connection with the remote server sending the ping won't time out. When any of these fields are changed in their source tables, the information is updated in the mt_trackback table.

trackback_rss_file

This field is currently unused. All TrackBack RSS files are named using the TrackBack ID and .xml.

trackback_entry_id and trackback_category_id

For each record, one of these two fields will contain the ID of the item that accepts incoming pings and the other will have a value of 0. The column in this table with the non-zero value (that is, a valid entry_id) determines whether the record is a category or entry TrackBack item.

trackback_passphrase

This field holds an optional passphrase chosen to protect a category enabled for pinging. The passphrase is held in clear text and is transmitted as part of the ping URL. For example, in the following URL, the trackback_id is 1 and whodooyoulove is the trackback_passphrase:

```
http://jayallen.org/mt/mt-tb.cgi/1/whodooyoulove
```

trackback_is_disabled

This Boolean field indicates whether a certain TrackBack item can receive pings or not. Like trackback_title et al, this value exists in mt_trackback only for lookup optimization. The value is the inverse value of entry_allow_pings and category_allow_pings.

Summary

Movable Type content ends up in a relational database as tables that contain a specific kind of information, including mt_comment for visitor comments, mt_entry for weblog entries, and mt_ipbanlist for IP addresses blocked from submitting comments and TrackBack pings.

You can work with these database tables from Movable Type plugins or external software, manipulating web content in whatever manner meets your needs.

Absolutely Necessary Database Tricks

At this point you know everything there is to know about how Movable Type stores your data. You understand that each table is a system object and that the fields in the table are simply its attributes. You are probably also now well familiar with the naming scheme. Therefore, the next question is, what can you do with that data?

The answer is, quite literally, "anything you can think of."

This chapter demonstrates just a handful of useful techniques that can make your life easier and your site richer. The examples herein are sometimes complex and intrinsically heavy on usage of Structured Query Language (SQL). However, even if you are a veritable newbie, the task-oriented, cookbook nature of this chapter, combined with the careful explanation of each SQL statement, will make it easy for you to follow along and join in the fun!

Before performing any of the feats in this chapter, please back up your database as described in Chapter 3. One command can erase a lifetime of content. It's always better to be safe than sorry.

Database Backup

Chapter 3 covered how to back up and restore your database. This is extremely important and useful information that must not only be understood, but also practiced regularly. Typically, the two biggest barriers to performing regular backups are the difficulty of the operation itself and remembering or consistently having the time to do it.

As previously shown, backing up a MySQL database is not difficult, but how can you make it so easy that you'll never forget and never lack the time to do it?

The answer is simple: *cron*.

Cron is every UNIX user's best friend. It is a program installed by default on all UNIX platforms that enables you to schedule jobs to run at a certain time in the future and to specify a frequency for execution.

Everything that you can do from the command line you can also do through cron. Each user has his or her own cron job schedule, otherwise known as a *crontab*. The UNIX system manages all of these jobs and executes them at the times specified by the owner.

In many cases, web-hosting companies offer crontab access through your account control panel. These web-based control panels offer a much easier editing interface than is available via the command line due to the fairly arcane format of the crontab. If you are not well versed in command-line basics and UNIX text editors, you may find this option preferable.

If you don't have control panel access to cron or you are at least somewhat familiar with UNIX, you can access cron from the command line. To list the jobs in your crontab, type the following:

```
crontab -l
```

If you want to edit your crontab, simply type the following:

```
crontab -e
```

At this point, your default editor will start and provide you with a space to enter or edit your scheduled jobs. When you quit your editor, your changes will be saved and scheduled in the system.

The Crontab Format

If you must go in through the shell, the crontab format can be a bit overwhelming. I will give you the very basics in order to get you started. You can read the manual pages for crontab, which describe the format in detail, by typing the following at the command line:

```
man 5 crontab
```

In short, each line of the crontab file is a command. Two types of commands are allowed in the crontab: job scheduling and environment setting commands.

Scheduling commands are divided into six fields that are space-delimited. The fields and their acceptable values are as follows:

```
minute          0-59
hour            0-23
day of month    1-31
month           1-12 (or names, see below)
day of week     0-7 (either 0 or 7 is Sun, or use names)
job command     See below
```

For all of the time and date fields, you can either specify a value from the preceding list or use an asterisk (*). Asterisks are wildcards that indicate that all of the values of that field are to be assumed. A better way to think of it, however, is that an asterisk indicates that there is no restriction for that field.

For example, if you wanted a command to run every day at 2:00 A.M., the date fields (we will get to the job command in a second) would look like this:

```
0 2 * * *
```

The 2 indicates the hour (on a 24-hour system) and the 0 indicates 0 minutes. Because this job will run every day, there are no restrictions on the other fields, so they contain asterisks.

The job command field is the command that you would issue if you were performing the action from the command line.

Scheduling the Backup

For the purposes of this tip, we only need to use a few of the fields above. How often you back up depends on how active your site is in terms of comments, TrackBacks, and entries. If you have a low-traffic site, backing up twice per month may be acceptable. Your entry in crontab would be as follows:

```
0 1 1,15 * *  mysqldump -a -u USERNAME -p PASSWORD DATABASE >
~/backups/`date +%Y%m%d`_backup.mysql
```

Replacing the all-caps placeholders with their actual values will produce a time-stamped (YYYYMMDD) dump of your database at 1:00 A.M. on the first and fifteenth of every month, placed in a previously created directory in your home directory called `backups`. Because each backup is time-stamped, your backups are never overwritten and you can download them at your leisure.

Putting your MySQL password in your crontab causes it to show up in the process listing (`ps -aux`) for the duration of the program execution. Because database dumps usually take only a second or two, I consider this an acceptable risk.

However, if you would prefer to avoid this, you can look into using the `expect` program installed on most versions of UNIX with which you can script an interactive session with MySQL.

TMTOWTDI with the MySQL Bible

The rallying cry of Perl mongers around the world is "There's more than one way to do it." That is also true with MySQL. If you've got a keen eye for SQL, you will recognize that the code I present is often not the easiest, most elegant, or optimized choice. However, aside from being useful, all of the examples were carefully chosen to illustrate a point to anyone less confident with their database hacking.

For those of you who are new to SQL or to MySQL's variety of it, you simply must bookmark MySQL.com. The site contains a wealth of information in its online manual, including comments by users detailing real-world solutions to real-world problems. You can find the manual at `http://dev.mysql.com/doc/mysql`.

If there is anything you don't understand (particularly some of the more complex functions), or if you simply want to modify or extend any of the examples in this chapter to suit your own needs, always make the manual your first stop.

By the way, have you backed up your database lately?

If you have a site with higher traffic, you may want to back up each night by changing the date fields to

```
30 4 * * *
```

and using the job command previously listed. This produces the same database dump nightly at 4:30 A.M.

After completing your job, cron will, by default, send an e-mail to your user account (login name plus server name) to let you know that it ran. It will also send you any output written to standard output, although in our case there is none.

If you would like to use an e-mail address other than the default, you can issue an environment setting command (the second of the two types of allowed crontab commands) and set the `MAILTO` environment variable right in the crontab:

```
MAILTO=fred@mydomain.com
0 1 1,15 * *  mysqldump -a -u USERNAME -p PASSWORD DATABASE >
~/backups/`date +%Y%m%d`_backup.mysql
```

For each job in the crontab, the `MAILTO` environment will be set to fred@mydomain.com.

Making Mass Changes

There are any number of reasons why you might want to make changes *en masse* directly through the database. There are some tasks that you simply cannot do from the MT admin interface. Issuing a single SQL statement is infinitely faster than slogging through page load after page load., checking checkboxes, clicking Submit buttons, and waiting for popup windows to pop to accomplish the same task. Being able to modify 10,000 records in less than one second is raw, unadulterated power.

Conversely, there is no safety net (unless of course, you've backed up). By issuing direct SQL commands, you are bypassing the benevolent protection of MT and taunting the terrible demon of catastrophic data loss. Luckily (or infuriatingly, depending on your perspective), MySQL is extremely finicky about syntax, so if you miss a quote mark you won't destroy the world; you'll simply get an error.

Practicing Safe SQL

In these exercises, you need to be very careful with two commands because they change the state of the database, potentially for the worse: `DELETE` and `UPDATE`.

To reduce the possibility of anything bad happening, there are a few best practices that you should try to keep in mind and observe as you experiment with the examples in this chapter.

Be SELECTive

Both of these commands are almost always issued with a `WHERE` clause to limit the scope of action to a subset of records in the table. That same `WHERE` clause can and should first be used in a `SELECT` statement (which is completely nondestructive) on the same table to ensure that you will only be deleting or updating the records intended.

For example, before doing this

```
DELETE FROM mt_comments WHERE comment_ip like '192.168%';
```

you should do something like this:

```
SELECT comment_id, comment_author FROM mt_comments
 WHERE comment_ip like '192.168%';
```

ID Is Key

Whenever you are deleting or updating only one row, you should always restrict the command in the WHERE clause on its primary key. This way, you avoid the possibility of accidentally selecting other matching rows, because the primary key is always unique in its table.

Good:

```
UPDATE mt_entry
 SET entry_keywords = 'Boring'
  WHERE entry_id = 62;
```

Bad:

```
UPDATE mt_entry
 SET entry_keywords = 'Boring'
  WHERE entry_title = 'What I ate for lunch today';
```

If you are deleting or updating several rows that are contiguous, you can restrict them to a range of values on the primary key with the BETWEEN operator (note that it's inclusive):

```
DELETE FROM mt_comment
 WHERE comment_id BETWEEN 249 AND 321;
```

LIMIT the Damage

If you are expecting to delete or update a specific number of records (which you may have attained from a SELECT count()), limit the number of possible rows acted upon with the LIMIT modifier:

```
DELETE FROM mt_comment
 WHERE comment_text LIKE '%You Suck!%'
  LIMIT 22;
```

Back Up Your Data

If you haven't gotten the hint by now, I will assume that you are either supremely confident in your abilities or not particularly fond of your data. In either case, this is your last reminder on my part to back up your database.

Closing Old Comments

Some people have found that closing comments on older entries has drastically cut down on the amount of comment spam they receive. Of course, I liken this to burning down your house to fix a termite problem or keeping a museum closed seven days per week to keep the floors clean for visitors. While your entries may be old to *you*, they are new to most people; and non-spam comments on older entries are no less valid than on newer ones.

If, however, your commitment to the common good is overcome by a barrage of spam and you want a passive way to control it, simply enter the following:

```
UPDATE mt_entry
 SET entry_allow_comments = 2
 WHERE entry_created_on < DATE_SUB(CURDATE(), INTERVAL 7 DAY);
```

This statement closes comments on all entries posted prior to one week ago. In English, the `WHERE` clause specifies entries whose `entry_created_on` date (see `mt_entry` in Chapter 4) is less than (that is, older than) the current date minus seven days. If run daily from your crontab, as discussed in the previous trick, you would have a rolling seven-day window of open comments, effectively keeping the floors of your museum clean for all of the visitors you aren't letting in.

The Forwarding Address

If a friend who frequently comments on your site switches domain names, you may want to change the e-mail and URL information on all of her comments:

```
UPDATE  mt_comment
SET
 comment_url = 'http://bigpinkcookie.com',
 email = 'notarealemail@bigpinkcookie.com'
  WHERE comment_url IN
    ('http://www.blahblahblog.com','http://blahblahblog.com');
```

The preceding code says change the URL to `http://www.bigpinkcookie.com` where the URL is either `http://www.blahblahblog.com` or `http://blahblahblog.com`. Note that when using the `IN` operator, the string must match one of the options exactly, which means that if there is even a single trailing slash the record will be skipped. Later in this chapter you will learn a much better method using the `REPLACE()` function.

For another example, suppose that you had a really bad breakup with your girlfriend, Kate, and you wanted to unpublish (set to draft) any entries that suggest her, regardless of whether it was actually her you were talking about:

```
UPDATE mt_entry
 SET entry_status = 1
  WHERE concat_ws(' ', entry_title, entry_text, entry_text_more)
   LIKE '%Kate%';
```

The preceding statement sets any entry to draft if the name Kate can be found in the title, entry body, or extended entry. For purposes of comparison, we concatenate the three fields together with a space as the separator. The percent sign (`'%'`) is a wildcard meaning that the word Kate can be surrounded by anything or nothing.

Cloning or Moving Your Install

This is a truly basic hint, but one that I rarely see talked about in the Movable Type community. If you have access to your database and can produce a full database dump as described in

Chapter 3, you can easily migrate an entire MT installation from one server to another, or clone it for development use.

As you may know, the export functionality in MT exports only entries and their comments. By using this functionality, you lose a great deal of information:

- Entry and comment IDs
- Author information and permissions
- Approved registered commenters
- Plugin configuration data
- TrackBacks
- Notification lists
- Templates

All of that information resides in the database; and because you already know how to dump and restore, it's a snap to clone or migrate your entire installation. The only thing you must do is change the filepaths and the URLs for the new site. Things that typically need to be changed include the following:

- Local site and archive paths for each blog
- Site and archive URLs for each blog
- Template outfile paths for each blog
- Template linked template paths for each blog
- Every internal link (those pointing to resources on your own site) posted in *any* of your entries

Were it not for that last item, changing everything within the MT admin interface could be considered palatable, but given that MT's internal search-and-replace leaves absolutely no room for error and no way of undoing damage, I have always considered this an unacceptable solution.

You could do this using MySQL (via the UPDATE statement, which is explained later in this chapter) to change the data in each field, but I find that for migration and cloning it's much easier to make the global changes in the dumped SQL file before importing into your new MySQL server. This way, you can change all of the outdated information at once, and in a way that is far safer and more recoverable.

Any basic text editor with a search-and-replace function will do the job admirably, but if you are working via the command line, the nifty but powerful UNIX utility `sed` makes things even easier. Among other things, `sed` — short for stream editor — takes text input, modifies it as instructed, and then spits it back out in its transformed state.

The `sed` command's syntax isn't too difficult aside from the use of regular expressions (which we're really not using here):

```
sed -e 's#OLD#NEW#g' INPUT_FILE > OUTPUT_FILE
```

The preceding command uses `sed` both to transform the `input_file` by executing (`-e`) the search and replace instructions in quotes and to put the results into the `output_file`. The execution instructions direct `sed` to substitute (`s`) all values of OLD with NEW and to do so globally (`g`).

Table 5-1 shows a migration I did about a year ago when I moved web host providers.

Table 5-1   Example Migration of an MT Database

	Site URL	*Site Path*
Old	http://openwire.com/	/home/openwire
New	http://jayallen.org/	/usr/home/jayallen

To begin with, I dumped the contents of my database to a file. The names of the output files in this example are arbitrary, but I choose mine to give me a sense of the changes each contains and the order in which they were processed.:

```
mysqldump -a -u jallen -p jay_mt > mt-0dump.mysql
```

First, I modified the filepaths from `/home/openwire` to `/usr/home/jayallen` and dumped the transformed content to `mt-1paths.mysql`:

```
sed -e 's#/home/openwire#/usr/home/jayallen#g' mt-0dump.mysql > mt-1paths.mysql
```

That was easy; however, the URLs are a bit more difficult. Because my site could be reached with and without the "www.", both must be transformed. Although this can be done with one step using regular expressions, I'll break it into two to make it more clear to those who aren't familiar with them:

```
sed -e 's#http://openwire.com#http://jayallen.org#g' mt-1paths.mysql >
mt-2urls.mysql
sed -e 's#http://www.openwire.com#http://jayallen.org#g' mt-2urls.mysql >
mt-3urls.mysql
```

With the preceding code, I have not only transformed all filepaths and URLs to their new values, but I also have three backup files (that is, `mt-dump.mysql`, `mt-1paths.mysql`, and `mt-2urls.mysql`) to which I can roll back if something got screwed up along the way. It's worth taking a look inside of these files just to make sure that everything went the way you expected. Often, just a simple `grep` will tell you what you need by showing you the matching lines that you can visually inspect for potential gotchas:

```
grep openwire.com mt-dump.mysql
grep /home/openwire mt-dump.mysql
```

In `mt-3urls.mysql`, we have a file that is ready to be imported into MySQL on the new server and which should run MT flawlessly with all of the information from the old server intact.

Editing TrackBacks

If you're a standards nut like myself, you are also most likely plagued by validation errors on your XHTML-Strict DOCTYPE pages caused by incoming TrackBacks that include characters that are not part of your specified character set. Unfortunately, there is no way to edit a TrackBack from within the Movable Type interface. Fortunately, we know a bit about the database.

As described in Chapter 4, incoming TrackBacks are stored in the `mt_tbping` table. If you don't want to simply delete the TrackBack, you can easily modify the `tbping_title` and/or `tbping_excerpt` fields. Once you know the `tbping_id` of the item, you can update the title and excerpt quite easily:

```
UPDATE mt_tbping
 SET tbping_title = '[From a Japanese weblog],
  tbping_except = '[Untranslatable Japanese text]'
   WHERE tbping_id = ID;
```

Simply change `ID` to the `tbping_id` of the incoming TrackBack and change the `tbping_title` and `tbping_excerpt` to whatever you like and you're back in compliance with standards.

Deleting TrackBack Abuse

The popularity of Movable Type makes it a ripe target for abuse from spammers who flood individual entries with bogus TrackBack pings and other unwanted junk.

Spammers seek to benefit from this practice in two ways: higher rankings in search engines such as Google, which factor in the number of pages linking to a site in their results, and higher traffic from visitors who click the TrackBack links.

Though the browser interface provides a way to remove pings by title, source, and IP address, you may find it faster and more flexible to employ direct database commands to get rid of them.

When you've received hundreds of junk pings, you can look for telltale phrases in the title and excerpts of these pings, such as "texas holdem," "totally nude," or "debt consolidation" to quickly find and delete them.

The following command deletes every ping with a title containing the phrase "phentermine":

```
DELETE FROM mt_tbping
  WHERE tbping_title LIKE '%phentermine%';
```

Similarly, here's a command to delete pings with a specific phrase in their excerpt fields:

```
DELETE FROM mt_tbping
  WHERE tbping_excerpt LIKE '%online casino%';
```

Deleted pings disappear from the database immediately, but do not disappear from your entries until they are rebuilt.

There's no way to undo these commands short of restoring the database from a backup, so take care not to delete pings with a phrase that may appear in legitimately submitted TrackBacks.

As stated earlier, to minimize the risk of deleting the wrong pings, a SELECT command can be tried first with the spam-hunting WHERE clause, as in this example command:

```
SELECT * FROM mt_tbping
  WHERE tbping_title LIKE '%Please visit%';
```

In response to this command, MySQL lists matching pings without deleting anything. The results can be skimmed to look for anything that should not be deleted.

Relocating Stray Comments

All too often, someone comments on my website in the wrong thread. Sometimes it's because they had multiple pages of my site opened in different windows and used the wrong one; other times they just didn't find the right thread. In any case, it's easy to relocate a comment from one entry to another.

The only connection between entry and comment is in the mt_comment table in the comment_entry_id field. Suppose someone named "Mom" commented in entry 2518 and you would like to move that to 2519:

```
SELECT comment_id, comment_entry_id, comment_author, comment_text
  FROM mt_comment
    WHERE comment_entry_id = 2518 AND comment_author = 'Mom';
```

I selected comment_text just to make sure that we were getting the right comment and that there was only one.

```
+------------+------------------+----------------+-------------------------+
| comment_id | comment_entry_id | comment_author | comment_text            |
+------------+------------------+----------------+-------------------------+
|       3114 |             2518 | Mom            | Don't forget to call!   |
+------------+------------------+----------------+-------------------------+
```

Now we update the comment_entry_id using the comment_id and a LIMIT restriction just to be on the safe side, and then rebuild:

```
UPDATE mt_comment
  SET comment_entry_id = 2519
    WHERE comment_id = 3114
      LIMIT 1;
```

Recovering Lost Passwords

Have you or another author forgotten your password only to find that the e-mail address and author hint in the profile were either empty, outdated, or forgotten? Without both of those, it's impossible to recover your password from the Movable Type web interface, but through

MySQL, it's a breeze. Replacing "JayAllen" in the following with the login ID of the user who is without access, you will retrieve the record:

```
SELECT author_id, author_name, author_email, author_hint
 FROM mt_author
  WHERE author_name = 'JayAllen';


+-----------+-------------+------------------+-------------+
| author_id | author_name | author_email     | author_hint |
+-----------+-------------+------------------+-------------+
|         1 | JayAllen    | jay@openwire.org |             |
+-----------+-------------+------------------+-------------+
```

An incorrect e-mail address and a blank author hint would be the problem, no doubt. Therefore, let's change both:

```
UPDATE mt_author
 SET author_email = 'mt@jayallen.org', author_hint = 'Idiota'
  WHERE author_id = 1
    LIMIT 1;
```

Now you can successfully recover your password through the web interface using the new author hint.

Global Search and Replace

As I showed you earlier, you can easily do a quick search and replace or `sed` transformation using a MySQL dumpfile. While this technique is quick and powerful, it doesn't enable you to easily specify the fields to which you want to limit your changes.

For example, suppose you wanted to change the wording of some phrase in all of your templates, but not touch your entries or comments. The fastest and easiest way to do that is using MySQL's `replace()` function:

```
UPDATE mt_template
 SET template_text = REPLACE(template_text, 'RSS feed', 'News feed');
```

This will change every instance of `'RSS Feed'` found in `template_text` to `'News feed'` for all templates in your installation. You could obviously use a `WHERE` clause to specify only templates in one of your blogs, or even a certain type of template (such as Main Index templates).

In the Forwarding Address example earlier in this chapter, you saw one way of changing a comment author's information retroactively:

```
UPDATE  mt_comment
SET
 comment_url = 'http://bigpinkcookie.com',
 comment_email = 'notarealemail@bigpinkcookie.com'
  WHERE comment_url IN
    ('http://www.blahblahblog.com','http://blahblahblog.com');
```

While valid, it requires that the URL be exactly as written in the preceding example and then
replaces the e-mail address despite what the comment author originally submitted. Using the
`replace()` function, you can do much better:

```
UPDATE mt_comment
 SET
  comment_url = REPLACE(comment_url, 'blahblahblog.com', 'bigpinkcookie.com'),
  comment_email = REPLACE(comment_email, 'blahblahblog.com',
'bigpinkcookie.com')
    WHERE comment_url LIKE '%blahblahblog.com%'
     OR comment_email LIKE '%blahblahblog.com%';
```

The preceding command looks for any record whose `comment_url` or `comment_email`
contains `'blahblahblog.com'` and changes each instance of that string to `big-
pinkcookie.com` in whichever field it exists.

Summary

The examples I've included in this chapter are just a small sample of the thousands of things
you could do with direct manipulation and selection of database data. By now, it should be
clear that access to the MT database gives you a lot of raw power. With it, you can make
changes both quickly and easily and do just about anything Movable Type can do.

The flip side, of course, is that you can also make mistakes quickly and easily if you aren't careful. The Movable Type code has safeguards and logic built into it that ensures that the data in
the database remains usable to the application. The Movable Type code also offers intrinsically
more intelligent data manipulation routines, such as text formatting plugins, and functions that
more easily cull data from different tables (for example, categories on an entry).

Later chapters will discuss some safer and more intelligent ways to interact with the MT system through use of Application Programming Interfaces (APIs). These interfaces are provided
as a way to interact programmatically with MT without having to manipulate the database
directly. APIs enable you to extend the capabilities of the program or to manipulate data as we
have done in this chapter, but within the confines (and protection) of the MT source code.

Using the APIs, you will learn to be an "MT law-abiding citizen," instead of a "database
renegade."

Hacking with APIs

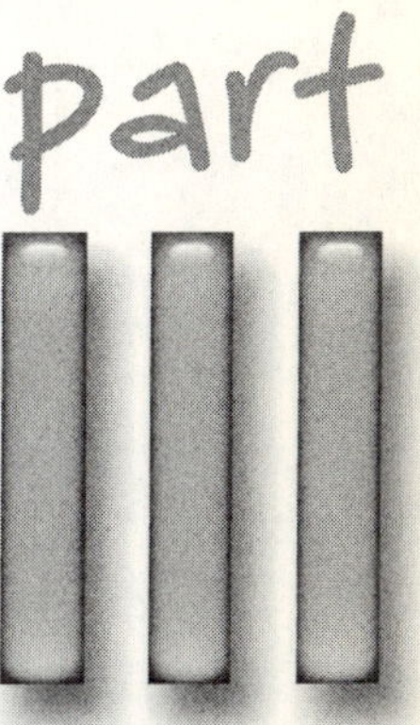

XML-RPC API

Arguably, the two features that make Movable Type so powerful are the internal and external Application Programmatic Interfaces (APIs). We will be dealing with the internal APIs in a later chapter. These next two chapters, however, deal with the ways in which external applications can interface with a Movable Type installation.

The oldest and most common way of doing this is via the XML-RPC interface. Three sets of commands are available: the Blogger API, the Metaweblog API, and the MT Extended API. Although there is some political squabbling surrounding these specifications, they all have their uses.

What Is XML-RPC?

Get thee to `http://xmlrpc.com/` and you'll see that Extensible Markup Language Remote Procedure Calls (XML-RPC) is a specification that enables different applications to talk to each other by throwing chunks of XML at each other. XML might seem to be quite a verbose way of doing it, but it does have a few advantages: it compresses easily, it's simple to use and debug, and should be — if the application designer is sensible — pretty much self-explanatory whenever you see a new call.

Note The full XML-RPC specification and a list of code implementations can be found at `http://xmlrpc.com/`.

Examples in this chapter use Perl, but of course you don't have to. In fact, this is one of the nice things about the MT XML-RPC APIs: You can code in pretty much any language you like. Interfacing with MT via a mix of Squeak and Flash is just as easy as doing so with Perl, if you feel the need.

An Example XML-RPC Call

Just to give you an idea of what is going on across the wire when you make a call, let's break an easy example down into its component parts. The call used is one of the 19 supported by MT: `blogger.getUsersBlogs`.

This call returns the list of weblogs within an MT installation to which the author has posting rights. The MT documentation says this:

- Description: Returns a list of weblogs to which an author has posting privileges
- Parameters: String `appkey`, String `username`, String `password`
- Return value: On success, array of structs containing String `url`, String `blogid`, String `blogName`; on failure, fault

The API call `blogger.getUsersBlogs` is part of the Blogger API suite of commands and was originally designed for use within Blogger itself. The `appkey` string is a Blogger-specific variable and is ignored by MT. You can make it equal to anything you like within your own code, but don't leave it out when you send the call the Movable Type. I like to make it equal `mt`, mostly out of habit.

In Perl, I like to use the XMLRPC::Lite module, as follows:

```perl
#!/usr/bin/perl -w

use strict;
use XMLRPC::Lite;

my $username = "Melody";
my $password = "Nelson";
my $url="http://192.168.16.52/mt-xmlrpc.cgi";

my $rpc_call = XMLRPC::Lite->new;

$rpc_call->proxy($url);

my $call_result = $rpc_call->call('blogger.getUsersBlogs' => 'MT',
$username, $password);

if ($call_result->fault) {
print "metaWeblog.newPost error code: ", $call_result->faultcode,
"\n\n", $call_result->faultstring, "\n\n";
} else {

my $call_result_array = $call_result->result();

foreach my $single_call_result (@$call_result_array) {
  print "BlogID: $single_call_result->{blogid} \n";
  print "Blog name: $single_call_result->{blogName} \n";
  print "Blog URL: $single_call_result->{url} \n";
}

}
```

XML-RPC versus Perl APIs

In writing this chapter, I've been running MT on my local machine, which is why all of the IP addresses in the examples are local ones. This is unusual in that the usual usage for these APIs is for a remote client to interface with MT (a desktop blogging application, for example).

However, this brings up an interesting debate; there are many occasions when you might want to post new entries, retrieve some data, or generally interface with your MT installation from the very same machine. The traditional way to do this would be with the Perl API, which you will see in Chapter 8, but I often prefer to use the XML-RPC interface, even on the local system. I find the code simpler and more portable. You may or may not agree. Either way, don't assume that the XML-RPC APIs are for remote machines only. The "LazyWeb" code on the next few pages is a good example of this.

–Ben Hammersley

Note that the variables set at the top of the script are for working on my test blog setup on my laptop; you need to change them to reflect your own target.

The call sends an XML document containing the meaningless appkey, the username, and the password, in that order. It looks like this:

```
<?xml version="1.0" encoding="UTF-8"?>
<methodCall>
 <methodName>blogger.getUsersBlogs</methodName>
  <params>
    <param>
     <value>
      <string>MT</string>
     </value>
    </param>
    <param>
     <value>
      <string>Melody</string>
     </value>
    </param>
    <param>
     <value>
      <string>Nelson</string>
     </value>
    </param>
  </params>
</methodCall>
```

The application — in this case, Movable Type — parses this document, retrieves the name of the method you wish to call and its associated inputs, performs the action associated with the call, and returns the result in XML:

```xml
<?xml version="1.0" encoding="UTF-8"?>
<methodResponse>
 <params>
  <param>
   <value>
    <array>
     <data>
      <value>
       <struct>
        <member>
         <name>blogid</name>
          <value>
           <string>1</string>
          </value>
        </member>
        <member>
         <name>blogName</name>
          <value>
           <string>First Weblog</string>
          </value>
        </member>
        <member>
         <name>url</name>
          <value>
           <string>http://192.168.16.52/</string>
          </value>
        </member>
       </struct>
      </value>
     </data>
    </array>
   </value>
  </param>
 </params>
</methodResponse>
```

As you can see, these documents are pretty big for what they contain, and if you're unused to seeing XML, they do look quite confusing. No worries, Perl has many modules to take the pain out of using XML-RPC. This chapter uses the XMLRPC::Lite module, available from CPAN mirrors everywhere.

The Supported Calls

Movable Type supports 19 different XML-RPC calls: 6 from the Blogger API, 5 from the Metaweblog API, and 8 of its own. These are documented in the online manual of your MT installation at `<SITEPATH>/mt-static/docs/mtmanual_programmatic.html`.

Using the Movable Type XML-RPC API

The following sections detail the various ways to post entries using the MT XML-RPC API.

Posting an Entry

An entry posting can be done with either the Blogger API's `blogger.newPost` call or the Metaweblog API's `metaWeblog.newPost` call. The Metaweblog call is much more powerful, providing access to all of the fields allowed in an MT entry, including extended entry, keywords, summary, comments, and pings on and off, and so on. For this reason, this is the one we'll be using.

Let's step through some code:

```perl
#!/usr/bin/perl -w

use strict;
use XMLRPC::Lite;
use Class::Struct;

# Set up variables
my $username = "Melody";
my $password = "Nelson";
my $url="http://192.168.16.52/mt-xmlrpc.cgi";
my $blogid = "1";
```

It starts off basically enough, with the good practice of use `strict`, and then the loading of `XMLRPC::Lite` and `Class::Struct`. You don't actually need `Class::Struct`; you can create the structs by hand, but as you will see in the next snippet, it makes for what I think is clearer code. Change the username and password to reflect your settings, and change the `$url` to equal the URL to your installation's `mt-xmlrpc.cgi` file. `$blogid`, too, should be changed to reflect your weblog:

```perl
my $struct;

struct( struct => {
title => '$',
description => '$',
dateCreated => '$',
mt_text_more => '$',
mt_excerpt => '$',
mt_keywords => '$',
mt_allow_comments => '$',
mt_allow_pings => '$',
mt_convert_breaks => '$',
mt_tb_ping_urls => '$'}
);

# Other code can go here
```

```perl
$struct->{'title'} "Put your title here";
$struct->{'description'} = "Put the main entry body here";
$struct->{'dateCreated'} = "Put a date here, optionally";
$struct->{'mt_text_more'} = "Extended entry body here,
optionally";
$struct->{'mt_excerpt'} = "The entry excerpt, optionally";
$struct->{'mt_keywords'}        = "Keywords, optionally";
$struct->{'mt_allow_comments'} = "1";
$struct->{'mt_allow_pings'} = "1";
$struct->{'mt_convert_breaks'} = "1";
$struct->{'mt_tb_ping_urls'} = "An array containing URLs to ping";
```

In this section, we've set up the struct and applied values to it. It is in the middle of this that we can place other code that will provide the data you want to put into the entry. Different uses are explained in a page or two, but now, let's post the thing:

```perl
# Post the message to the blog
my $rpc_call = XMLRPC::Lite->new;
$rpc_call->proxy($url);

my $call_result = $rpc_call->call('metaWeblog.newPost' => $blogid,
$username, $password, $struct, 1);

if ($call_result->fault) {
print "\n\nThere was a problem.\n\nmetaWeblog.newPost error code:
", $call_result->faultcode, " \n\n", $call_result->faultstring,
"\n\n";
}
else {
    print "\n\nPost '$struct->{'title'}' published.\n\n";
}
```

This invokes the XMLRPC::Lite module and sends the call. You're passing the `blogid`, your `username` and `password`, the `struct` containing the post, and then finally a Boolean value of 1 or 0 denoting whether you wish the post to be published or not. As you will discover in the next few pages, this value is ignored by all versions of MT post 2.11.

Posting an Entry to the LazyWeb

Let's look at actually using the framework code on a site. One site that uses it is the LazyWeb (`www.lazyweb.org`). This site, for web developers and other such technological reprobates, enables its readers to post their ideas to it in the hope that others will already know of a solution or be inspired to take up the coding challenge. It works by utilizing the TrackBack autodiscovery system built into MT. The front page contains the TrackBack RDF snippet, so whenever anyone links to it, MT will automatically request that page, pull out the snippet, realize it is TrackBackable, and then send off the ping. The TrackBack snippet, however, doesn't point to the usual MT TrackBack code, but to our own script, which parses the TrackBack ping and posts it as a new entry on the site. It does this via the XML-RPC interface.

Consider the mapping of the data. The TrackBack specification, found at `www.movabletype.org/docs/mttrackback.html`, states that a TrackBack ping contains four parameters:

- **Title** — The title of the entry.

- **Excerpt** — An excerpt of the entry. In the Movable Type implementation, if this string is longer than 255 characters, it will be cropped to 252 characters, and ... (ellipses) will be added to the end.

- **url** — The permalink for the entry. Like any permalink, this should point as closely as possible to the actual entry on the HTML page, as it will be used when linking to the entry in question.

- **blog_name** — The name of the blog in which the entry is posted.

`Title` and `Excerpt` map beautifully onto Title and Main Body, but the `url` and `blog_name` don't really fit. Having this data, however, is useful, especially having it in a way that enables you to use it within the MT templates. Therefore, let's use the extended entry and keywords fields for them. If we do that, our mapping looks like this:

    title -> title

    excerpt -> description

    url -> mt_text_more

    blog_name -> mt_keywords

Following is our existing code with a TrackBack listener added in. Happily, TrackBack acts just like the submission of a CGI form, so this is very simple:

```perl
#!/usr/bin/perl -w
use strict;
use CGI qw( :standard );
use XMLRPC::Lite;
use Class::Struct;

# Set up variables
my $username = "YOUR NAME HERE";
my $password = "YOUR PASSWORD HERE";
my $url="http://YOUR URL HERE/mt-xmlrpc.cgi";
my $blogid = "YOUR BLOGID HERE";
my $struct;

struct( struct => {
title => '$',
description => '$',
dateCreated => '$',
mt_text_more => '$',
mt_excerpt => '$',
mt_keywords => '$',
mt_allow_comments => '$',
```

```perl
mt_allow_pings => '$',
mt_convert_breaks => '$',
mt_tb_ping_urls => '$'
}
);

my $i = { map { $_ => scalar param($_) } qw(title excerpt url
blog_name) };

$struct->{'title'} = "$i->{title}";
$struct->{'description'}        = "$i->{excerpt}";
$struct->{'mt_text_more'} = "$i->{url}";
$struct->{'mt_keywords'}        = "$i->{blog_name}";

# Post the message to the blog
my $rpc_call = XMLRPC::Lite->new;
$rpc_call->proxy($url);

my $call_result = $rpc_call->call('metaWeblog.newPost' => $blogid,
$username, $password, $struct, 1);

print "Content-Type: text/xml\n\n";
print qq(<?xml version="1.0" encoding="iso-8859-1"?>
\n<response>\n);
if ($call_result->fault) {
        printf qq(<error>1</error>\n%s\n), xml('message',
$call_result->faultstring);
} else {
        print qq(<error>0</error>\n) . ($_[1] ? $_[1] : '');
}
print "</response>\n";
```

Making Everything Much Easier with Net::Blogger

Calling the interface directly, whether by using XMLRPC::Lite or any other standard XML
RPC module or toolkit is simple enough, but it can be made even easier. A Perl module
available on CPAN provides an even simpler interface, which abstracts away even that:
Aaron Straup Cope's Net::Blogger (`http://search.cpan.org/~ascope/`
`Net-Blogger-0.87/`).

You'll remember that MT supports three XML-RPC commandsets: Blogger, Metaweblog,
and the MovableType Specific. Net::Blogger deals with all of these. In practice, however, you
will probably find that your application starts to use a combination of Net::Blogger and your
own bespoken XMLRPC::Lite code. This is not a problem at all. It shows a pleasing sense of
the baroque.

Anyhow, Net::Blogger provides access to all of the available MT XML-RPC commandsets. As
an example, let's rewrite the relevant bits of the previous LazyWeb code:

```perl
#!/usr/bin/perl -w
use strict;
use CGI qw( :standard );
```

```perl
use Net::Blogger;

my $mt = Net::Blogger->new(engine=>"movabletype");

# Set up variables
$mt->proxy("http://YOUR URL HERE/mt-xmlrpc.cgi");
$mt->Username("YOUR NAME HERE");
$mt->Password("YOUR PASSWORD HERE");
$mt->BlogId("YOUR BLOGID HERE");

my $i = { map { $_ => scalar param($_) } qw(title excerpt url
blog_name) };

# Post the message to the blog
$mt->metaWeblog()->newPost(title=>"$i->{title}",
                           description=>"$i->{excerpt}",
                           mt_text_more=> "$i->{url}",
                           mt_keywords=> "$i->{blogname}",
                           publish=>1);

# The rest of the code would continue here.
```

As you can see, it's much shorter and simpler this way. The specific line that is important to Movable Type is this:

```perl
my $mt = Net::Blogger->new(engine=>"movabletype");
```

Indeed, Net::Blogger has extensions for many weblogging packages. Invoking the `engine=>"movabletype"` makes all of the Movable Type interface methods available. If you don't specify an engine, to use Aaron Straup Cope's term, the module will default to the vanilla Blogger interface, which is workmanlike, but dull.

You do have to pay attention to the commandset in which the method you are calling is found, however. Note the difference between these two calls:

```perl
$mt->newPost(postbody=>"hello world",publish=>1)
```

```perl
$mt->metaWeblog()->newPost(description=>"hello world",publish=>1);
```

They do the same thing, with the top line using the Blogger API, and the bottom line using the Metaweblog. Because Net::Blogger considers the Metaweblog API an additional vocabulary to the default Blogger API, you have to call the `metametaWeblog()` method first. If you're deep into object-oriented programming, you'll be excited to know that it returns an object. If you're cutting and pasting a script together, just remember to stick the additional `metaWeblog()->` into every line that calls a Metaweblog method. Actually, this is the beautiful thing about using this module over XMLRPC::Lite; it produces eminently reusable/stealable code.

To access the MT Specific commandset, the additional method is `mt()`. To call the MT Specific `getTrackbackPings()` method, you would write a script similar to the following:

```perl
my $mt = Net::Blogger->new(engine=>"movabletype");
...
$mt->mt()->getTrackbackPings(postid=>"1234");
```

With those little additional flourishes understood, Net::Blogger behaves exactly as you might expect. The method names are exactly the same as their counterparts in the XML-RPC APIs themselves, and they take exactly the same variables. Using Net::Blogger, once you understand how to invoke a Net::Blogger object as previously demonstrated, is really just like addressing the XML-RPC API directly. You can code directly from the Movable Type manual's listing of the supported calls.

As a reminder, you will find the Movable Type manual's listing of supported calls at `www.movabletype.org/docs/mtmanual_programmatic.html#xmlrpc%20api`.

Don't forget that `appkey` has no meaning in MT, but still needs to be set to something. Use it to store a message of secret love to your beau. Whatever, MT won't look or care.

Because the list of commands is so long, and so admirably covered by the MT and Net::Blogger documentation itself, we won't go into the calls individually. Instead, let's look at what you can't do with the available APIs, and what you can do about that.

Post Status: A Problem

Movable Type's XML-RPC interfaces, indeed any interfaces using the Blogger or Metaweblog APIs, have a serious limitation: They can't tell you the status of an entry. Generally, this is not surprising; there is no standard set of post statuses across the content management system world, so it's difficult to build a standard interface for them. However, as we are concentrating on an individual toolkit, we can build nonstandard calls to help us out. MT already does this, with its suite of `mt.*` calls, but sadly none of them enable you to retrieve the status of an entry.

Let's recap: Movable Type 3.0D has four separate status codes available internally for an entry, only two of which (at the moment) are in use. These four are 1, 2, 3, and 4 and are defined as follows:

- **"1" HOLD** — Draft, store but do not publish
- **"2" RELEASE** — Publish
- **"3" REVIEW** — Unused at present
- **"4" FUTURE** — Unused at present

At this point, it is also very important to note the following comment from the MT source code:

```
## In 2.1 we changed the behavior of the $publish flag. Previously,
## it was used to determine the post status. That was a bad idea.
## So now entries added through XML-RPC are always set to publish,
## *unless* the user has set "NoPublishMeansDraft 1" in mt.cfg, which
## enables the old behavior.
```

As it stands, with a stock build of MT3.0D, it's impossible to author a draft post over XML-RPC, or to check whether a post is draft or not, or to publish it if you somehow find that it is.

The only way to do this over XML-RPC is to modify the MT code itself to include the requisite additional calls. We'll call them `mt.getStatus` and `mt.setStatus`.

Adding a Call to the Interface

The callable methods available to the XML-RPC interface are delivered out of `/lib/MT/XMLRPCServer.pm`. This is a very simple file to understand, with each call simply being its own subroutine, accepting inputs and returning results to `mt-xmlrpc.cgi`, which deals with the whole XML-RPC aspect of the transaction. We needn't worry about these mechanics; we just need to add our own subroutines to `XMLRPCServer.pm` and they become available to the outside world.

Here's an example of one of the existing calls, `mt.getCategoryList`:

```
sub getCategoryList {
    my $class = shift;
    my($blog_id, $user, $pass) = @_;
    my $mt = MT::XMLRPCServer::Util::mt_new();    ## Will die if
MT->new fails.
    my($author, $perms) = $class->_login($user, $pass, $blog_id);
    die _fault("Invalid login") unless $author;
    die _fault("Author does not have privileges")
        unless $perms && $perms->can_post;
    require MT::Category;
    my $iter = MT::Category->load_iter({ blog_id => $blog_id });
    my @data;
    while (my $cat = $iter->()) {
        push @data, {
            categoryName => SOAP::Data->type(string => $cat-
>label),
            categoryId => SOAP::Data->type(string => $cat->id)
        };
    }
    \@data;
}
```

Stepping through this code, you can see that it takes the three arguments `blog id`, `username`, and `password`, checks that the username and password are correct, whether the user has the right, and shows the data on the requested `blog id`. If all is okay, it iterates through each category assigned to that blog, returning two strings, the label, and its category id.

I won't say any more about this code — for the full details about exactly how this code works, the chapters on the Perl API and plugin design will prove extremely useful — except to say that it is extremely simple stuff. For our `mt.getStatus` call, we need only add this code snippet to `XMLRPCServer.pm`:

```perl
sub getStatus {
    my $class = shift;
    my($entry_id, $user, $pass) = @_;

    my $mt = MT::XMLRPCServer::Util::mt_new();
    require MT::Entry;

    my $author = $class->_login($user, $pass);
    my $entry = MT::Entry->load($entry_id)
        or die _fault("Invalid entry ID '$entry_id'");
    my($author, $perms) = $class->_login($user, $pass, $entry-
>blog_id);
    die _fault("Invalid login") unless $author;
    die _fault("No posting privileges") unless $perms && $perms-
>can_post;
    { status => SOAP::Data->type(string => $entry->status)};
}
```

This call takes the entry id, username, and password and returns a struct containing the status
code, or an error code on failure. A successful exchange looks like this:

```xml
<?xml version="1.0" encoding="UTF-8"?>
 <methodCall>
 <methodName>mt.getStatus</methodName>
 <params>
 <param>
 <value><int>8389</int></value>
 </param>
 <param>
 <value><string>Ben Hammersley</string></value>
 </param>
 <param>
 <value><string>SekretPassword</string></value>
 </param>
 </params>
 </methodCall>
```

The server replies coyly:

```xml
<?xml version="1.0" encoding="UTF-8"?>
 <methodResponse>
 <params>
 <param>
 <value>
 <struct>
 <member>
 <name>status</name>
 <value><string>2</string></value>
 </member>
 </struct>
 </value>
 </param>
 </params>
 </methodResponse>
```

Use Case Hardening

The code you're looking at here is really the code running LazyWeb.org—more or less. In real life, real users and real abusers demanded that I include code to ignore empty entries, and to pass the data through Jay's MT-Blacklist. This sort of sanity checking is trivial, however, so I've left it out of this code for the sake of clarity. If you're going to use the code as is on the open web, spend a few minutes considering the possibility of abuse. My main problem was that the site showed only the last entry, and the RSS feed the last five. A curious Denial of Service attack started, where someone would make five quick, empty submissions, effectively emptying my site of content. Preventing this sort of use-case-specific abuse is worth thinking about.

To install it, just add that subroutine inside the `XMLRPCServer.pm` file next to the others. I dropped it in at line 702, for example. (In future releases of MT, the line numbers might change, and this might appear to be a daft place to put it, but I thought I'd take a flier.) You can now use the XML-RPC interface to query for each weblog entry's status. We shall be using this in combination with the `getRecentPosts` call in the following section.

But first, having ascertained the status of a post, what if you want to change it? For that we're going to need another call: `mt.setStatus`. Again, it uses Perl API commands covered elsewhere in this book, so we'll go straight to the code:

```perl
sub setStatus {
    my $class = shift;
    my($entry_id, $user, $pass, $status) = @_;
    my $mt = MT::XMLRPCServer::Util::mt_new();    ## Will die if
MT->new fails.
    require MT::Entry;
    my $entry = MT::Entry->load($entry_id)
        or die _fault("Invalid entry ID '$entry_id'");
    my($author, $perms) = __PACKAGE__->_login($user, $pass,
$entry->blog_id);
    die _fault("Invalid login") unless $author;
    die _fault("Not privileged to edit entry")
        unless $perms && $perms->can_edit_entry($entry, $author);
    $entry->status($status)
        or die _fault("Status change failed: " . $mt->errstr);
    $entry->save
            or die _fault("Saving entry failed: ". $entry->errstr);
    $mt->rebuild_entry( Entry => $entry, BuildDependencies => 1 )
        or die _fault("Rebuild after status change failed: " .
$mt->errstr);
    SOAP::Data->type(boolean => 1);
}
```

This, when placed inside `XMLRPCServer.pm`, will take four inputs: username and password, entry id, and the code for the status. That can be 1, 2, 3, or 4 for draft, publish, and the currently unused review and future, respectively. Changing the status code on an entry will cause it, and any connected indexes, to be rebuilt. Therefore, if you set a draft post to status code 2, publish, it will appear in the indexes. If you set a published post to code 1, it will disappear from the indexes; however, it will not be removed from the site's archive directory. If anyone remembers it is there, they will still be able to retrieve it. This may or may not be a problem for you and your site's workflow. If it is a problem, it's easy to add another call to `XMLRPCServer.pm` (or convert an existing call) to delete the file itself.

A Mobile Article Trigger

By way of example, let's build a little application that uses the calls we now have available to us. Imagine, if you will, that you're a journalist on assignment at an awards ceremony. There are four shortlisted candidates, and you've prepared an article on each of them in advance. All you need to know is which one has actually won and which article to put up live on the web.

What we'd like is a small CGI application that prints the title and entry id of all of the posts and enables the user to select an entry id, which will then be published. Here is the code:

```perl
#!/usr/bin/perl -w
use strict;
use XMLRPC::Lite;
use XML::Simple;
use Net::Blogger;
use CGI;

# Set up variables
my $username = "Ben Hammersley";
my $password = "joe90";
my $url="http://www.mediacooperative.com/mt-xmlrpc.cgi";
my $blog_id = "3";

my $cgi = CGI::new();
my $post_to_publish = $cgi->param('publish');

if ($cgi->param('publish')) {
                    my $publish_result = publish_post($cgi-
>param('publish'));
                    print $cgi->header();
                    print $cgi->start_html(-
title=>"Publication Result");
                    print $cgi->h1('Publication Result');
                    print $cgi->p("Result: $publish_result");
                    print $cgi->end_html();
                } else {
                    print $cgi->header();
                    print $cgi->start_html(-title=>"Drafts to
Publish");
                    print $cgi->h1('Drafts to Publish');
                    my $retrieve_last_20_posts_test_result =
retrieve_last_x_posts();
                    print "<ul>";
```

```perl
                              for my $entry(@$retrieve_last_20_posts_
test_result) {
                              my $retrieve_post_status_test_result =
retrieve_post_status($entry->{postid});
                              if ($retrieve_post_status_test_result
eq "1") {
                                    print '<li><a
href="'.'remotepublishdrafts.cgi?publish='."$entry-
>{postid}".'">'."$entry->{title}</a></li>";
                              }
                        }
                  print "</ul>";
                  print $cgi->end_html();
            }


sub retrieve_last_x_posts {
    my $rpc_call = Net::Blogger->new(engine=>"movabletype");
    $rpc_call->Proxy($url);
    $rpc_call->Username($username);
    $rpc_call->Password($password);
    $rpc_call->BlogId($blog_id);
    my $recent_posts = $rpc_call->mt()->getRecentPostTitles();
    return ($recent_posts);
}

sub retrieve_post_status {
    my $post_id = shift;
    my $rpc_call = XMLRPC::Lite->new;
    $rpc_call->proxy($url);
    $rpc_call->outputxml(1);
    my $call_result = $rpc_call->call('mt.getStatus' => $post_id,
$username, $password);
    my $raw_xml_result = XMLin($call_result);
    my $parsed_result = $raw_xml_result->{params}->{param}-
>{value}->{struct}->{member}->{value}->{string};
    return ($parsed_result);
}

sub publish_post {
    my $post_id = shift;
    my $rpc_call = Net::Blogger->new(engine=>"movabletype");
    $rpc_call->Proxy($url);
    $rpc_call->Username($username);
    $rpc_call->Password($password);
    $rpc_call->BlogId($blog_id);
    my $publish_call = $rpc_call->mt()->publishPost($post_id);
    return ($publish_call);
}
```

This is not the most beautiful use of `CGI.pm`, but it shows a basic framework. If the page is accessed without a parameter, it throws itself over to the `retrieve_last_x_posts` subroutine:

```perl
sub retrieve_last_x_posts {
    my $rpc_call = Net::Blogger->new(engine=>"movabletype");
    $rpc_call->Proxy($url);
    $rpc_call->Username($username);
    $rpc_call->Password($password);
    $rpc_call->BlogId($blog_id);
    my $recent_posts = $rpc_call->mt()->getRecentPostTitles();
    return ($recent_posts);
}
```

This uses the Net::Blogger module to make the `getRecentPostTitles` call and returns the resulting array. We use this call because we only want the titles (for the user) and the entry ids (for the rest of the program) — the other call that would give us the same information, `getRecentPosts`, would be overkill.

The subroutine returns the result, an array, which we then step through:

```perl
my $retrieve_last_20_posts_test_result = retrieve_last_x_posts();
print "<ul>";
for my $entry(@$retrieve_last_20_posts_test_result) {
    my $retrieve_post_status_test_result =
retrieve_post_status($entry->{postid});
    if ($retrieve_post_status_test_result eq "1") {
        print '<li><a
href="'.'remotepublishdrafts.cgi?publish='."$entry-
>{postid}".'">'."$entry->{title}</a></li>";
                                }
```

It takes every entry in the array and sends the `entry_id` over to the `retrieve_post_status` subroutine:

```perl
sub retrieve_post_status {
    my $post_id = shift;
    my $rpc_call = XMLRPC::Lite->new;
    $rpc_call->proxy($url);
    $rpc_call->outputxml(1);
    my $call_result = $rpc_call->call('mt.getStatus' => $post_id,
$username, $password);
    my $raw_xml_result = XMLin($call_result);
    my $parsed_result = $raw_xml_result->{params}->{param}-
>{value}->{struct}->{member}->{value}->{string};
    return ($parsed_result);
}
```

Because this uses the `getStatus` call that we've hacked into the MT source, we have to use XMLRPC::Lite to make the call, and XML::Simple to parse the result. That result is just a string: 1, 2, 3, or 4.

If that returns with a status of 1– (remember that this means the entry is a "Draft"), the main code prints the entry title and id as a link, with a parameter of the entry id.

We then move onto the next entry in the array, and so on, until the resultant page is closed off and the script ends. If one of the links that we produced is clicked, the script is called again, this time with the parameter in place. That triggers the final subroutine, `publish_post`:

```
sub publish_post {
    my $post_id = shift;
    my $rpc_call = Net::Blogger->new(engine=>"movabletype");
    $rpc_call->Proxy($url);
    $rpc_call->Username($username);
    $rpc_call->Password($password);
    $rpc_call->BlogId($blog_id);
    my $publish_call = $rpc_call->mt()->publishPost($post_id);
    return ($publish_call);
}
```

This uses Net::Blogger again to call the `publishPost` method on the XML-RPC interface and publish the post.

With this script, simple as it is, you can see how you can use the XML-RPC interface to create additional interfaces to your Movable Type installations. Indeed, the desktop clients now available for webloggers do their job in exactly this way.

Summary

This chapter showed how Movable Type's XML-RPC interface enables you to post, retrieve, and edit entries from within other programs. You can now use these skills to create your own new interfaces to MT, or to have other applications create weblog posts automatically. However, you've also seen that the XML-RPC API is quite limited. The next chapter looks at the new generation of weblogging APIs: the Atom Publishing Protocol.

Atom API

One of the major additions to the Movable Type codebase included with version 3 was the introduction of the Atom API. This new standard aims to take the place of the more disparate XML-RPC APIs explored in Chapter 6. It is part of a larger project that also includes the Atom syndication format, and it looks set to become a widely supported specification, by standards bodies as well as programmers.

This chapter looks at using the version of the Atom API supported by MT. At the time of writing, Atom is not yet finalized, so it would be wise to check the latest documentation, both for Movable Type and for Atom itself. This chapter was written using MT 3.01D, Atom API spec document `draft-ietf-atompub-protocol-01.txt`, and the Perl module XML::Atom 0.09. Chances are good that these have all been updated.

You can find Atom's main development documentation at `www.intertwingly.net/wiki/pie/FrontPage`, while the latest specifications are archived at `http://bitworking.org/projects/atom/`.

Introducing the Atom API

The Atom API uses the native functions of HTTP to provide a system to create, retrieve, edit, delete, and upload new web resources. It does this, with either REST or SOAP style requests, by using the standard HTTP verbs:

- **GET** — Used to retrieve a representation of a resource, or the resource itself as a read-only request
- **PUT** — Used to update a resource
- **POST** — Used to create a resource
- **DELETE** — Used to remove a resource

These verbs are directed at five standard URIs:

- **EditURI** — Takes PUT, GET, and DELETE. This is used to edit a single entry and is unique to that entry. Every editable entry has one.
- **PostURI** — Takes POST. This is used to create an entry. POSTing a properly formed Atom entry to this URI will create one or more resources (the individual entry archive in HTML and in Atom, for example).

- **FeedURI** — Takes GET. This is used to retrieve a representation of the resource in the Atom syndication format. There are three different types of FeedURIs for MT: the entire installation, a single weblog, or a single entry.

- **UploadURI** — Takes POST. This is used to upload a file to the weblog. It doesn't create an entry, but merely moves a file.

- **CategoryURI** — Takes GET. This is used to retrieve a list of the categories within a weblog.

Current Toolkits

There are currently only a few toolkits for working with the Atom API (there are far more for the Atom syndication format), but looking at `www.atomenabled.org/everyone/ atomenabled/index.php?c=7` will enable you to find more.

For our purposes, we shall be using the XML::Atom Perl module, written by Ben Trott. It's the library that powers Movable Type's side of the API, so we know it's robust; and being a web API, it really doesn't matter what language you write your client code in.

Security and Authentication Under MT

Currently, the authentication system that Atom uses is incompatible with the way that Movable Type stores its passwords internally. This means that you can't use your usual MT password to authenticate yourself with Atom. Rather, you must use your usual username and the "Atom Authentication Token" that is given on your Author Details page. You can find this by going to the main MT menu and looking for your name at the top right. Click on it and scroll down the resulting page. It's about halfway down.

This value, not your usual password, is what you need to log into Movable Type's Atom API.

Using the Atom API with Movable Type

Although everything is very new, we can use the Atom API to interact with Movable Type today. In fact, at the time of this writing, Movable Type has the best support for the Atom API to be found anywhere.

Retrieving Weblog Information

For our first foray into Atom land, let's retrieve information about the weblog by running a GET request to the FeedURI. Remember, there are three possible FeedURIs within Movable Type: the FeedURI for the whole installation, the FeedURI for a single weblog, and the FeedURI for a single entry.

Retrieving Information from an Entire Installation

The FeedURI for an entire installation is `http://PATH.TO.MT/mt-atom.cgi/weblog/`.

This code will access that and print out the result as XML:

```perl
#!/usr/bin/perl -w
use strict;
use XML::Atom::Client;

my $username = "Ben Hammersley";
my $password = "XXXXXXXX";
my $FeedURI = "http://www.mediacooperative.com/mt-
atom.cgi/weblog/";

my $api = XML::Atom::Client->new;
$api->username($username);
$api->password($password);

my $feed = $api->getFeed($FeedURI);

if ($feed) {
    print $feed->as_xml;
        } else {
    print $api->errstr;
}
```

The result for my own weblog is as follows:

```xml
<?xml version="1.0"?>
<feed xmlns="http://purl.org/atom/ns#">
  <link xmlns="http://purl.org/atom/ns#"
type="application/x.atom+xml" rel="service.post"
href="http://www.mediacooperative.com/mt-
atom.cgi/weblog/blog_id=3" title="Ben Hammersley's Dangerous
Precedent"/>
  <link xmlns="http://purl.org/atom/ns#"
type="application/x.atom+xml" rel="service.feed"
href="http://www.mediacooperative.com/mt-
atom.cgi/weblog/blog_id=3" title="Ben Hammersley's Dangerous
Precedent"/>
  <link xmlns="http://purl.org/atom/ns#"
type="application/x.atom+xml" rel="service.upload"
href="http://www.mediacooperative.com/mt-
atom.cgi/weblog/blog_id=3/svc=upload" title="Ben Hammersley's
Dangerous Precedent"/>
  <link xmlns="http://purl.org/atom/ns#"
type="application/x.atom+xml" rel="service.categories"
href="http://www.mediacooperative.com/mt-
atom.cgi/weblog/blog_id=3/svc=categories" title="Ben Hammersley's
Dangerous Precedent"/>
  <link xmlns="http://purl.org/atom/ns#"
type="application/x.atom+xml" rel="service.post"
```

```
href="http://www.mediacooperative.com/mt-atom.cgi/weblog/
blog_id=5" title="Lazyweb"/>
  <link xmlns="http://purl.org/atom/ns#" type="application/
x.atom+xml" rel="service.feed"
href="http://www.mediacooperative.com/mt-atom.cgi/weblog/
blog_id=5" title="Lazyweb"/>
  <link xmlns="http://purl.org/atom/ns#" type="application/
x.atom+xml" rel="service.upload"
href="http://www.mediacooperative.com/mt-atom.cgi/weblog/
blog_id=5/svc=upload" title="Lazyweb"/>
  <link xmlns="http://purl.org/atom/ns#" type="application/
x.atom+xml" rel="service.categories"
href="http://www.mediacooperative.com/mt-atom.cgi/weblog/
blog_id=5/svc=categories" title="Lazyweb"/>
  <link xmlns="http://purl.org/atom/ns#" type="application/
.atom+xml" rel="service.post"
href="http://www.mediacooperative.com/mt-atom.cgi/weblog/
blog_id=19" title="BHDP Static Pages"/>
  <link xmlns="http://purl.org/atom/ns#" type="application/
x.atom+xml" rel="service.feed"
href="http://www.mediacooperative.com/mt-atom.cgi/weblog/
blog_id=19" title="BHDP Static Pages"/>
  <link xmlns="http://purl.org/atom/ns#" type="application/
x.atom+xml" rel="service.upload"
href="http://www.mediacooperative.com/mt-atom.cgi/weblog/
blog_id=19/svc=upload" title="BHDP Static Pages"/>
  <link xmlns="http://purl.org/atom/ns#" type="application/
x.atom+xml" rel="service.categories"
href="http://www.mediacooperative.com/mt-atom.cgi/weblog/
blog_id=19/svc=categories" title="BHDP Static Pages"/>
</feed>
```

As you can see, I have three weblogs within my installation that I care to share with you, and each one has four URIs associated with it. The fifth type, the EditURI, is only associated with individual entries, and so doesn't get listed here.

Being in XML, I can use a variety of tools on the results that the Atom API throws back at me. XML::Atom requires either XML::LibXML or XML::XPath as a prerequisite to it being installed, so straight away you can use DOM or XPath to do your querying. (Or, you can load up something like XML::Simple and use that — whatever you are most comfortable with. This is Perl, remember.)

In this case, we're really interested in my main site, titled "Ben Hammersley's Dangerous Precedent," so we need to pull out the specific FeedURI for that from the result we have now.

Using the standard XML::LibXML interface, you can do it like this:

```perl
#!/usr/bin/perl -w
use strict;
use XML::Atom::Client;

my $username = "Ben Hammersley";
```

```perl
my $password = "XXXXXXXX";
my $FeedURI = "http://www.mediacooperative.com/mt-atom.cgi/
weblog/";

my $api = XML::Atom::Client->new;
$api->username($username);
$api->password($password);

my $feed = $api->getFeed($FeedURI);

if ($feed) {
    my @links = $feed->{doc}->getElementsByTagNameNS('http://purl.
org/atom/ns#', 'link');
    foreach my $link (@links) {

      my $link_rel = $link->getAttribute('rel');
      my $link_title = $link->getAttribute('title');
      my $link_href = $link->getAttribute('href');

      if (($link_rel eq 'service.feed') && ($link_title eq
"Ben Hammersley\'s Dangerous Precedent")) {
        print "$link_href";
              }
    }
        } else {
    print $api->errstr;
}
```

This will print out the FeedURI for that specific weblog, which turns out to be www.
mediacooperative.com/mt-atom.cgi/weblog/blog_id=3.

Let's move on and use it.

Retrieving Information from a Single Weblog

GETting the FeedURI for a single weblog will return the last 20 entries, in descending
chronological order. Again using XML::Atom, and the FeedURI previously found above, this
is simply as follows:

```perl
#!/usr/bin/perl -w
use strict;
use XML::Atom::Client;

my $username = "Ben Hammersley";
my $password = "XXXXXXXX";
my $FeedURI = "http://www.mediacooperative.com/mt-atom.cgi/weblog/
blog_id=3";

my $api = XML::Atom::Client->new;
$api->username($username);
$api->password($password);

my $feed = $api->getFeed($FeedURI);
```

```
if ($feed) {
    print $feed->as_xml;
        } else {
    print $api->errstr;
}
```

The outcome is the same as before, but with the longer FeedURI. This results in a more complicated document. It's a complete Atom feed, just like the Syndication standard, containing details of the last 20 entries on that blog. Here's a cut-down version with only one `<entry>` where usually there would be 20:

```
<?xml version="1.0"?>
<feed xmlns="http://purl.org/atom/ns#">
<link xmlns="http://purl.org/atom/ns#" type="text/html"
rel="alternate" href="http://www.benhammersley.com" title=""/>
<title>Ben Hammersley's Dangerous Precedent</title>
<link xmlns="http://purl.org/atom/ns#"
type="application/x.atom+xml" rel="service.post"
href="http://www.mediacooperative.com/mt-
atom.cgi/weblog/blog_id=3" title="Ben Hammersley's Dangerous
Precedent"/>

<entry xmlns="http://purl.org/atom/ns#">
 <title>Perl really can do everything</title>
 <summary/>
 <content mode="xml">
 <div xmlns="http://www.w3.org/1999/xhtml">The perils of coding
and bittorrenting at the same time.
<code>perl -MCPAN -e 'install CSI::Miami'</code>
More coffee needed. I repeat, more coffee needed.</div>
 </content>
 <author>
  <name xmlns="http://purl.org/atom/ns#">Ben Hammersley</name>
  <url
xmlns="http://purl.org/atom/ns#">http://www.benhammersley.com</url
>
  <email
xmlns="http://purl.org/atom/ns#">ben@benhammersley.com</email>
 </author>
 <issued>2004-07-13T14:17:40+0100</issued>
 <id>tag::post:8588</id>
 <link xmlns="http://purl.org/atom/ns#"
type="application/x.atom+xml" rel="service.edit"
href="http://www.mediacooperative.com/mt-
atom.cgi/weblog/blog_id=3/entry_id=8588" title="Perl really can do
everything"/>
 </entry>
</feed>
```

Parsing this document for the details of each post is very easy indeed. As you can see, it's straightforward XML.

You will notice, however, that this feed does not give the public URL for the entry. You can't take this data and expect to be able to produce proper URLs for public display. Neither does it include the category under which the entry has been posted. These are serious drawbacks to the current Atom implementation, but they may have been fixed by the time you read this.

To edit an entry, you must call the EditURI for the entry itself. Notice there's a pointer to it at the bottom of the <entry>.

We would parse this value out using our own favorite XML technique, and declare it thus:

```
http://www.mediacooperative.com/mt-
atom.cgi/weblog/blog_id=3/entry_id=8588
```

Now we can find out all about an installation, a single weblog, and an entry. Before moving on to more interesting things, here is a nice entry to play with.

Posting an Entry

Posting an entry is merely a matter of POSTing correctly formed content to the correct PostURI. Within MT, PostURIs are formed like so:

```
http://URL.TO.MT/mt-atom.cgi/weblog/blog_id=X
```

Once again, we turn to XML::Atom. With this module, you create an XML::Atom::Entry object and push it at the server.

Let's look at some code that will post an entry, and work from there:

```perl
#!/usr/bin/perl -w
use strict;
use XML::Atom::Client;

my $username = "Ben Hammersley";
my $password = "XXXXXXXXXXXXX";
my $PostURI = "http://www.mediacooperative.com/mt-atom.cgi/weblog/
blog_id=3/";

my $api = XML::Atom::Client->new;
$api->username($username);
$api->password($password);

my $entry = XML::Atom::Entry->new;
$entry->title('And it shall render my doubts asunder');
$entry->content('If this works, I shall be unto an Atom API
wrangling god. Oh yes.');

my $EditURI = $api->createEntry($PostURI, $entry);

if ($EditURI) {
print $EditURI;
} else {
print $api->errstr;
}
```

When run, this produces an entry and returns the new entry's EditURI to the script. This is `www.mediacooperative.com/mt-atom.cgi/weblog/blog_id=3/entry_id=8644`; we'll save that for later.

As you can see, you can invoke various methods on the object that give it the attributes you want. In other words, you can do any combination of these, with the `content()` call being compulsory:

```
$entry->title('This is the title');
$entry->content('This is the main entry body');
$entry->summary('This is the excerpt');
```

Setting the Posting Date

```
$entry->issued('2004-08-06T00:12:34Z');
```

Currently, under MT3.01D, MT will only accept the issued date set as Zulu. It's simple to change the date, however; just invoke the issued method with the new date in the format shown.

Setting the Category

Categories within the raw XML of an Atom request are denoted by the use of the trusty old Dublin Core element `<dc:subject>`, perhaps already familiar to you from RSS.

The code to do this is useful to know, as it can be changed to fit any namespaced element, should they be introduced:

```
my $dc = XML::Atom::Namespace->new(dc => 'http://purl.org/dc/
elements/1.1/');

$entry->set($dc, 'subject', 'your_category');
```

Note that the category must already exist within your weblog for the entry to take it on. If it doesn't, the call will throw an error and the post will not be made. For a remote client, therefore, you need to either know the categories or be able to get MT to tell you what they are.

Remembering categories is a job best left to computers. Happily, Movable Type provides an Atom method to retrieve the categories it knows about. Remember when we retrieved the FeedURI for the entire installation? One of the lines for my own weblog was this:

```
<link xmlns="http://purl.org/atom/ns#" type=
"application/x.atom+xml" rel="service.categories"
href="http://www.mediacooperative.com/mt-atom.cgi/weblog/
blog_id=3/svc=categories" title="Ben Hammersley's Dangerous
Precedent"/>
```

We can parse this to get the following CategoryURI:

```
http://www.mediacooperative.com/mt-atom.cgi/weblog/blog_id=3/
svc=categories
```

We can then run a GET request on the CategoryURI, like so:

```perl
#!/usr/bin/perl -w
use strict;
use XML::Atom::Client;

my $username = "Ben Hammersley";
my $password = "XXXXXXXXXXXXX";
my $FeedURI = "http://www.mediacooperative.com/mt-atom.cgi/
weblog/blog_id=3/svc=categories";

my $api = XML::Atom::Client->new;
$api->username($username);
$api->password($password);

my $feed = $api->getFeed($FeedURI);

if ($feed) {
    print $feed->as_xml;
        } else {
    print $api->errstr;
}
```

A file like this is returned:

```xml
<?xml version="1.0" encoding="utf-8"?>
<categories xmlns="http://sixapart.com/atom/category#">
  <subject xmlns="http://purl.org/dc/elements/1.1/">Movable
Type</subject>
  <subject xmlns="http://purl.org/dc/elements/1.1/">RDF and
FOAF</subject>
  <subject xmlns="http://purl.org/dc/elements/1.1/">Renaissance
Art</subject>
  <subject xmlns="http://purl.org/dc/elements/1.1/">Social
Software and Virtual Communities</subject>
  <subject xmlns="http://purl.org/dc/elements/1.1/">Urban
Theory</subject>
  <subject
xmlns="http://purl.org/dc/elements/1.1/">Weblogging</subject>
</categories>
```

This is very straightforward indeed to parse, and we leave that as an exercise for the reader.

Setting the Author and Other Things

Currently, although the toolkits may allow it, Movable Type does not recognize or react in any way to any other payload within an entry creation call. XML::Atom, for example, has a very nice object for the author of a post, but setting it within a new post will have no effect at all.

Incidentally, you can look at the code that interacts with an incoming Atom call yourself. It's at `/lib/MT/AtomServer.pm` — however, please be conscientious and back it up before tinkering with it.

Editing an Entry

So now that we've created an entry, and it has given us the EditURI for a single entry, we can do some more interesting stuff, such as load up an entry, change something, and send it back.

First, we load the entry like so:

```perl
#!/usr/bin/perl -w
use strict;
use XML::Atom::Client;

my $username = "Ben Hammersley";
my $password = "XXXXXXXXXXXXX";
my $EditURI = "http://www.mediacooperative.com/mt-atom.cgi/weblog/
blog_id=3/entry_id=8588";

my $api = XML::Atom::Client->new;
$api->username($username);
$api->password($password);

my $entry= $api->getEntry($EditURI);

if ($entry) {
print $entry->as_xml;
} else {
print $api->errstr;
}
```

This will print out the XML of the entry, which in our case appears as follows:

```xml
<?xml version="1.0"?>
<entry xmlns="http://purl.org/atom/ns#">
  <title>Perl really can do everything</title>
  <summary/>
  <content mode="xml">
    <div xmlns="http://www.w3.org/1999/xhtml">The perils of coding
and bittorrenting at the same time.

<code>perl -MCPAN -e 'install CSI::Miami'</code>

More coffee needed. I repeat, more coffee needed.</div>
  </content>
  <author>
    <name xmlns="http://purl.org/atom/ns#">Ben Hammersley</name>
    <url
xmlns="http://purl.org/atom/ns#">http://www.benhammersley.com</url
>
    <email
xmlns="http://purl.org/atom/ns#">ben@benhammersley.com</email>
  </author>
  <issued>2004-07-13T14:17:40+0100</issued>
  <id>tag::post:8588</id>
</entry>
```

This is very similar indeed to the <entry>s inside a FeedURI result. So now we know what we're dealing with. Fortunately, there is no need to mess around with the raw XML. The XML::Atom module provides a good object-oriented interface to the entry.

At this point, however, I should mention that in version 3.01D, with which I am writing this chapter, there is a bug that prevents the Edit Entry functionality from working. It's easy to fix, however. At line 432, you should change

```
$entry->text($atom->content);
```

to read

```
$entry->text($atom->content()->body());
```

This problem may have been fixed in later versions, but if you find your calls failing weirdly, check this out. Another problem, mentioned before, is that you can't retrieve the current category, although you can set a new one. If you're thinking of writing code to show the current category and then change it to something else, you will need to wait for Six Apart to fix this before you can do the first bit.

Anyhow, you can load the Entry object, and you can place new values into the Entry's attributes. Then you just send the updated Entry object back to MT, doing that with the XML::Atom function updateEntry(), which takes the EditURI and the Entry object.

That is pretty much it: Load the entry, change it, and put it back. However, there are a couple things to notice about XML::Atom:

- Calling the method with no argument gives you the current value, whereas setting an argument changes the value, as in the following example:

```
$entry->title(); # will return the current title.
$entry->title('new title'); # will set the title to
'new title'.
```

- Although it is not mentioned in the current XML::Atom documentation, the content body is an exception to this. You retrieve the body text like this:

```
my $current_entry_body = $entry->content()->body();
```

but set it like this:

```
$entry->content("$new_entry_body");
```

Put all of that together and you get something like this:

```
#!/usr/bin/perl -w
use strict;
use XML::Atom::Client;
use XML::Atom::Entry;

my $username = "Ben Hammersley";
my $password = "XXXXXXXXXXXXXX";
my $EditURI = "http://www.mediacooperative.com/mt-atom.cgi/weblog/
blog_id=3/entry_id=8588";
```

```perl
my $api = XML::Atom::Client->new;
$api->username($username);
$api->password($password);

my $entry = $api->getEntry($EditURI);

my $current_entry_title = $entry->title();
my $current_entry_body = $entry->content()->body();

my $new_entry_body = "$current_entry_body". "Update: Atom Rocks!";

$entry->title("$current_entry_title - UPDATED");
$entry->content("$new_entry_body");

my $post_result = $api->updateEntry($EditURI, $entry);
```

This will load the entry, change the title, append the text "Update: Atom Rocks!" to the current body text, and send it back to MT.

Note If you have architected your site in the way recommended in Chapter 1, changing the entry title will change the permalink of that entry.

Uploading a File

Sometimes you want to upload files to MT: images, for example, or other types of media files. This is done using the UploadURI, denoted within the whole installation feed as `service.upload`. As we discovered earlier, for my site this is `www.mediacooperative.com/mt-atom.cgi/weblog/blog_id=3/svc=upload`.

This URI takes a POST call, with the binary contents of the file as the content entry, its filename as the entry title, and the file's mime type as entry content type. It returns a 1 on success or an error message. It's easy to work out the URL of the uploaded file, as MT will automatically save it into the weblog's root directory. This cannot be changed. You can then place that URL inside a new entry.

Here's some code that takes a local image file and throws it onto the server:

```perl
#!/usr/bin/perl -w
use strict;
use XML::Atom::Client;

my $username = "Ben Hammersley";
my $password = "XXXXXXXXXXXXXXX";
my $UploadURI = "http://www.mediacooperative.com/mt-atom.cgi/weblog/blog_id=3/svc=upload";

my $name = "image.gif";
open my $fh, $name or die $!;
binmode $fh;
```

```perl
my $data = do { local $/; <$fh> };
close $fh;


my $api = XML::Atom::Client->new;
$api->username($username);
$api->password($password);

my $entry = XML::Atom::Entry->new;

# The title is the filename
$entry->title('exampleimage.gif');
$entry->content($data);
$entry->content()->type('image/gif');

my $link = $api->createEntry($UploadURI, $entry);
```

If the file already exists, it won't be overwritten. Instead, it will have an underscore and a number appended to it, like this:

```
exampleimage.gif

exampleimage_1.gif

exampleimage_2.gif
```

Note that, in old school style, the numbering starts from zero.

Deleting Entries

Deleting an entry is merely a matter of sending a DELETE request to the entry's EditURL. You can do this within the XML::Atom module with the `deleteEntry()` function, like so:

```perl
#!/usr/bin/perl -w
use strict;
use XML::Atom::Client;

my $username = "Ben Hammersley";
my $password = "XXXXXXXXXXXXXXX";
my $EditURI = "http://www.mediacooperative.com/mt-atom.cgi/weblog/blog_id=3/entry_id=8644";

my $api = XML::Atom::Client->new;
$api->username($username);
$api->password($password);

my $entry= $api->deleteEntry($EditURI);

if ($entry) {
print $entry;
```

```
} else {
print $api->errstr;
}
```

This will also return 1 on success, or an error message.

Summary

From this chapter, you should have learned how to post, retrieve, and edit entries using the Atom API, and you will have used the interface to upload other files. Movable Type's support for the Atom API is, like the API standard itself, still in its infancy, but it is already quite powerful. Be sure to keep track of the Movable Type documentation to see how it develops in future versions.

Perl API

The Movable Type Perl API is an excellent example of object-oriented Perl development. That makes MT extremely accessible, whether you are creating external tools or plugins that extend its capabilities.

This chapter delves into this powerful API and explores how you can use it to control Movable Type yourself. It assumes you are familiar with Perl programming and general object-oriented programming concepts.

Overview of the Class Hierarchy

Movable Type's codebase is stored in the `lib` subdirectory of a typical installation. Let's take a closer look at how these modules relate to one another. Figure 8-1 displays the physical location of each of the MT Perl modules (this excludes the files from the `extlib` and `plugins` directories, which are outside of the core Movable Type API).

Figure 8-2 is a view of the MT Perl API, showing the class hierarchy and relationships between the classes. The `MT::ErrorHandler` class is a base class for many of the objects, but it provides little function other than the capability to store an error status in the case of an exception within the MT framework.

Figure 8-3 shows the same set of modules as Figure 8-2, but this time they're grouped by their functionality.

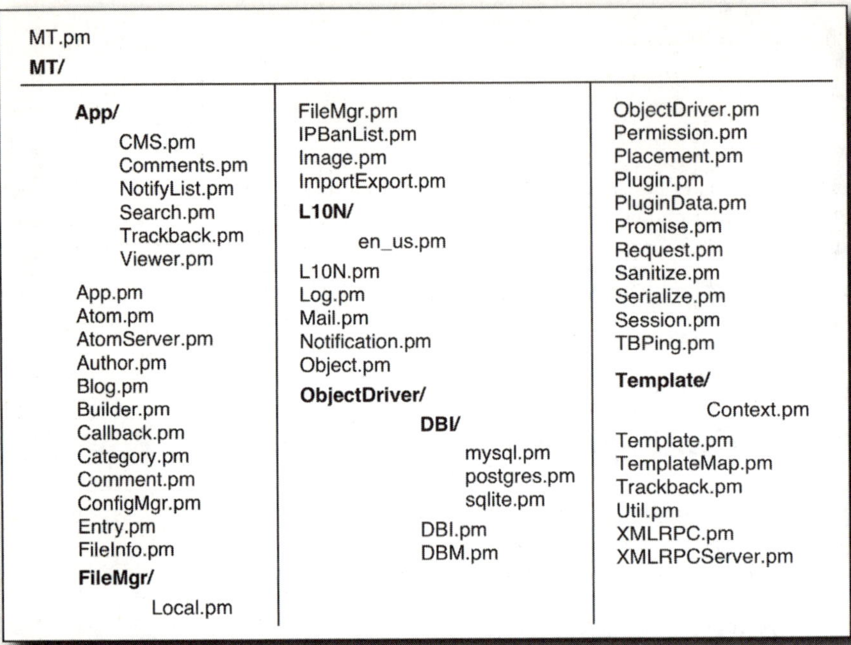

FIGURE 8-1: Movable Type's Perl API, filesystem view

The MT Class

The MT class is the ancestor of MT::App and handles the startup of the Movable Type environment. This includes loading the configuration file (mt.cfg) and initialization of installed plugins. The MT class also provides hooks and management routines for the Movable Type callback architecture. Additionally, the MT class includes much of the weblog rebuilding operations because most any MT subclass (particularly applications) will be rebuilding weblog elements.

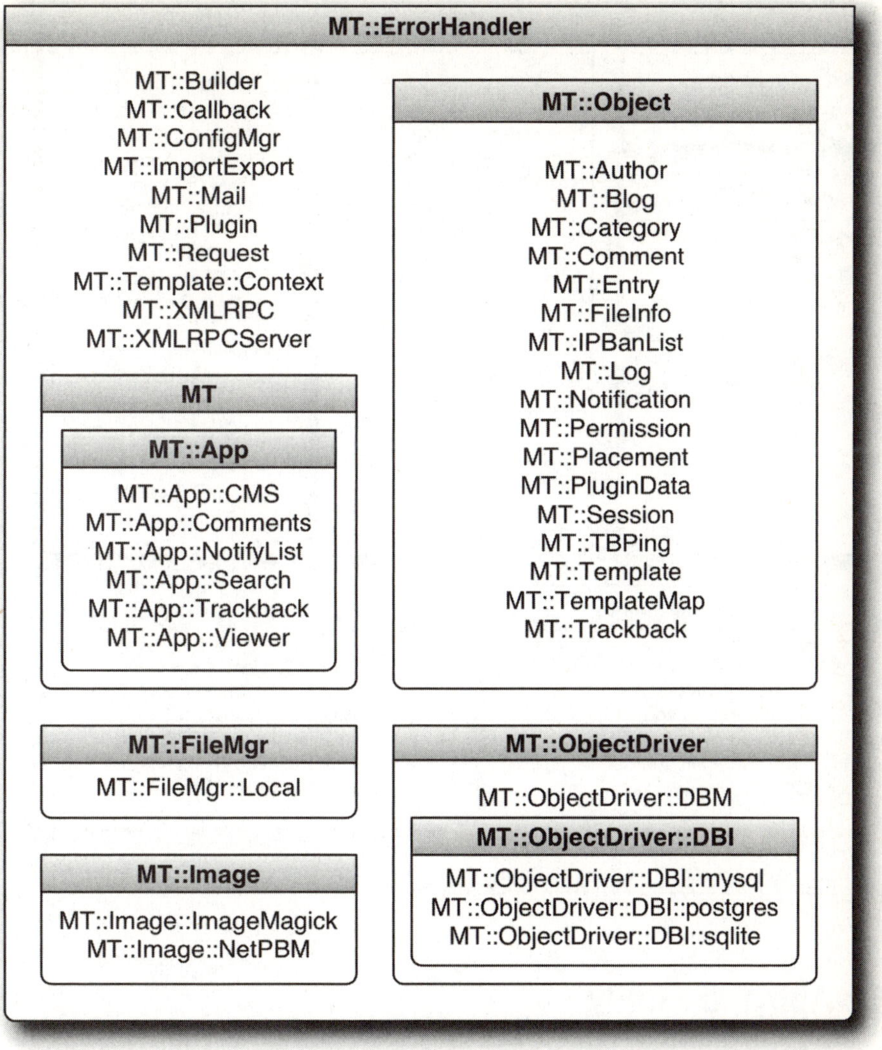

FIGURE 8-2: Movable Type's Perl API, hierarchical view

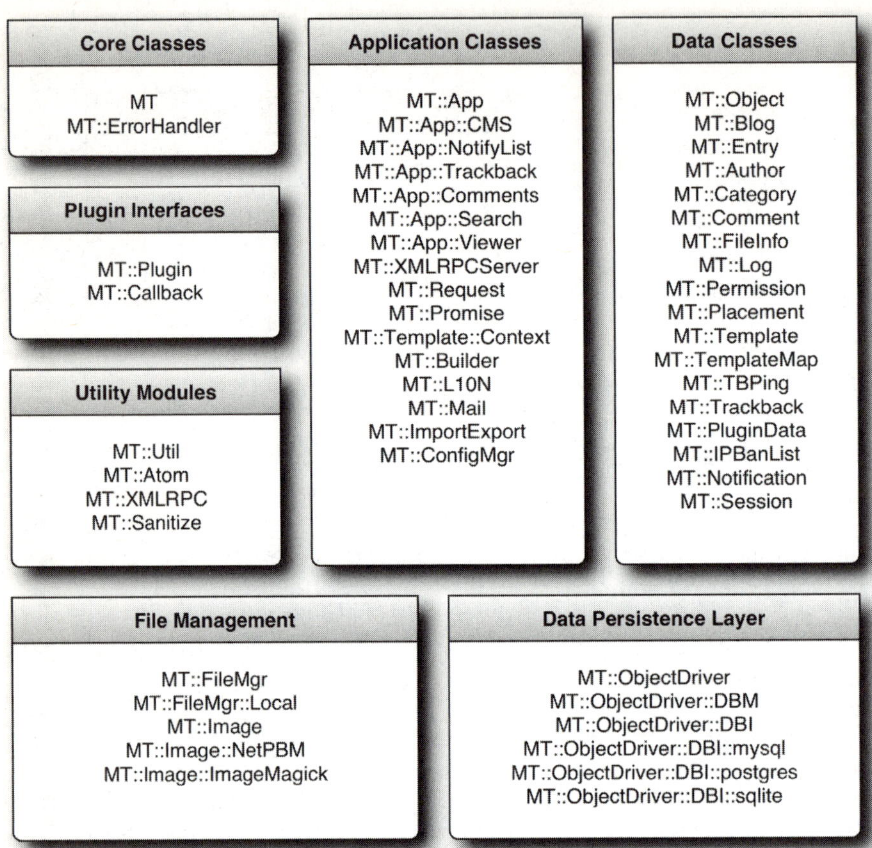

FIGURE 8-3: Movable Type's Perl API, functional view

MT::App and Family

The `MT::App` class is a descendant of the `MT` class and establishes a framework for applications. Most of Movable Type's CGI applications are implemented as a subclass of the `MT::App` class. Table 8-1 shows the relationship between the `MT::App` descendants and the CGI files that invoke them.

Table 8-1   MT::App Subclasses

CGI Filename	MT::App Subclass	Purpose
mt.cgi	MT::App::CMS	Primary MT application
mt-comments.cgi	MT::App::Comments	Handles comment submissions
mt-add-notify.cgi	MT::App::Notify	Handles weblog subscription requests
mt-search.cgi	MT::App::Search	Handles search requests
mt-tb.cgi	MT::App::Trackback	Receives TrackBack submissions
mt-view.cgi	MT::App::Viewer	Generates pages dynamically

You will want to inherit the functionality provided by MT::App when writing your own MT extensions, particularly if they have a web interface of their own. The MT::App class enables you to enforce a login to access the application. You can also leverage the cookie management, templating, and error handling support MT::App provides.

MT::App Structure

Creating your own MT-based applications is pretty simple. You first create a Perl package that defines a new MT::App subclass. At a minimum, it should implement the init method and define a default handler. Listing 8-1 illustrates a minimal MT::App subclass.

Listing 8-1: A Minimal MT::App Subclass

```perl
# store in extlib/MT/App/MyApp.pm
package MT::App::MyApp;

use strict;
use base 'MT::App';

sub init {
    my $app = shift;
    $app->SUPER::init(@_) or return;
    $app->add_methods('main' => \&main,
        'time' => \&show_time);
    $app->{default_mode} = 'main';
}


sub main {
    my $app = shift;
    # return HTML to the browser
    return '<html><body>Hello, world!</body></html>';
}
```

Continued

Listing 8-1 (continued)

```perl
sub show_time {
    my $app = shift;
    my $time = localtime(time);
    return qq{<html><body>Server time is $time</body></html>};
}


1;
```

The other element you need is a way to invoke your application class. If you are using traditional CGI on your server, you need to write a small script to launch the application. The code should look something like what is shown in Listing 8-2.

Listing 8-2: Launch Code for Invoking Your Application Class

```perl
#!/usr/bin/perl -w
use strict;

# establish the directory we're running from and
# add the 'lib', 'extlib' directories to the Perl
# search path
my($MT_DIR);
BEGIN {
    if ($0 =~ m!(.*[/\\])!) {
        $MT_DIR = $1;
    } else {
        $MT_DIR = './';
    }
    unshift @INC, $MT_DIR . 'lib';
    unshift @INC, $MT_DIR . 'extlib';
    # add any other Perl library paths you require here...
}

eval {
    # load application package
    require MT::App::MyApp;
    # instantiate application
    my $app = MT::App::MyApp->new(Config => $MT_DIR . 'mt.cfg',
                                  Directory => $MT_DIR )
        or die MT::App::MyApp->errstr;
    local $SIG{__WARN__} = sub { $app->trace($_[0]) };
    $app->run;
};
if ($@) {
    print "Content-Type: text/html\n\n";
    print "Got an error: $@";
}
```

Once you have your CGI, you can execute requests to your application package from your browser. For example, if you placed your CGI in the MT directory, the URL for your request might look like this:

```
http://localhost/cgi-bin/mt/myapp.cgi
```

This will invoke the "main" handler in MT::App::MyApp, because it is defined as the default application mode. To request other modes, such as time, the URL would look like this:

```
http://localhost/cgi-bin/mt/myapp.cgi?__mode=time
```

The __mode parameter is what you use to segment the functionality of your application into different subroutines. The MT::App package directs the requests to the appropriate handler based on the given mode.

Extending MT Applications

Extending MT applications is very easy to do with the object-oriented framework. For example, you can create a package that inherits from the MT::App::CMS package (the main MT application). If you do that, you can add additional functionality and override existing behavior, as illustrated in Listing 8-3.

Listing 8-3: Adding Additional Functionality

```perl
package MT::App::MyCMS;

use strict;
use base 'MT::App::CMS';

sub init {
    my $app = shift;
    # important, since it populates all the standard MT
    # application methods
    $app->SUPER::init(@_) or return;
    # now we can customize the method list; note that
    # redefining an existing method is okay too.
    $app->add_methods(
        'my_mode' => \&my_mode,        # new mode
        'list_blogs' => \&list_blogs # overridden mode
    );
    $app;
}

sub my_mode {
    return '<html><body>Hello, world!</body></html>';
}

sub list_blogs {
    my $self = shift;
    my $html = $self->SUPER::list_blogs(@_);
    # now do something with $html
```

Continued

Listing 8-3 (continued)

```
    # finally, return html
    return $html;
}

1;
```

To use this package, you would create a copy of the standard `mt.cgi` script that invokes `MT::App::MyCMS` instead of `MT::App::CMS`.

Accessing the HTTP Environment

Once you're ready to move beyond "Hello, world," you will want to start doing real communication with the browser. The data sent by the browser can be accessed through the following methods. (The `$app` variable here is the instance of your `MT::App` subclass. Plugins can also retrieve this object using the `MT->instance()` method.)

- `$app->query_string` — Returns any data from the URL, following the ? character.

- `$app->cookie_val` — Retrieves the value of a particular browser cookie.

- `$app->{query}` — Holds the original CGI object. Use this to retrieve individual parameters, process uploaded files, and retrieve other information sent to the CGI from the request.

- `$app->get_header` — Retrieves the value of a particular HTTP header.

- `%ENV` — Perl's global hash variable for accessing environment variables. It's also useful for determining whether you are executing in a `mod_perl` environment, because `$ENV{MOD_PERL}` will be assigned.

- `$app->path_info` — Returns any characters following the CGI name that are not part of the query string (for example, returns `/path` from a request like `http://localhost/mt/myapp.cgi/path`).

The handlers of your application respond to HTTP requests by returning a scalar with the content to be returned to the client. The content is usually HTML (or XHTML), but could also be RSS or Atom, among others. To adjust the content type header that is returned to the client, use the `send_http_header` method of the application object:

```
$app->send_http_header("image/jpeg");
```

Application Callbacks

Movable Type 3 introduced a callback system, which enables plugins to hook into various points of the MT application. MT exposes the application callback entry points listed in Table 8-2.

Table 8-2   Application Callback Entry Points

Callback Name	Application Class	Purpose
AppPostEntrySave	MT::App::CMS	Invoked upon saving an entry and all objects related to that entry
CommentThrottleFilter	MT::App::Comments	Enables plugins to control whether an e-comment is denied based on a throttle rule
CommentFilter	MT::App::Comments	Enables plugins to intercept an inbound comment and either accept, deny, or moderate it
TBPingThrottleFilter	MT::App::Trackback	Enables plugins to control whether a TrackBack ping is denied, based on a throttle rule
TBPingFilter	MT::App::Trackback	Enables plugins to intercept an inbound TrackBack ping and either accept or deny it

The comment and TrackBack callbacks in particular are excellent means for developing your own comment filtering plugins. Attaching a method to one of these callbacks is demonstrated in Listing 8-4.

Listing 8-4: Attaching a Method to a Callback

```perl
# attach to the AppPostEntrySave callback
use MT;
MT->add_callback( 'AppPostEntrySave', 2, undef,
    \&post_entry_save_handler );

sub  post_entry_save_handler {
    my ($cb, $app, $entry) = @_;
    # do something with $entry
}
```

The parameters given to the `add_callback` method are as follows:

- `method` — The name of the callback to which you are attaching.

- `priority` — A number from 1 to 10 that controls the order of execution for your callback. This is particularly useful when you register multiple callbacks for the same method and one is expecting the other to be run first. The callbacks are executed in order by priority, starting from priority 1.

- `plugin` — You can optionally pass in an `MT::Plugin` (or descendant of `MT::Plugin`) object reference here.

- `code` — A code reference to the callback handler.

The `$cb` object that is passed to your callback routine is an object of type `MT::Callback`. The object also operates as a Perl hash reference and the hash contains the following keys:

- method

- priority

- plugin

- code

As you can see, these are the same elements that were registered with the `add_callback` method.

Object Persistence

Movable Type is all about data. `MT::Object` is the core class that Movable Type uses to manage data as it is stored and retrieved from the database. In programming terms, the `MT::Object` class is what you would call an *abstract class,* meaning that it isn't usable by itself. Movable Type's other data classes derive from `MT::Object`, which supplies their core functions. Refer to Figure 8-2 for a list of the `MT::Object` descendant classes.

MT::Object

The `MT::Object` class provides all of the basic methods necessary to store and retrieve the data from the object itself. A separate class named `MT::ObjectDriver` (and child classes for each supported database, such as MySQL, Postgres, and BerkeleyDB) is used to marshal these objects to and from the underlying database.

MT::Object Data Access Methods

Basic operations on all persistent object data is done through the methods shown in Table 8-3.

Table 8-3   MT::Object Methods

Method Name	Operation
count	Counts all or a subset of objects
exists	Checks if a particular object exists
load	Retrieves one or more objects
load_iter	Incrementally retrieves objects

Method Name	Operation
save	Saves an object to the database
remove	Removes a single object
remove_all	Removes all objects of this class

The MT::Object->load Method

One of the more significant methods of `MT::Object` is the `load` method. Because Movable Type supports several different types of databases, the `load` method provides a vendor-neutral mechanism for retrieving data from a database. That means that regardless of whether you are using the BerkeleyDB as your database or a SQL-based database such as MySQL or PostgreSQL, you code the same way for all of them. You don't have to worry about what happens underneath, it just works.

The `load` method can retrieve either a single object or a list of objects. Another method, `load_iter`, is used to retrieve multiple objects one row at a time. Here's how you might use the `load` method to retrieve a `MT::Blog` object with an ID of 1:

```
use MT::Blog;
my $blog = MT::Blog->load(1);
```

When called with a single numeric parameter, the `load` method assumes it to be the unique ID of the object to be loaded. However, you aren't limited to selecting objects by their ID. The `load` method is quite flexible and can select based on other column values as well (as long as they are indexed columns — a limitation of the BerkeleyDB database). You pass a hash reference in this form. This provides the search terms for the `load` method. You provide the column names and values for the selection:

```
use MT::Blog;
my $terms = { name => "Bloghappy" };
my $blog = MT::Blog->load( $terms );
```

If the `load` method cannot find the object requested, it will return an `undef` value, which you should test for in your code:

```
use MT::Blog;
my $blog = MT::Blog->load({ name => "Unknown Blog" });
return $self->error("Could not load 'Unknown Blog'")
    unless defined $blog;
```

The second parameter for the `load` method is another hash reference, which provides additional search arguments. The argument's hash reference may include the following elements:

- `sort` — Use to sort by an individual column (for compatibility with all supported databases, this must be an indexed column):

  ```
  # selects all blogs, sorting them by name in ascending order
  my $args = { sort => 'name' };
  my @blogs = MT::Blog->load(undef, $args);
  ```

- `direction` — Use to define an ascending (ascend) or descending (descend) sort order. The default is `ascend`:

```
# selects all blogs, sorting by name in descending order
my $args = { sort => 'name', direction => 'descend' };
my @blogs = MT::Blog->load(undef, $args);
```

- `limit` — Use to specify a maximum number of rows to return. The default is to return all available rows:

```
# selects the first 10 blogs
my $args = { limit => 10 };
my @blogs = MT::Blog->load(undef, $args);
```

- `offset` — Use to specify an offset for your record selection. The default is no offset:

```
# selects the 10 entries following the first 10
my $args = { offset => 10, limit => 10 };
my @entries = MT::Entry->load(undef, $args);
```

- `start_val` — Use to define the start of the selection of records to return. This argument is used in combination with the `sort` argument. The column the `start_val` value is compared against is the column specified with the `sort` argument:

```
# select blogs with a blog_id of 11 or more
my $args = { sort => 'id', start_val => 10 };
my @blogs = MT::Blog->load(undef, $args);
```

- `range` — Use to select a range of records. The value of the `range` argument is a hashref that identifies which of the terms specified are to be used this way. The value of the search term in this case is not a scalar value but an array reference that contains the low and high value boundaries of the range:

```
# selects all MT::Entry records who have an entry_id
# between 20 and 40 (but does not include entry_id 20
# or entry_id 40; this is an exclusive range operation).
my $terms = { 'id' => [ 20, 40 ] };
my $args = { range =>  { 'id' => 1 } };
my @entries = MT::Entry->load($terms, $args);
```

- `range_incl` — Similar to the `range` argument, but used to select an inclusive range of records:

```
# selects all MT::Entry records who have an entry_id
# between and including 20 and 40.
my $terms = { 'id' => [ 20, 40 ] };
my $args = { range_incl =>  { 'id' => 1 } };
my @entries = MT::Entry->load($terms, $args);
```

- `join` — Use to join one table with another. This is the most complicated argument of the `load` method, because there are so many options for it. This argument enables you to select and sort on one table of data, but return matching objects from another table. The format of the `join` argument is as follows:

```
join => [ (class), (column), (terms), (arguments) ]
```

The MT documentation provides an excellent example of a join, listing entries that have been recently commented on. What is returned is an array of MT::Entry objects that are related to the MT::Comment objects selected with the join criteria:

```
# selects the last 10 recently commented-on entries
my $args = {
        'join' => [ 'MT::Comment', 'entry_id',
                      { blog_id => $blog_id },
                      { 'sort' => 'created_on',
                        direction => 'descend',
                        unique => 1,
                        limit => 10 } ]
    };
my @entries = MT::Entry->load(undef, $args);
```

- unique — Use in conjunction with the join argument to ensure that only a single instance of any object is returned in the lookup.

To load a collection of objects, you can either call the load method with an array receiving the return value (which tells the load method to return an array of all matches), or you can use the load_iter method instead. The former is best for cases in which you know you are fetching just a few objects. The latter is best when you are operating on an unknown number of objects or when you're processing all of the available objects:

```
use MT::Blog;
# immediately loads all MT::Blog objects into @blogs array
my @blogs = MT::Blog->load();

# loads all MT::Blog objects one at a time using an
# iterator
my $iter = MT::Blog->load_iter();
while (my $blog = $iter->()) {
    # do something with $blog
}
```

Accessing Data

Now that you can load objects from the MT database, you will probably want to access or change the data they contain. All of the MT::Object child classes use a method named install_properties to establish the column names. This method is invoked when the object module is loaded initially. The data can then be retrieved or assigned by calling methods that are named after the properties that were installed. For example, the MT::Blog class defines a name property that gets and sets the weblog name:

```
# retrieve name of blog
my $name = $blog->name;

# assign weblog name and save it
$blog->name("My weblog");
$blog->save;
```

The `save` method will save your updated object back to the database. Removing objects is just as easy. Simply load the object first and then use the `remove` method to delete it.

Object Callbacks

Another noteworthy component of the `MT::Object` class is the callback system. Object callbacks were introduced with Movable Type 3 and they add a whole new way for plugins to interact with Movable Type. A callback is a way to ask Movable Type to run a piece of custom code whenever a particular event happens. In the case of `MT::Object` callbacks, these events include those listed in Table 8-4.

Table 8-4　MT::Object Callbacks Events

Callback Name	*Function*
pre_load	Before loading an object (called from load, load_iter methods)
post_load	After loading an object (called from load, load_iter methods)
pre_remove	Before removing an object
post_remove	After removing an object
pre_remove_all	Before removing all objects
post_remove_all	After removing all objects
pre_save	Before saving an object
post_save	After saving an object

A callback can be associated with any of the `MT::Object` descendant classes. It is important to know that these callbacks have no control over the event; they cannot prevent or roll back an operation in progress. Callbacks are covered in more detail in Chapter 11.

Extending MT::Object

If you need to store objects of your own, you must create a subclass of `MT::Object`. Suppose you wanted to create a list of weblogs to automatically ping (to a target TrackBack ping URL, perhaps a category TrackBack URL) for each post you create. Listing 8-5 provides such an example.

Listing 8-5: Creating a List of Weblogs to Ping for Each Post

```perl
package BlogPal;

use strict;
use base 'MT::Object';
```

```perl
__PACKAGE__->install_properties ({
    columns => [
        'id', 'blog_id', 'name', 'ping_url',
    ],
    indexes => {
        name => 1,
        blog_id => 1
    },
    datasource => 'blogpal',
    primary_key => 'id',
});


1;
```

With this package, it is instantly usable when run on a BerkeleyDB database, but for SQL-based databases, you will need to create the table first. For MySQL databases, the SQL to create this table would look like this:

```sql
create table mt_blogpal (
    blogpal_id integer not null auto_increment primary key,
    blogpal_blog_id integer,
    blogpal_name varchar(100),
    blogpal_ping_url varchar(100),
    index (blogpal_name),
    index (blog_id)
);
```

With your object class defined, you would use it just as you would any other `MT::Object` subclass:

```perl
my $pal = new BlogPal;
$pal->blog_id( $blog_id );
$pal->name("Foo Bar's Blog");
$pal->ping_url("http://foobarblog.com/mt/mt-tb.cgi/10");
$pal->save;
```

Then, your plugin or extension would hook into the `pre_save` callback for `MT::Entry`:

```perl
use MT::Entry;
MT::Entry->add_callback('pre_save', 1, undef,
    \&blogpal_entry_pre_save);


sub blogpal_entry_pre_save {
    my ($cb, $obj, $entry) = @_;

    require BlogPal;
    my @pals = BlogPal->load( { blog_id => $entry->blog_id } );
    return 1 unless @pals;

    my %to_ping = map {$_ => 1} @{ $entry->to_ping_url_list };
```

```perl
    my %pinged = map {$_ => 1} @{ $entry->pinged_url_list };
    foreach (@pals) {
        # add each blog pal ping url to the entry "to ping"
        # list unless the url has already been pinged.
        my $pal_ping_url = $_->ping_url;
        $to_ping{$pal_ping_url} = 1
            unless exists $pinged{$pal_ping_url};
    }
    $entry->to_ping_urls(join "\n", keys %to_ping);
    return 1;
}
```

Plugin API

Movable Type has a very rich and extensible plugin architecture. The plugin API has grown
significantly with Movable Type 3. The plugin API is touched on here because it is a key component of the Perl API, but also refer to Chapter 10 and Chapter 11, dedicated to writing
Movable Type plugins.

MT::Plugin

Movable Type 3 provides a new package that should be the basis for any MT plugin that tar-
gets version 3 or later. The `MT::Plugin` package enables your plugin to identify itself formally
with Movable Type. `MT::Plugin` descendants are visible in the MT web interface and can
provide URLs for configuring the plugin as well. A typical plugin package utilizing
`MT::Plugin` looks like what is shown in Listing 8-6.

Listing 8-6: A Typical Plugin Package Utilizing MT::Plugin

```perl
package MyPlugin;

use strict;
use MT;
use base qw(MT::Plugin);

my $plugin = new MyPlugin({
    name => 'My Plugin',
    description => 'Dices, slices with the greatest of ease',
    doc_link => 'docs/index.html',
    config_link => 'myplugin.cgi'
});
MT->add_plugin($plugin);

1;
```

The `config_link` and `doc_link` parameters passed to the `MT::Plugin` constructor should be relative paths (relative to the directory in which the plugin is installed). The plugin object you create can also be used when registering for MT object and application callbacks.

Plugins register themselves with the Movable Type application in several ways. Table 8-5 identifies attachable entry points.

Table 8-5   Plugin Registration Methods

Package	Method	Purpose
MT	add_plugin	Registers a plugin so that it is visible in the Movable Type main menu
MT	add_plugin_action	Registers a plugin action link so that it appears on the target page
MT	add_callback	Used to hook into application callbacks
MT	add_text_filter	Used to register a text-processing filter
MT::Object (or descendant)	add_callback	Used to hook into object callbacks
MT::Template::Context	add_tag	Registers a new MT template tag
MT::Template::Context	add_container_tag	Registers a new MT template container tag
MT::Template::Context	add_conditional_tag	Registers a new conditional MT container tag
MT::Template::Context	add_global_filter	Registers an MT template global tag attribute

MT::PluginData

If your plugin has data it needs to store in the MT database, it can utilize the `MT::PluginData` package for this. The `MT::Plugin` package provides some convenience methods for storing configuration data. The following example demonstrates how to save a configuration setting:

```
$my_plugin->set_config_value( 'preference', $setting );
```

Loading a previously saved setting is even easier:

```
my $setting = $my_plugin->get_config_value( 'preference' );
```

You may want to assign a default in the event that the configuration element cannot be found:

```
$setting = $default_setting if !defined $setting;
```

If you need to store things besides configuration data, you can create your own `MT::PluginData` records. Here's a method that will read and write data for a particular key

into `MT::PluginData` objects in the database. This would be a method for your
`MT::Plugin` descendant class:

```perl
sub data($key, $data) {
    my $self = shift;
    my $key = shift;
    require MT::PluginData;
    my $pd = MT::PluginData->load({ plugin => $self->name(),
        key => $key });
    if (@_) {
        my $data = shift;
        unless ($pd) {
            $pd = new MT::PluginData;
            $pd->plugin( $self->name() );
            $pd->key($key);
        }
        $pd->data($data);
        $pd->save;
    }
    $pd->data;
}
```

As with any other `MT::Object` class, you can also delete `MT::PluginData` records using
the `remove` method:

```perl
sub remove_all_data {
    my $self = shift;
    require MT::PluginData;
    my @data = MT::PluginData->load({plugin => $self->name()});
    $_->remove foreach @data;
}
```

MT::Session

The `MT::Session` class provides a place to hold temporary data. It has an ID column that
can hold up to 80 characters. The `kind` column is a two-character column you would populate
with a signature that is unique to your plugin. This enables you to segregate your session data
from any others, avoiding the possibility of overwriting data belonging to other plugins or to
MT itself.

The following example demonstrates how you would create a new session record:

```perl
my $sess = MT::Session->new;
# note that IDs can be non-numeric for session data.
$sess->id('some_unique_identifier');
$sess->kind('ex');
$sess->data('data to be stored');
# be sure to record the time it was created
$sess->start = time;
$sess->save;
```

Normally, session data is used to avoid doing some lengthy or resource-intensive operation over and over again. A good example would be fetching data from a remote server. In cases like this, you would check the session table to determine whether the data is available, and if not, you would do the expensive operation to gather the data and then save it to the session table. When fetching your session data, instead of using the `load` method, you will want to use the `get_unexpired_value` method. It is identical to the `MT::Object::load` method, but adds an additional parameter used to specify the timeout period, specified in seconds. If rows are found that exceed the timeout period, they are automatically removed. If a row that is within the timeout period is found, it is returned:

```perl
# the first parameter to get_unexpired_value is the timeout,
# in this case, 300 seconds or 5 minutes.
my $sess = MT::Session::get_unexpired_value( 300, { id => $id,
                kind => 'ex' } );
my $data;
if ($sess) {
    $data = $sess->data;
} else {
    $data = some_timeconsuming_process();
    my $sess = MT::Session->new;
    $sess->id($id);
    $sess->data($data);
    $sess->kind('ex');
    $sess->start(time);
    $sess->save;
}
```

MT Publishing Mechanics

When Movable Type starts a page build procedure, it uses the following packages to manage the process:

- `MT::Template` — Holds the MT template text itself and invokes the build process.

- `MT::Template::Context` — Responsible for matching MT tags to Perl handlers. Also provides the data necessary for each tag, such as the current weblog and the date range being processed.

- `MT::Builder` — Provides two primary methods:

    - `compile` — Converts MT template text into a series of tokens.

    - `build` — Processes a set of template tokens and returns the "built" result.

The example in Listing 8-7 demonstrates how you can invoke these classes programmatically. Normally, you would use the `MT::Template::build` method to do much of this work, but in this case, we will parse a plain string rather than an `MT::Template`.

Listing 8-7: Invoking These Classes Programmatically

```perl
# make sure these packages are all loaded
use MT::Blog;
use MT::Builder;
use MT::Template::Context;

# our mini-template to demonstrate
my $tmpl = q{<MTBlogName>};

# a builder object for compiling and executing the template
my $builder = new MT::Builder;

# a context which we will populate with the target weblog
my $ctx = new MT::Template::Context;

# here we will just place the first weblog we find
$ctx->stash('blog', MT::Blog->load_iter()->());

# compile the template into a series of tokens (an array
# of data that is easy and fast to process by the builder's
# build method)
my $tokens = $builder->compile($ctx, $tmpl);

# finally, build the tokens and print the result
print $builder->build($ctx, $tokens);
```

The Stash

During the page build process, Movable Type uses a state storage object called the *stash*. The stash is essentially just a Perl hash table, where you can store one value for any element name. The implementation of Movable Type's stash adds some extra capabilities. As pages are published, the stash is populated with the contextual information needed by Movable Type's template tags.

The stash becomes the dumping ground for MT tag handlers. Container tags typically store data in the stash for use by tags that are used within them. For example, the `<MTEntries>` container tag sets an `entry` element in the stash that points to the active `MT::Entry` instance. Other entry tags such as `<$MTEntryTitle$>` refer to the `entry` element on the stash and use it as the entry context for the title or whatever they output.

Some MT tag plugins (such as Other Blog or Whole System) replace particular elements in the stash to extend MT's capabilities. For instance, by setting the blog stash element, you can change which weblog MT is looking at when it fetches entries or other weblog-related data.

The `MT::Template::Context` package provides access to the stash. Tag and text-processing plugins receive a `Context` object. The following is a small plugin that will output an incrementing counter with each use. It stores the counter in the stash:

```
use MT::Template::Context;
MT::Template::Context->add_tag( 'Counter' => &CounterHandler );

sub CounterHandler {
    my ($ctx, $args, $cond) = @_;
    my $counter = $ctx->stash('counter') || 1;
    $ctx->stash('counter', $counter + 1);
    $counter;
}

1;
```

With container tags, you deal with the stash a little differently. Because the stash only holds one value for any given named slot, it is up to the developer to preserve the value previously assigned to that slot (if any). For example, container tags such as `<MTOtherBlog>` change the blog element of the stash, but upon the closing `<MTOtherBlog>` tag, you would expect the active blog to return to what it was:

```
Before: <MTBlogName>
Inside: <MTOtherBlog blog_id="2"><MTBlogName></MTOtherBlog>
After: <MTBlogName>
```

If `<MTOtherBlog>` did not save and restore the active blog, the last `<MTBlogName>` tag would output the blog name of blog #2. There is an easy way to accomplish this with Perl, using the `local` statement:

```
local $ctx->{__stash}->{blog} = $new_blog;
```

In this manner, we assign to the stash directly, rather than through the stash method of the `MT::Template::Context` package. This is a shortcut, however. Accessing private member data of an object is generally frowned upon. Therefore,, if you're a purist, you may want to do things the proper way, by retrieving the existing value using the `stash` method and then assigning it back with the `stash` method just prior to exiting your handler routine.

MT::Promise and Lazy Loading

Movable Type 3 introduced a new technique for putting items in the stash. The `MT::Promise` class enables you to put a key into the stash without having to include the value. However, if the key is requested, the value will be produced.

Suppose you want to place some data in the stash for later use:

```
use MT::Entry;
my @entries = MT::Entry->load();
$ctx->stash('all_entries', \@entries);
```

Granted, this is a very contrived example, but it helps illustrate what `MT::Promise` is good for, which is to make data available only if it is necessary. If the `all_entries` element is never requested from the stash, it would never have been necessary to load all those entries into memory. Therefore, we will use a `MT::Promise` instead:

```
use MT::Promise qw(delay);
use MT::Entry;
my $promise = delay(sub {
    my @entries = MT::Entry->load();
    return \@entries;
});
$ctx->stash('all_entries', $promise);
```

The delay routine creates an `MT::Promise` object whose instance is bound to the code provided. In this case, fetching all of the available entries is potentially a time and resource-consuming process. Because we do not know if this stash element will be used or not, we provide the data through a promise. When the stash receives a request for an `all_entries` element, it will see that the value is an `MT::Promise` object and will run the code that was associated with the object. Once the code associated with the promise has been invoked, the result of that operation will be used for any subsequent requests for that stash element.

MT::Request and Object Caching

Another time-saving mechanism is the `MT::Request` package. `MT::Request` provides a place to store data that lives for the duration of the active HTTP request. The following example demonstrates how you might cache lookups for some data into the `MT::Request` object:

```
my $id = shift;
require MT::Request;
my $request = MT::Request->instance;
my $data = $request->cache( $id );
if (!$data) {
    $data = build_data($id);
    $request->cache( $id, $data );
}
# by this point, $data is properly assigned and cached for
# the next lookup.
```

Caching data once per HTTP request can be particularly time-saving if you plan to use it multiple times, even across multiple templates. If you need to cache data across HTTP requests, you should use the `MT::Session` or `MT::PluginData` package.

Error Handling

For any custom tag handlers you write, you should always make a point to surface any errors that users experience. You would do this by returning an error message in the `MT::Context` object you receive:

```
sub my_tag_handler {
    my ($ctx, $args, $cond) = @_;
    my $result = do_something_risky();
    if (!defined $result) {
        return $ctx->error("A useful error message");
    }
    return $result;
}
```

Background Tasks

Movable Type 3 introduces a new subroutine to the `MT::Util` package that enables you to invoke background tasks. Because this capability is not available on every platform (and is not available if you're running MT using `mod_perl`), it is disabled by default. To enable background tasks, add this to your Movable Type configuration file (`mt.cfg`):

```
LaunchBackgroundTasks  1
```

Movable Type currently uses this whenever a comment or TrackBack ping is issued. In the case of comments, it saves your visitor the time MT needs to rebuild the index pages and issue the notification e-mail.

You can use this capability in your own MT plugins and extensions. If you need to run some intensive process that doesn't require user interaction, you can execute it as a background process instead:

```
MT::Util::start_background_task(sub {
    # code for some lengthy, involved process
});
```

Note that even when background tasks are not available for a given MT installation, the `start_background_task` routine will simply execute the task immediately, rather than run it in the background.

Logging and Communication Using MT::Log

The `MT` class (and descendants) provide a log method that is used to store records in the application's log table. These records can be viewed through the MT web interface using the View Activity Log link from MT's main menu. To store log records, use the `log` routine in the main MT package:

```
MT::log("Today is a good day to die -- severe error");
```

Or, if you have a reference to the application object, you can invoke it that way if you prefer:

```
$app->log("Today is a good day to die -- severe error");
```

Debugging Techniques

The following sections detail a couple of techniques for debugging software.

Messaging

One of the simplest (and effective) techniques for debugging software is *messaging*. Simply exposing the value of a variable can be quite revealing. With MT, debugging plugins is problematic because it is a web-based application, usually running on a different computer entirely. With messaging, you have a means to output values of variables or to record how many times a particular routine is called, and the amount of detail you expose is entirely in your hands.

There are several ways to do messaging with MT. From your code, you can issue messages using Perl's `warn` and `die` statements. The `warn` statement will cause a message to display in the web browser (usually at the bottom of the page). A Perl `die` statement will cause the application to halt (unless the `die` statement happened in the context of an `eval` operation, which would trap it). Your web server may be configured to log error messages from CGI scripts to the error log for your site. If this is the case, you can simply print debugging information to `stderr` and it will be sent to the log file. For example:

```
print STDERR "The value of X is $x\n";
```

You may want to output the state of the MT stash to see what it contains:

```
use Data::Dumper;
print STDERR Dumper($ctx->{__stash});
```

Yet another way to debug through messages is to embed them in your templates. Sometimes it is helpful to see what is going on within a particular part of your template. The `WarnDie` plugin enables you to return those Perl warn messages through your templates:

```
<MTWarn>Now building entry: <$MTEntryTitle$></MTWarn>
```

Debugging through messaging is simple, very effective, and easy to do. Just remember to remove any logging instructions you've added once you're done.

Debugging with ptkdb

A much more interactive way to debug your MT extensions and/or plugins (or any Perl code for that matter) is to use a Perl debugging package called `Devel::ptkdb`. A few components are required in order to use this debugger. An X11 server must be running on the computer you are using to access Movable Type. If you're using Linux or Mac OS X, you likely already have X11 installed. For Windows, you can download an X11 server from `http://xfree86.org/`. This package also requires installation of the Tcl/Tk scripting package, which is freely available for most platforms. Tcl/Tk should be installed on the web server on which Movable Type is running. You can find the latest version from `http://tcl.tk/`. Once Tcl/Tk is installed, you would also install the Perl `Tk` and `Devel::ptkdb` packages, again on the web server that runs MT. Once this is done, you would modify the `mt.cgi` script, changing the first line to read as follows:

```
#!/usr/bin/perl -d:ptkdb
```

Then add these lines immediately after that:

```
# Now, add a BEGIN block that defines the X11
# display to use for the debugger:
BEGIN {
    # assign the IP of your workstation here in place of
    # '127.0.0.1' if the web server is not running on your
    # workstation:
    $ENV{DISPLAY} = '127.0.0.1:0.0';
}
```

This works best when everything is running on the same network or on the same computer. Otherwise, you may have to deal with potential firewall rules to enable the X11 connections to come through to your workstation.

For the Windows platform, ActiveState provides a number of development tools for building Perl applications, including CGI applications.

Practical Examples

This section provides you with some practical examples for using Movable Type's Perl API.

Booting Up Movable Type

You can use Movable Type's Perl API in two ways. You can develop extensions for Movable Type through its plugin architecture, or you can create external tools or full applications that use the Movable Type API. If you are creating your own tools or applications, you need to properly initialize Movable Type's framework before you can use any of the MT objects. The initialization process loads the Movable Type configuration file and establishes MT's home directory:

```
my $mt = MT->new(Config => '/path/to/mt.cfg',
                 Directory => '/path/to/mt_home');
```

The `Directory` initialization parameter provides Movable Type with a base location for looking for the other files it needs to function, such as templates, search templates, CSSs, and so forth. These directories can also be defined in the `mt.cfg` file. Without a `Directory` parameter, MT will assume it is the same folder that contains the `mt.cfg` file, or will use the current working directory.

Whether you are creating your own tools or developing plugins, the MT Perl API is used the same way. The following examples will give you a feel for how to use these objects.

Programmatically Creating Users, Weblogs, Categories, Whatever

Creating new authors through Perl is a good place to start. Why would you want to do this? Well, for some uses of Movable Type, you may want to dynamically create new authors. For example, perhaps you have a community blog site where anyone can submit entries for publication. All they have to do is register. Perhaps your registration process uses a Perl CGI to process the registration form. That CGI could use the Movable Type API to add the new registrant as an author to the community blog. The code in Listing 8-8 uses constants to demonstrate the API usage. Your CGI would use CGI post data to populate the author values instead.

Listing 8-8: Using the Movable Type API to Add New Authors

```perl
#!/usr/bin/perl
use strict;

use MT;
use MT::Author qw(AUTHOR);
use MT::Permission;

# initialize Movable Type framework:
my $mt = MT->new(Config => 'mt.cfg');

# create new author
my $author = new MT::Author;
$author->name("Mr. Blog");
$author->nickname("Mr. B");
$author->email("mrb@blog.com");
$author->type(AUTHOR);
$author->set_password("blogging");
$author->save;

# now, assign this new user to be an author
# for the 'Bloghappy' weblog:
my $blog = MT::Blog->load({ name => 'Bloghappy' });
my $perm = new MT::Permission;
$perm->blog_id($blog->id);
$perm->author_id($author->id);
$perm->can_post(1);
$perm->save;

# now redirect the user to the MT interface...
my $cfg = MT::ConfigMgr->instance;
print "Location: ".$cfg->CGIPath."mt.cgi\n\n";
```

At this point, this user could log in to the Movable Type application itself. She would only have access to the community blog "Bloghappy." She can post new entries (and edit ones she's created), but that's all.

Inserting a New Entry

Naturally, creating entries can also be done through the Perl API. There are lots of reasons why you may want to create entries for your weblog through an external script. A few uses include the following:

- You have a script that creates entries upon receiving e-mails to a specific e-mail address.

- You aggregate news from other sources and then republish them.

- You have a custom interface enabling authors to submit and edit their entries.

Regardless of your reasons for doing it, the technique is the same, as shown in Listing 8-9 (again, using constants here for the sake of demonstration).

Listing 8-9: Creating New Entries

```perl
#!/usr/bin/perl
use strict;

use MT;
use MT::Author;
use MT::Entry;

# initialize Movable Type framework:
my $mt = MT->new(Config => 'mt.cfg');
my $blog = MT::Blog->load({ name => 'Bloghappy' })
    or die "Could not load blog";
my $author = MT::Author->load({ email => 'mrb@blog.com' })
    or die "Could not load author";

my $entry = new MT::Entry;
$entry->blog_id($blog->id);
$entry->author_id($author->id);
$entry->title("Some interesting title");
$entry->text("Content of entry");
$entry->status(MT::Entry::RELEASE());
$entry->save;
$mt->rebuild_entry(Entry => $entry,
                   BuildDependencies => 1);
```

Assigning an Entry to Categories

Assigning entries into categories requires the use of three classes:

- `MT::Entry`
- `MT::Category`
- `MT::Placement`

The first two are obvious, but the `MT::Placement` package may not be. Because entries can be assigned to multiple categories, the `MT::Placement` class is used to relate the two together. Listing 8-10 shows how to use them to add categories to an existing entry.

Listing 8-10: Adding Categories to an Existing Entry

```
# load the primary, secondary category and entry
# these can be created from scratch or simply loaded
# as we're doing here...
my $primary_cat = MT::Category->load({ name => "Journal" });
my $secondary_cat = MT::Category->load({ name => "Weather" });
my $entry = MT::Entry->load({ title => "Rainy day" });

my $place = MT::Placement->new;
$place->entry_id($entry->id);
$place->category_id($primary_cat->id);
$place->is_primary(1);
$place->save;

$place = MT::Placement->new;
$place->entry_id($entry->id);
$place->category_id($secondary_cat->id);
$place->is_primary(0);
$place->save;

# at this point, you may wish to rebuild since the entry
# has changed
my $mt = MT->instance();
$mt->rebuild_entry(Entry => $entry,
                   BuildDependicies => 1);
```

Invoking a Rebuild

Finally, you may want to execute rebuild operations independently of the application. Perhaps you have an element in your template(s) that needs to be updated from time to time (but not necessarily upon every page view from your website). Or perhaps you use MT to pull content from other websites or web services and you want to refresh that content on a periodic basis.

You already learned in the last example how to rebuild for a particular entry:

```perl
$mt->rebuild_entry(Entry => $entry,
                   BuildDependencies => 1);
```

There are also rebuild methods available to rebuild your archives or even your entire weblog:

```perl
# rebuild the individual archives for blog ID 1.
$mt->rebuild(BlogID => 1, ArchiveType => 'Individual');

# rebuild the entire weblog for blog ID 1
$mt->rebuild(BlogID => 1);

# rebuild all archives, but not the index templates:
$mt->rebuild(BlogID => 1, NoIndexes => 1);

# rebuild everything. All weblogs are processed:
my @blogs = MT::Blog->load;
$mt->rebuild(BlogID => $_->id) foreach @blogs;
```

You can use simple scripts to force MT to rebuild pages like this. Timely, scripted rebuild operations can give you many of the benefits of dynamic pages, even if you are publishing a static website.

Summary

Movable Type has become a playground for Perl programmers because of its well-designed and comprehensive Perl API. Anyone who can code in Perl can extend the capabilities of the software with plugins and other enhancement scripts.

The plugin framework transforms a nice browser-based content management system into a truly ambitious publishing and information-gathering tool.

Ideally, a plugin should integrate so seamlessly with Movable Type that it feels as if it were part of the software's standard installation.

Hacking with Plugins

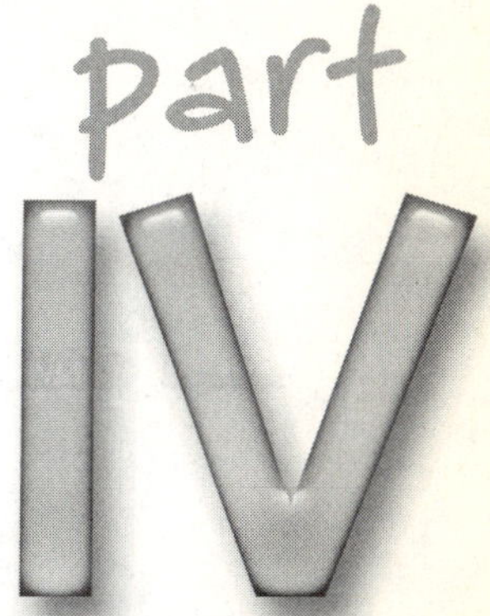

The Wonderful World of Plugins

Movable Type is a very powerful application, but its real power isn't to be found in the built-in features. For the majority of users, the real power of MT is found in plugins.

Over one hundred plugins have been written since MT's birth, and they continue to add greater and deeper capabilities to the core system. This chapter details where most of these plugins live, explains how to install them, and then looks at some of our favorites.

Finding the Available Plugins

Thanks to what is undoubtedly one of the truly heroic efforts of the weblogging world, it is very easy to find plugins for your installation. You only need turn to the MT Plugins Directory.

Founded by Kristine Beeson, known on the Movable Type support board as "Kadyellebee," the site has now been taken under the wing of Six Apart and can be reached at www.sixapart.com/pronet/plugins.

From that page you will find the vast majority of all MT plugins ever written, catalogued by how they are used.

The Different Types of Plugins

At their most basic, plugins provide a collection of new template tags with new capabilities for outputting data from your Movable Type installation. At their most powerful, they can completely customize the way the application runs.

The basic types of plugins are as follows:

- Plugins that provide new access to internal data in the form of template tags
- Web services plugins that provide access to external data
- Text formatting plugins that modify your entry text
- Plugins that give you facilities to enable basic programming
- Plugins that modify the way the internal functions work

The following sections introduce examples of most of these categories.

How We Chose the Plugins

Between us (the authors of this book), we have built countless Movable Type–based sites, most of which simply couldn't have been built without the help of certain plugins. These were obvious choices.

Other plugins we chose because of their necessity in maintaining a healthy site. These are typically spam-related and have saved us countless hours reducing our spam load.

A third group of plugins we chose are those that do something uniquely interesting but not necessarily life-saving. These plugins were chosen because they make the web a better place in general.

General Conventions for This Chapter

Every description includes directions for installation. Installing plugins requires uploading certain files to particular locations and sometimes setting permissions so that the plugin will operate. In general, we list locations of the programs using two variables:

- `MT_DIR` — Your main MT directory, where `mt.cgi` is located
- `MT_STATIC` — Your static directory, which, by default, is the same as your `\N`, but different if you have moved it elsewhere and specified that location in `mt.cfg`

Therefore, if you are required to upload `plugin.css` to your static directory and `plugin.pl` to your MT plugins (Perl) directory, it will be written like this:

- `MT_DIR/plugin.pl`
- `MT_STATIC/plugin.css`

In some cases, you will be required to create a directory if you have not already done so.

Static versus Dynamic Plugins

With the advent of MT 3.1, Movable Type included dynamic publishing as an option for templates selected by the user. Unfortunately, any template tags provided by plugins could not be used as is on the dynamic side because they were written in Perl and not PHP.

Shortly after MT 3.1's debut, a conversion campaign was started to get the most widely used plugins compatible with PHP as well as Perl. This process is ongoing, so some plugins documented in this chapter may lack PHP support. A plugin that only supports Perl cannot be employed on dynamically published pages.

For each plugin we detail in the following sections, we will indicate whether it is compatible with dynamic publishing.

SimpleComments

The SimpleComments plugin, written originally by Adam Kalsey and ported to PHP for dynamic templates by Brad Choate, merges the idea of a comment and a TrackBack. If you think about it, a TrackBack is really just a comment that someone has chosen to place primarily on their own weblog instead of yours; but it is still a comment, and it can be considered as such within your own templates. SimpleComments provides template tags that enable just this.

SimpleComments is PHP-compatible.

How to Install It

Installation is simple. Download the plugin (`v1.32`) from `http://kalsey.com/tools/simplecomments` and unarchive it. Put the files in the archive in `MT_DIR/plugins/` and the `MT_DIR/php/plugins` directories into the corresponding directories in your main MT directory. Doing so completes the installation.

How to Use It within a Template

SimpleComments provides seven new template tags, which work the same for both static and dynamic templates. Within an entry context, you can use any of the tags that follow:

- `<MTSimpleComments>` — This is the main container tag. This tag will create a list of comments and TrackBack pings, by default, sorted by date. This is effectively a combination of the effects of the built-in `<MTComments>` and `<MTPings>` container tags. Just as with those two standard elements, the `sort_order` attribute works to display the comments and TrackBacks in chronologically ascending or descending order. The `lastn="N"` attribute also works as normal to limit the total number of comments and pings displayed. Under MT3.x, only approved comments are displayed. If you want to show unapproved comments as well, add an attribute of `moderate="0"`.

- `<MTSimpleCommentCount>` — This gives a unified count of both your comments and TrackBack pings. For example, if an entry has three comments and two pings, `MTSimpleCommentCount` will display five.

- `<MTSimpleCommentNumber>` — This displays the numeric order of the current comment or TrackBack ping. For the first SimpleComment, it reads 1. For the second, 2, and so on.

- `<MTSimpleCommentOdd>` — This returns 1 if the current SimpleComment is odd, and 0 if it is even. This is useful for setting alternating background colors with a CSS, for example — use code such as `class="commentbg<MTSimpleCommentOdd>"` and then have CSS classes named `"commentbg0"` and `"commentbg1"`.

- `<MTSimpleCommentIfTrackback>` — The contents of this tag will only be displayed if the current item in the comment list is a TrackBack.

- `<MTSimpleCommentIfComment>` — The contents of this tag will only be displayed if the current item in the comment list is a Comment.

- `<MTSimpleCommentEntry>` — This container tag works just like the `MTCommentEntry` tag and contains the entry on which the comment or TrackBack was made. Using this tag, you can use `MTEntry` tags to get entry data for that SimpleComment.

Put these together and you have something like what is shown in Listing 9-1, a simple example of using SimpleComments on an entry page.

Listing 9-1: Using SimpleComments on an Entry Page

```
<MTSimpleComments>
<MTSimpleCommentIfTrackback>
<div id="trackback">
<em><MTPingBlogName></em> commented on this post:<br/>
<blockquote cite="<$MTPingURL$>"><MTPingExcerpt></blockquote>
Read more <a href="<$MTPingURL$>">here</a></p>
</div>
</MTSimpleCommentIfTrackback>

<MTSimpleCommentIfComment>
<div id="comment">
<$MTCommentBody sanitize="0" validable="1" smarty_pants="1"
acronym="1"$>
<span class="permalink">Posted by: <$MTCommentAuthorLink
show_email="0"$> <MTCommentAuthorIdentity> on
<$MTCommentDate$></span>
</div>
</MTSimpleCommentIfComment>
</MTSimpleComments>
```

Using this in your template will intermingle the comments left directly on your blog with TrackBacks, but it will also enable you to style the two items differently. In Listing 9-1, the plugin wraps the TrackBack and the comment in `div` blocks of the corresponding label, and adds the correct data about the origin of the comment. Using CSS to style these `div`s differently is dead simple, as shown in Listing 9-2.

Listing 9-2: CSS Styling of Comments and TrackBacks

```
body#comment {
        /* Normal page content styling */
        }
body#trackback {
        border: 1px solid #DD9963;
        padding: 6px;
        }
```

The plugin can also be used on the main index page, which is best in conjunction with the MT-Switch plugin, to provide grammatically correct invitations to comment. Listing 9-3 shows this.

Listing 9-3: Using SimpleComments with MT-Switch

```
<p class="tools">
<MTSwitch value="[MTSimpleCommentCount]">
  <MTSwCase value="0">
    <a href="<$MTEntryPermalink$>">
    No comments as yet.</a>
  </MTSwCase>
  <MTSwCase value="1">
    <a href="<$MTEntryPermalink$>">
    1 Comment - Add another.</a>
  </MTSwCase>
  <MTSwDefault>
    <a href="<$MTEntryPermalink$>">
    <$MTSimpleCommentCount$> comments - Add more.</a>
  </MTSwDefault>
</MTSwitch>
</p>
```

The Result

Figure 9-1 shows the result of the SimpleComments plugin used together with MT-Switch (as in Listing 9-3) on a site. In this author's opinion, this is a much cleaner design than the standard template's way of showing Comments and TrackBacks as separate values.

Adam Kalsey October 24, 2004 9:05 AM

Arvind: Use either one. I've included Brad's in the download because it's released under the same license as my original and because Brad wrote it with the intention of making it part of the product.

Both dynamic plugins do essentially the same thing, you can use either one.

Trackback from **Movable Type Plugin Directory**
October 25, 2004 12:11 AM
Simple Comments
Excerpt: 1.1 SimpleComments can now be used outside an entry. 1.32 adds dynamic option, along with some fixes and easier installation....

FIGURE 9-1: The effect of the SimpleComments plugin

Textile and Markdown

There's no doubt that a long entry can be easily made much longer and more tedious to write by including reams of HTML markup. All of those quotes, equals signs, angle brackets, and slashes are enough to make anyone curse the semantic web. Still, there's nothing that replaces strong emphasis, and good luck trying to embed a picture without a little markup magic — unless, of course, you have the right tools: text-formatting plugins.

A text-formatting plugin is a special type of plugin that transforms the entry text you input into some other desired output. There are a number of text-formatting plugins, but the two most useful are Textile and Markdown, written by Brad Choate and John Gruber, respectively (with PHP versions by Arvind Satyanarayan for dynamic pages).

Both of these plugins (based on the markup formats by the same name) enable you to write content that is utterly devoid of HTML and yet is marked up correctly when the page is published or displayed. It does this by equating actual markup constructs for pneumonic text-based counterparts commonly found in plaintext e-mail or wikis.

What's truly awesome, however, is that both Textile and Markdown features are a superset of Movable Type's built-in "Convert breaks" text formatting. What that means is that your current entries are *already* in Textile/Markdown format (with a few gotchas, which are explained shortly). You can, in fact, use as much or as little of the special formatting features as you like, and you can even use regular HTML. Really, they are superior in almost every way imaginable to the default formatting. Get them now.

How do you choose? There is some overlap in syntax (covered briefly in a second), but for the most part, they are different languages, both with their benefits and shortcomings. In general, Markdown markup tends to be simpler and highly readable, while Textile is more powerful but slightly kludgier and harder on the eyes. The one you choose depends on how much power you need. Take a look at Markdown first. The only thing really missing from Markdown is tables and the capability to specify class or ID CSS selectors for certain tags (images, links, and so on).

Both Markdown and Textile are PHP-compatible.

How to Install Them

For Textile with static templates, download the plugin from `www.bradchoate.com/mt-plugins/textile`. Install the `textile2.pl` file into `MT_DIR/plugins`. Put the `Textile.pm` file into `MT_DIR/extlib/Text`. Create either if they do not exist.

For Markdown, download the plugin archive from `http://daringfireball.net/projects/markdown`. Unpack the archive and upload `Markdown.pl` to `MT_DIR/plugins`.

For Textile or Markdown with dynamic templates, download the plugin from `www.movalog.com/archives/dynamic/breaking-plugins.php`. Put all of the files into `MT_DIR/php/plugins`.

How to Use Them within a Template

If you only want to use Textile or Markdown conversion in your entry body and extended body or your comments, you don't have to make any changes to your templates. However, both can be used on any arbitrary tag using the `filters` attribute. For example, if you wanted to mark up your weblog's description (set in Weblog Config ⇨ Preferences) you would insert it into your templates as follows:

```
<$MTBlogDescription filters="markdown"$>
```

If you are using Textile, you would replace the `"markdown"` in the preceding code with `"textile_2"`.

The Result

For example, if you wanted to write

```
I am <em>stylish</em> while you are <strong>bold</strong>.
```

you would write this in Markdown:

```
I am *stylish* while you are **bold**.
```

In Textile, you would write the following:

```
I am _stylish_ while you are *bold*.
```

The full Textile syntax can be found at `www.bradchoate.com/mt/docs/mtmanual_textile2.html`. Markdown's syntax can be found at `http://daringfireball.net/projects/markdown/syntax`.

Never again will you forget to close a link tag.

Blacklist

MT-Blacklist is the Swiss-army knife of anti-spam plugins for Movable Type. Written by Jay Allen, this plugin was awarded the grand prize in the Movable Type Plugin Developer's Contest in 2004 and has become the most crucial plugin to have in your arsenal.

True to its name, Blacklist works in part by enabling a user to block or force moderate comments and TrackBacks that contain certain strings (not IP addresses). Usually, these strings are domains of spammers, but sometimes using an e-mail address can be surprisingly effective. It also enables the user to match patterns (specified by regular expressions, either anchored to a link or not), which delivers broad protection against a multitude of spammish domains.

However, MT-Blacklist is more than just a blacklist. It also enables a user to force moderate comments with too many URLs or those placed on older entries. Both of these are excellent indicators of spam and work to keep spam off of your site entirely. What's more, it also blocks duplicate pings.

The options available to users in controlling external feedback on their site are numerous and the plugin's administration interface will be immediately familiar to any Movable Type user.

MT-Blacklist is PHP-compatible.

How to Install It

To install MT-Blacklist, download the archive appropriate to your version of Movable Type from `www.jayallen.org/projects/mt-blacklist/`. Unpack the archive and upload the Blacklist directory to the `MT_DIR/plugins/Blacklist/`. The other files are placed as follows:

- `MT_STATIC/mt-blacklist-styles.css`

- `MT_STATIC/mt-blacklist.js`

- `MT_STATIC/docs/Blacklist/`

- `MT_STATIC/images/Blacklist/`

Finally, run `http://YOURSITE.COM/plugins/Blacklist/mt-bl-load.cgi` to initialize the program. The initialization process will add a couple of tables to your database but will not touch your existing Movable Type tables. Still, it is always a good idea to back up your data first before running it.

When the initialization is done, you will be directed to the MT-Blacklist configuration screen. After setting up the options to your liking, you are protected against spam.

No template changes are required in order to use MT-Blacklist.

The Result

The result is, undoubtedly, that you will block a mind-bending amount of spam. An explanation of how MT-Blacklist works follows.

Encapsulation

At runtime, Movable Type includes into memory all of its own code as well as that of the installed plugins. Before the actual request from the client is processed, it executes all of the plugin code to register each plugin's callbacks.

This is where MT-Blacklist moves to encapsulate the MT system (as shown in Figure 9-2) to intercept comments/TrackBacks before they ever get processed by Movable Type and after Movable Type's processing is complete to handle responses to the client and comment notifications.

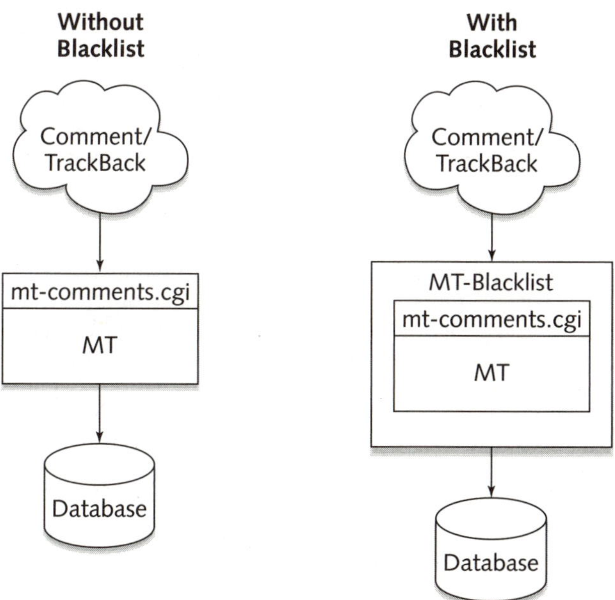

FIGURE 9-2: Blacklist's interaction with Movable Type

Blacklist Matching

After the plugin has control, it checks the comment or TrackBack for matches to its blacklist. The plugin supports three different types of blacklist entries:

- Strings
- Regular Expressions
- URLPatterns

Strings

Blacklist strings are the most straightforward type. The program will attempt to exactly match all Blacklist strings that you add against every field submitted by the commenter (Name, Email, URL, and comment) or in a TrackBack (Blog Name, URL, Excerpt). This is most often used to block submissions containing links to particular domains, but can also be used as a general word filter. Exact string matching is superfast and incurs relatively little overhead in terms of processing.

You should note two things. First, matching is done in a case-insensitive way, so the following are true:

- cat equals cat
- Dog equals DOG
- Snake equals sNaKe

Second, you must be careful with your Blacklist strings because if your item is a substring of a string found in the comment, it will be matched. For instance, a very popular Blacklist string could be `cialis`. Unfortunately, cialis would catch the word "specialist" because it is contained within it. Be on the lookout for substrings.

Regular Expressions (Regexes)

Blacklist strings are excellent for battling a persistent spammer who is trying to get one domain or a limited number of them onto your site. However, it's well known that spammers have more domains in their arsenal than you can imagine, and trying to add each of them as a Blacklist string is nothing more than an unwinnable arms race. For example, one spammer may have

- texas-holdem.com
- texas-hold-em.com
- texas--hold--em.com
- texas-hold-em-000.com

. . . and a thousand more like them. There are a mind-boggling number of permutations that a spammer could use while still maintaining a relatively comprehensible domain name, especially if you take into account all of the top-level and country code domains.

So how do you stay ahead? Regular expressions. A *regular expression* is a carefully crafted text string with metacharacters that act as wildcards for other characters, enabling you to match a number of different strings all in one. The most commonly used metacharacters for MT-Blacklist users are shown in Table 9-1.

Table 9-1   Commonly Used Metacharacters

Character	Definition
.	Any character
*	Zero or more
?	One or zero
+	One or more
[ ]	Character class
\b	Word boundary
\s	A space
\S	Anything but a space

Therefore, to block that Texas Hold-em guy and his 10,000 domains, you only need to add the following as a Blacklist regex:

```
texas\S\*hold\S\*em
```

This matches any comment with the substrings `texas`, `hold`, and `em` with no intervening spaces between them. By ensuring that the intervening characters are not spaces, you avoid matching something like the following phrase: The **Texas** Legislature is **hold**ing a November referendum.

There's a lot more to regular expressions that is outside the scope of this book. Luckily, you don't really need many regular expressions to use Blacklist effectively. You'll see why in the next section.

URLPatterns

You know that MT-Blacklist can block just about anything that you want. The question is, what do you block? Because spammers typically do their thing to get their domains posted on your site and usually do so to get a higher ranking in search engine algorithms, the best thing that you can target is their domain names. By blocking domain names, you cost the spammer time and money in registering new ones, which increases their cost of doing business.

Because we are interested almost solely in spammer domain names, Blacklist provides URLPatterns, a shortcut to doing some of the magic necessary to specify that you only intend to match URLs.

URLPatterns are regular expressions just like Blacklist regexes, except they match URLs only. By using URLPatterns, you don't have to worry about matching small substrings throughout the comment as we did in the preceding Texas Hold-em example. If it's not included in the URL, it won't match.

Using the previous example, but crafting it as a URLPattern, you would get the following:

```
texas.*hold.*em
```

That specifies the strings `texas`, `hold`, and `em` joined by zero or more of anything, but only in URLs, because URLs don't have spaces.

While this URLPattern isn't significantly different from the Regex version, the important point is that you will cut down on accidental false positives because the pattern must be found in one particular URL.

Anyway, the real power of URLPatterns is banning or force moderating single words that would be found in URLs you don't want on your site.

After the Match

If you were lucky enough for one of the items on your blacklist to be matched (and I promise you will), the plugin gives you two options for what to do with that submission (configured when you added the item to the blacklist): block or moderate.

Setting an item to block is an excellent choice when it's the domain of a known spammer or a URLPattern containing a word that has just about zero possibility of being found in a legitimate URL. I could list a few here but spammers are a crude lot and there might be children reading this. You probably already know what I mean.

Moderation provides a wonderful cushion — a purgatory, if you will — that enables you to be hyper-aggressive in your blacklisting. Each Blacklist item can be set individually to block or moderate any matching comments. The program will continue searching through the blacklist for a blocking match even if a moderating one has been found, with the idea that the strongest rule always applies.

By blocking obviously spammy things and moderating "possibly spammy" things, you essentially have a much more flexible (and hence powerful) defense — one that will enable you to reach the initial goal of keeping spam off of your site.

Finally, and most important to your own sanity, there is no need to clean up items in moderated status right away. If something is in a moderated state, it can be left there for an hour, a day, a week, or forever. Get used to the idea of letting spam sit in moderation instead of constantly and quickly despamming your blog after each addition and you'll live a much longer and happier life. Incidentally, moderation also offers you a good way to test certain blacklist items. Think of it as training wheels.

Max URL and Old Entry Checks

If the submission makes it through the gauntlet of blocked and moderated blacklist items, the plugin tallies the number of URLs to determine whether it has surpassed your configured limit. It also checks the posting date of the target entry for the comment or TrackBack to determine whether it's outside of your commenting window. If either of these conditions is true, the comment is moderated. Note that because TrackBacks cannot currently be moderated, this step is only applicable to comments. Still, this works very well in catching nearly all of the spam not matched by your blacklist because spammers have a tendency to hit old entries and cram tens or hundreds of URLs into a comment.

Duplicate Check

The plugin also does a simple check to ensure that the same comment or TrackBack wasn't submitted to the same entry or category (in the case of a category ping). If one exists, it is silently rejected. This feature wasn't created so much to combat spam as it was to solve an issue that annoyed thousands.

Wrapping It Up

Finally, when a comment or TrackBack is submitted successfully, Blacklist gives you the option of receiving enhanced notifications with a link to "de-spam" the submission if it's spam. Once you do that, you can optionally submit the found domains to a master blacklist that all MT-Blacklists use to update their own listings.

A whole bevy of other features are included with MT-Blacklist, but that should be enough to emphasize the importance of having it to keep your blog spam-free and to get you started in using it effectively.

MT-Notifier

The MT-Notifier plugin, written by Chad Everett, is more than just a simple plugin for the Movable Type content management system. It is very nearly an application in its own right.

While Movable Type comes with a basic notification system, it is lacking in several areas. MT-Notifier extends that process to its logical conclusion, offering subscriptions to individual entries, categories, or even an entire blog. This enables your readers to keep up with an individual thread, anything in a particular category, or even your entire blog — all automatically, without you having to lift a finger.

You can download MT-Notifier from `http://downloads.everitz.com/ MT-Notifier.zip`.

MT-Notifier is PHP-compatible.

How to Install It

Installation is very straightforward. First, download the most recent version of the plugin. When the download completes, unarchive the package and upload to the following locations:

- `MT_DIR/mt-notifier.cgi`

- `MT_DIR/extlib/jayseae/notifier.pm`

- `MT_DIR/plugins/Notifier.pl`

- `MT_DIR/tmpl/cms/notifier.tmpl`

- `MT_DIR/tmpl/cms/view_log.tmpl` (overwrites MT template)

- `MT_DIR/tmpl/email/notification.tmpl`

Create any directories that do not exist and set the permissions of `mt-notifier.cgi` to 755. Unlike the other files, this one must be executable, because it needs to be executed to access the MT-Notifier management interface. The management interface is protected by requiring a Movable Type login, so not just anyone will be able to access this script.

How to Use the Management Interface

MT-Notifier provides a full-featured management interface to access the functions of the plugin:

- Configure — This option enables you to set a default sender address for your notifications (the default is to use the author e-mail address), indicate the type of notifications you would like to send (comments, entries, or both), and indicate whether you'd like to send entry notifications when entries are updated or only on the initial save. Many people make changes to their entries after publishing; if this describes you, keep in mind that each time you save the entry, a new notification will be sent unless you set this last option to only send notifications one time.

- Install — To process subscriptions from a comment form (more on that shortly), you'll need to integrate MT-Notifier with your MT installation. Do not fear this process. It is as simple as clicking a link in this menu. This menu also enables you to turn on (or turn off) the comment notification for each blog. Comment notification must be turned on in MT for MT to send notifications for that blog.

- Manage — If you want to set up new subscriptions, view existing subscriptions, or even set options on a per-blog, per-category, or per-entry basis, this is the place. You can add new subscriptions to any of the notification types; you can switch subscriptions so that they provide opt-out (never send) records instead; and you can set options for each of the subscription types. This is easily the most frequently used menu of the management interface.

- Purge — When you decide to get rid of some records, you'll want to visit this menu. The basic purge enables you to remove records that are invalid or records of subscriptions for people who have opted out and no longer want to receive notifications. The advanced purge provides much more granular control over the purge, including being able to select the type of records to purge, as well as the location from which to purge (blog, category, or entry). You can even specify an e-mail address so that only records containing that address are removed.

- Transfer — If you have subscriptions elsewhere, you'll likely want to check out the transfer menu. This menu provides options to transfer subscription records from several other notification programs, including Movable Type and MT-Notifier version 1.x! More options are added all the time, so if you don't see the program you use, contact Chad and ask him to add it.

- User Administration Interface — Each notification that is sent includes a link to that user's administration page, where they can change their subscription to their heart's content (subject to the parameters you specify, of course). They will only be able to access their own subscription page, because each user subscription has a unique key that is required to access the interface.

How to Use It within a Template

MT-Notifier can be used for notifications on just about anything within the Movable Type system. For example, you can do the following:

- Use it on an individual entry so that your readers will receive updates whenever a new comment is placed on that entry.

- Place one on your home page and people will be notified about anything new, anywhere on the site.

- Add it to each category and let people know when you add information to that topic.

You'll notice that each of the following subscription forms is remarkably similar. This is by design. The only thing you need to change — aside from the obvious changes to the text to indicate exactly what is being subscribed to — is the key used for the subscription.

Subscribe to a Blog

Say you want to provide a subscription form to your blog so that your readers will know whenever something has been updated. You'll need to create this form with some basic information that is required to create the subscription. Specifically, you need to provide a key and the e-mail address subscribing. Place the template code from Listing 9-4 onto any page that Movable Type produces.

Listing 9-4: Blog Subscription Form

```
<form method="get" action="<$MTCGIPath$>mt-notifier.cgi">
<input type="hidden" name="dkey" value="<$MTBlogID$>:0" />
Subscribe Without Commenting<br/ ><br />
<input name="mail" />
<input type="submit" class="button" value="Go" />
</form>
```

Subscribe to a Category

To provide your visitors with a subscription to your categories so that they are notified when an entry is posted to the category they subscribe to, add the code from Listing 9-5 in a part of any template that has category context (for example, within an `<MTCategories>` loop).

Listing 9-5: Category Subscription Form

```
<form method="get" action="<$MTCGIPath$>mt-notifier.cgi">
<input type="hidden" name="dkey" value="<$MTCategoryID$>:C" />
Subscribe to entries in <$MTCategoryLabel$><br/ ><br />
<input name="mail" />
<input type="submit" class="button" value="Go" />
</form>
```

Of course, the most natural place to put this form is on your category archive pages, which, ironically, lack the sufficient category context needed for `MTCategoryID` and `MTCategoryLabel`. To resolve this, you could use the CategoryOfArchive plugin (`www.sixapart.com/pronet/plugins/plugin/categoryofarchi`) in conjunction with Notifier, as shown here (replacing the line in the preceding listing containing `<$MTCategoryID$>`):

```
<input type="hidden" name="dkey"
value="<MTCategoryOfArchive><$MTCategoryID$></MTCategoryOfArchive>
:C" />
Subscribe to entries in <$MTArchiveCategory$><br/ ><br />
```

Subscribe to an Entry (Standalone Form Method)

Just as with the blog and entry subscription forms, you can create a form to enable users to subscribe to an entry. The format, shown in Listing 9-6, is eerily similar and should be placed on your individual archive page or on any template within an entry context (for example, within an `<MTEntries>` loop).

Listing 9-6: Entry Subscription Form

```
<form method="get" action="<$MTCGIPath$>mt-notifier.cgi">
<input type="hidden" name="dkey" value="0:<$MTEntryID$>" />
Subscribe to comments/TrackBacks on this entry<br/ ><br />
<input name="mail" />
<input type="submit" class="button" value="Go" />
</form>
```

Subscribe to an Entry (En Passant Method)

You may not always want a subscription form all by itself. Often, it is much easier to have the user check a box on the comment form and have the subscription processed automatically. Before you can do this, you must have run the Integrate step within the Install menu described earlier in this chapter.

Luckily, making this work is very simple indeed. Just add the following code to your comment form, or something very much like it (make sure you keep the name `"subscribe"`):

```
<input name="subscribe" type="checkbox" /> Notify me of new
comments on this entry
```

There are, unfortunately, a few things to take care of when using this method. First, if the user previews his or her comments, the value of this checkbox will be lost. Second, if you use the `MTCommentFields` method of generating your comment forms, there is no way for you to edit the contents of that field, and you will not be able to add this checkbox to the form.

MT-Moderate

The MT-Moderate plugin, written by Chad Everett, both addresses a critical flaw in Movable Type and adds functionality to an existing function. The critical flaw is that while comments can be moderated and the options for managing them work quite well, the same cannot be said about TrackBacks. TrackBacks are pings sent from one weblog to another to form a sort of interconnected whole across the Internet. In addition, moderating every single comment that comes into your system isn't always the best solution. Sometimes you would prefer to moderate only certain comments. MT-Moderate to the rescue.

Note   MT-Moderate is not PHP-compatible.

How to Install It

Installing MT-Moderate is quite simple. Download the most recent version of the plugin from `http://downloads.everitz.com/MT-Moderate.zip`. When the download completes, unarchive the package. When you do, the directory structure will be created for you, which enables you to easily see where each piece needs to reside on your server:

- `MT_DIR/plugins/jayseae/moderate.pl`

- `MT_DIR/plugins/jayseae/lib/moderate.pm`

- `MT_DIR/plugins/jayseae/lib/moderate/comments.pm`

- `MT_DIR/plugins/jayseae/lib/moderate/trackbacks.pm`

- `MT_DIR/tmpl/cms/list_ping.tmpl` (overwrites the MT template)

Installing on Windows Servers

If your site is hosted on a Windows server, you must follow some slightly different steps because of the way plugins are handled by MT on a Windows server.

Do not create any subdirectories under the plugins directory. Instead, place the `moderate.pl` file directly in the plugins directory:

- `MT_DIR/plugins/moderate.pl`

- `MT_DIR/extlib/jayseae/moderate.pm`

- `MT_DIR/extlib/jayseae/moderate/comments.pm`

- `MT_DIR/extlib/jayseae/moderate/trackbacks.pm`

- `MT_DIR/tmpl/cms/list_ping.tmpl` (overwrites the MT template)

How to Use MT-Moderate

Perhaps the best part about MT-Moderate is that it's already running. Any incoming comments or TrackBacks are already being routed through MT-Moderate prior to posting. If the entry receiving the post is older than seven days, the comment or TrackBack will be moderated (so that you cannot see it on your blog).

Additionally, any comment posted will check the entry to find the most recent comment. If the most recently approved comment is one day old (or less), the new comment will be allowed too. This permits ongoing conversations to continue, even though the entry itself is out of date.

Only Moderate Comments or TrackBacks

MT-Moderate does not have to moderate both incoming comments and incoming TrackBacks. If you decide not to moderate one or the other, simply remove the corresponding module from your server. If you don't want to moderate comments because you are handling them some other way, remove the `comments.pm` file from your server. To allow TrackBacks, remove the `trackbacks.pm` module from the server.

Changing the Moderation Window

Within the `moderate.pm` file, you will find two constants that define the period used for moderation. Simply change these values to the ones you like and MT-Moderate will do the rest. By default, MT-Moderate checks for an age of seven days (or less) on entries, and an age of one day (or less) when looking for comments. Use a value of 0 to allow incoming comments and TrackBacks only on the same day, or a value of -1 to moderate everything.

TechnoratiTag

Tag classification was a big hit in 2004, spurred on by services such as Flickr and del.icio.us, which enabled users to easily label pieces of information with keywords. Unlike hierarchical categorization, which tries to put things into the perfect bucket, tags describe everything that a piece of data could be, allowing searching on any number of facets (tags are an ad hoc implementation of faceted classification, and while there are books written on such distinctions, this is not one).

Opening this practice up to people other than the creator of the content unleashed a new term of the weblog community: *Folksonomies*. This bottom-up view of what a piece of data is, built collaboratively by content creator and consumer, changes the way we think about it and, more important, how we search for it.

In January 2005, Technorati, a leading blog search engine, introduced Technorati tags, which are a way to indicate to Technorati specifically what a piece of data is and to allow tag-based search. You can find the most popular ones at `www.technorati.com/tag/technorati`.

Photos from Flickr and links from del.icio.us are automatically pulled in by Technorati, but you can also link any blog post to one or more tags just by placing a link for that tag on the individual archive page and pinging Technorati when you post a new entry.

The format for the link is as follows:

```
<a href="http://technorati.com/tag/[tagname"
rel="tag">tagname]</a>
```

Not a day or two after this feature was released, George Hotelling came out with the TechnoratiTags plugin, which introduces a new template tag, `<$MTTechnoratiTags$>`.

Note   TechnoratiTags is not PHP-compatible.

This tag displays in the proper format any of the tags entered into the Keywords field of the entry.

PHP/Dynamic Template Option

If you are using Dynamic templates for your individual archive template (or whichever template you choose to put this on), you cannot use the TechnoratiTags plugin. However, you can easily get the same functionality with the following PHP snippet inserted into the appropriate place in your template:

```php
<?php

/* PARSING ENTRY KEYWORD FIELD INTO TECHNORATI TAGS */


$tags = explode(" ", $this->tag('MTEntryKeywords'));

if (! empty($tags[0])) {

    print "<p><strong>Tags:</strong> ";

    foreach ($tags as $tag) {

        print '<a href="http://technorati.com/tag/'.

            $tag.'" rel="tag">'.$tag.'</a> ';

    }

    print "</p>";

}

?>
```

How to Install It

First, download and unpack the archive found at `http://george.hotelling.net/ 90percent/projects/technoratitags.php`. Upload to `MT_DIR/plugins/ TechnoratiTags.pl`.

Next, select Weblog Config ➪ Preferences and, in the section labeled Publicity/Remote Interfaces/TrackBack, check the box for technorati.com. This will cause Technorati to be pinged anytime you create a new entry in that blog.

Finally, make sure that the Keywords field is displayed on your new entry screen. If it is not, click the Customize This Page link near the bottom of the entry form fields and select Keywords, along with any other fields you desire for display.

How to Use It within a Template

Add keywords for your post, separated by spaces. For example, the TechnoratiTags plugin might get these tags: technorati tags MovableType. (Note that Movable Type was turned into one word: MovableType. If it had been spelled with the space, the entry would have been tagged with Movable and Type but not Movable Type.)

In your Individual Archive template, add the following somewhere between the MTEntries tags (for example, near the entry's byline):

```
<MTIfNonEmpty tag="MTEntryKeywords">
<p><strong>Tags:</strong> <$MTTechnoratiTags$></p>
</MTIfNonEmpty>
```

By default, the hyperlinks will be given the CSS class of "TechnoratiTags," which is useful for differentially styling them. If you'd prefer to change that, you could use the `class` attribute to MTTechnoratiTags:

```
<$MTTechnoratiTags class="MyTagClass"$>
```

The Result

With the preceding template code, if you create a new entry and tag it with "hacking" and "MovableType" in the Keywords field, the following will be output:

```
<p><strong>Tags:</strong> <a
href="http://technorati.com/tag/hacking" rel="tag"
class="TechnoratiTags">hacking</a> <a
href="http://technorati.com/tag/MovableType" rel="tag"
class="TechnoratiTags">MovableType</a></p>
```

If, on the other hand, you don't include any tags, nothing will be output.

By tagging your entry as such, anyone searching Technorati using the keywords "hacking" or "MovableType" will find your post.

MultiBlog

The MultiBlog plugin, written by David Raynes based on his OtherBlog plugin and the GlobalListings plugin by Stepan Riha, provides users with the capability to include templated content from other blogs in their Movable Type installation. In addition, it enables users to define rebuild triggers, because normally posts to one blog do not cause rebuilding in another that might be including content from it.

Note MultiBlog is not PHP-compatible.

How to Install It

Download the latest version of the plugin from www.rayners.org/plugins/multiblog. Create a directory in your MT_DIR/plugins/ directory named MultiBlog, and unpack the plugin into it. Then make sure that the permissions of the multiblog-config.cgi file are set correctly (on a UNIX system, that means 755).

Getting started with MultiBlog is as easy as clicking the MultiBlog link in the Configure Active Plugins section of MT's main menu screen.

Rebuild Control

One of the most important features of MultiBlog is the capability to create rules that will cause other blogs to rebuild their indexes when another blog has an entry posted to it.

To set up these rules, locate the Configuration portion of the Rebuild Control section of the config page. Select the blog to which posting should trigger the rebuild first, followed by the blog whose indexes should be rebuilt and what event should trigger that rebuild, and then click the Set button.

To remove that dependency later, locate the Current Ruleset portion of the Rebuild Control section, and locate the blog that triggers the rebuild in the left column. All the blogs whose indexes will be rebuilt are listed in the right column. To remove the rebuild rule for one of them, just click the Remove link next to the blog name.

How to Use It within a Template

MultiBlog provides a multitude of tags for your templated enjoyment:

- MTMultiBlog — MTMultiBlog is a container tag that will loop over a list of blogs. Within the container, the blog used by all of the template tags will be the current blog in the loop and not the blog for which the template is being built. MTMultiBlog takes one of two arguments: either include_blogs (which will take precedence if both are used) or exclude_blogs. The format for both arguments is a list of blog ids (for example, "2,3,5"). If neither is included, the default will be to select all the blogs to which the current blog has access.

- MTMultiBlogIfLocalBlog and MTMultiBlogIfNotLocalBlog — MTMultiBlogIfLocalBlog and MTMultiBlogIfNotLocalBlog are conditional tags that enable you to determine whether or not the current blog within whatever MultiBlog tag you are currently in is the overall blog for which the template is being built.

- MTMultiBlogObject tags — The MTMultiBlogObject tags enable you to select one particular entry, comment, category, or ping from across all blogs for which the current blog has access (just replace Object in the tag name with Entry, Comment, Category, or Ping). They take only a single argument: id.

- MTMultiBlogObjectCount tags — The MTMultiBlogObjectCount tags return the total count for the specified object type (Entry, Comment, Category, or Ping again) for all of the blogs specified with either `include_blogs` or `exclude_blogs`, just like the `MTMulitBlog` tag.

- `MTMultiBlogObjects` tags — The `MTMultiBlogObjects` tags are MultiBlog versions of their nonglobal counterparts. They accept the same arguments as the corresponding core tags, in addition to `include_blogs` and `exclude_blogs`.

The Result

Because MultiBlog is so powerful, it would be impossible to detail all of its possible uses. However, a few useful examples may be illustrative of the types of things you can do with it.

The first example, shown in Listing 9-7, is including content from one blog onto another. This is most often done for link blogs where categories in the primary blog are already heavily used so as not to pollute the category hierarchy.

Listing 9-7: Entries in a Side Blog

```
<h3>Side Blog</h3>
<MTMultiBlog include_blogs="7">
<MTEntries lastn="10">
<div class="entry">
<h4><$MTEntryTitle$></h4>
<p><MTEntryBody></p>
</div>
</MTEntries>
</MTMultiBlog>
```

Another example is local blog aggregation. Suppose you have a number of blogs in the system but want to provide your users with a system view of all blog entries (this is especially great as a syndication feed). Listing 9-8 provides code to aggregate the last 15 entries, total, from blogs 2, 3, and 5 (not 15 each, but 15 overall).

Listing 9-8: Local Blog Aggregation

```
<MTMultiBlogEntries include_blogs="2,3,5" lastn="15">
<div class="entry">
<h3><a href="<MTBlogURL>"><MTBlogName></a>: <a
href="<MTEntryPermalink>"><MTEntryTitle></a></h3>
<MTEntryBody>
</div>
</MTMultiBlogEntries>
```

Workflow

The Workflow plugin, written by David Raynes, is a masterful plugin that enables one author to pass along an entry to another and enforces author permissions for publishing an entry to the blog.

As you can imagine, this plugin is essential for anyone working in a collaborative environment with divisions of labor among writing, editing, and publishing.

Workflow is PHP-compatible.

How to Install It

Download the latest version of the plugin from `www.rayners.org/plugins/workflow`, create a directory in your `MT_DIR/plugins/` directory named `Workflow`, and unpack the plugin into it. Make sure that the permissions of the `workflow.cgi` file are set correctly (on a UNIX system, that means 755).

If all you wish to do is transfer entries from one author to another, the setup is already complete. If, however, you wish to enable the publishing permissions system, there is a further step. Browse to the blog for which you want to set up permissions and click the Administer Publish Permissions link provided. If you currently have permission to edit all posts for that particular blog, you will be given some setup options for the permissions.

You can choose to use the current settings (meaning anybody who can currently post to the blog will still be able to), in which case, you can then trim the list to who can publish afterward. Or, you can select the restricted setting (meaning anybody who can edit all of the posts will still be allowed to publish, but nobody else will), in which case, you can then build up the list of authors who are allowed to publish.

No template changes are required to use Workflow's features.

The Result

From then on, whenever an author who does not have permission to publish for that blog saves an entry with the status set to Publish, the entry status will be reset to Draft by the plugin, effectively denying publishing.

Transferring an Entry

This procedure could not be simpler. Browse to the entry edit page for the entry you wish to transfer and click the Transfer Ownership of This Entry link at the bottom. You will then be given a list of authors to which the entry can be transferred. Select one and send it their way. They will be sent an e-mail notifying them of their new responsibility.

KeyValues 1.53

Movable Type's roots are in blogging and of that there is no doubt. Just looking at the new entry screen, the input fields make it patently evident: entry body, extended entry, excerpt, keywords, and category. Of course, as hackers, we all know that Movable Type is far more than just a blogging application — it's a publishing platform. Imaginative people have created link blogs, photoblogs, project management tools, merchant catalogs, to-do lists, day planners, and more just by thinking outside the box and using the existing fields creatively as containers for things that are published on the other side, with no attention paid to the label above the box.

Still, all of us have run into the problem of needing just a few more fields. This is why the KeyValues plugin was developed. KeyValues, written by Brad Choate, enables you to overload any input field on the entry editing screen with key-value pairs, essentially providing you with an infinite number of fields. With KeyValues, Movable Type breaks out of blogging and becomes a powerful front-end database access tool.

KeyValues is not PHP-compatible.

How to Install It

Download the archive from `www.bradchoate.com/weblog/2002/07/27/keyvalues`. You will also have to download the Regex plugin, also written by Brad Choate, to use a couple of the tags. You can find the Regex plugin at `www.bradchoate.com/weblog/2002/07/27/mtregex`.

After unpacking each archive, you should upload the following files to the locations listed:

- `MT_DIR/plugins/keyvalues.pl`
- `MT_DIR/plugins/regex.pl`
- `MT_DIR/extlib/bradchoate/regex.pm`
- `MT_DIR/extlib/bradchoate/postproc.pm`
- `MT_DIR/extlib/bradchoate/keyvalues.pm`

You may have to create the `bradchoate` directory if it doesn't exist inside of `extlib`.

How to Use It within a Template

KeyValues provides you with several tags for use within your templates that enable you to access the entry information in different ways:

- `MTKeyValues` — Container tag for accessing your key/value data in an iterative manner.
- `MTKeyValuesHeader` — The contents of this container block will be printed at the start of a KeyValues block.

- `MTKeyValuesFooter` — The contents of this container block will be printed at the end of a KeyValues block.

- `MTIfKeyExists` — Given a key name, this conditional block tests whether a key exists.

- `MTIfNoKeyExists` — Given a key name, this conditional block tests whether a key does not exist.

- `MTIfKeyMatches` — This conditional block tag will test the name of a key against a value or pattern.

- `MTIfKeyNotMatched` — Outputs contained text if a given key is not matched using an `IfKeyMatches` tag.

- `MTKeyName` — Outputs the name of a key (only useful when iterating over key/value pairs).

- `MTKeyValue` — Outputs the value of a key. Can output value by name or will output the value of the current key when iterating over key/value pairs.

- `MTKeyValuesStripped` — Outputs the source of your key/value pairs without the key/value data. This enables you to retain the use of your field(s) for regular blog data and use them to store key/value data at the same time.

Now that you have the overview, let's look at all of those in detail.

MTKeyValues

The following attributes are allowed:

- `delimiter` — Defaults to =

- `pattern` — Only processes key/value pairs matching the regular expression provided. (Requires the Regex plugin — see the previous installation instructions.)

- `source` — Defines the source of the key/value pairs. Default source is the current entry's Additional Text field.

- `iterate` — If this attribute is given (iterate="1"), the contained data is output for each key/value pair that exists.

This tag has two modes of operation. The normal way it works is to output anything contained within the tag once (regardless of the key/value pairs you have defined). The other way is to output the contained data multiple times for as many keys as you have defined.

For example, this extended entry text

```
Blah blah blah. Blah blah blah.... This is the regular text
followed by the key/value pairs which are in the form of
key=value.
rating=3
link=http://www.bradchoate.com/
name=Brad Choate
```

and a portion in an Individual Archive Template such as

```
<MTKeyValues>
Extended entry (without key value data):
[[<MTEntryMore>]]<br />

Name: <MTKeyValue key="name"><br />
Link: <a href="<MTKeyValue key="link">">
    <MTKeyValue key="link"></a><br />
<MTIfKeyExists key="rating">
Rating: <MTKeyValue key="rating"><br />
</MTIfKeyExists>
<MTIfKeyExists key="favorite">
This is my favorite site!<br />
</MTIfKeyExists>
</MTKeyValues>
```

will output the following:

```
Extended entry (without key value data):
[[Blah blah blah. Blah blah blah.... This is the regular text
followed by the key/value pairs which are in the form of
key=value.]]<br />

Name: Brad Choate<br />
Link: <a href="http://www.bradchoate.com/">
    http://www.bradchoate.com/</a><br />
Rating: 3<br />
```

The other way to use KeyValues is like this:

```
<MTKeyValues iterate="1">
<MTKeyName>: <MTKeyValue><br />
</MTKeyValues>
```

This will output (again using our preceding sample data) the following:

```
name: Brad Choate<br />
link: http://www.bradchoate.com/<br />
rating: 3<br />
```

Now you might want to just output some of those key/value pairs:

```
<MTKeyValues iterate="1" pattern="m/a/">
<MTKeyValuesHeader>
Here are the keys with 'a' in their name:<br />
</MTKeyValuesHeader>
<MTKeyName>: <MTKeyValue><br />
</MTKeyValues>
```

The preceding code will output all keys with 'a' in their name:

```
Here are the keys with 'a' in their name:<br />
name: Brad Choate<br />
rating: 3<br />
```

The `source` attribute enables you to define where your key/values are coming from. The default is the additional entry text field for your blog entries. However, you can put key/value pairs anywhere. You might want to store some in your blog description. If you do, this is how you would extract them (note that for the `source` attribute, you use [and] instead of < and > to delimit the MT tags):

```
<MTKeyValues source="[MTBlogDescription]">
<body bgcolor="<MTKeyValue key="bgcolor">">
</MTKeyValues>
```

That might look weird, but if you have `bgcolor=#ff0000` in your blog description, this will produce the following:

```
<body bgcolor="#ff0000">
```

A red background — not recommended for those with a weak stomach. You can also write multiline values. You can use this syntax in your entry data:

```
address==
123 Anywhere Street
Anytown USA
==address
```

Or substitute your delimiter of choice for =. (You just use two instead of one to indicate the multiline format.) To be recognized, there shouldn't be any blank space to the right of the opening ==, and the closing == should be at the start of the line. If you want to assign the value of your delimiter to a key, you'll have to write it like this:

```
mykey==
=
==mykey
```

MTKeyValuesHeader

This tag may be used within the KeyValues tag to produce a header if there are keys available. This is only useful when using the `iterating` attribute of the KeyValues tag.

MTKeyValuesFooter

This tag may be used within the KeyValues tag to produce a footer if there are keys available. This is only useful when using the `iterating` attribute of the KeyValues tag.

MTIfKeyExists

This tag enables you to test for the existence of a particular key.

The `key` attribute identifies the name of the key:

```
<MTKeyValues>
<MTIfKeyExists key="somekey">
  'somekey' exists!
</MTIfKeyExists>
</MTKeyValues>
```

MTIfNoKeyExists

This tag enables you to test that a particular key does not exist. The `key` attribute represents the name of the key to look for:

```
<MTKeyValues>
<MTIfNoKeyExists key="somekey">
  'somekey' doesn't exist!
</MTIfNoKeyExists>
</MTKeyValues>
```

MTIfKeyMatches

This tag enables you to test whether or not a given key matches a particular value or whether the value matches a given pattern. These attributes are allowed:

- `key`: Name of the key to test

- `value`: Value to compare against

- `pattern`: Regular expression pattern to test the value against

```
<MTKeyValues>
<MTIfKeyMatches key="color" value="blue">
  Color is blue
</MTIfKeyMatches>
<MTIfKeyMatches key="color" value="red">
  Color is red
</MTIfKeyMatches>
<MTIfKeyMatches key="color" value="green">
  Color is green
</MTIfKeyMatches>
<MTIfKeyNotMatched key="color">
  Color is not red, green or blue
</MTIfKeyNotMatched>
</MTKeyValues>
```

Here's how you would use the `pattern` attribute:

```
<MTKeyValues>
<MTIfKeyMatches key="color"
  pattern="m/(red|green|blue)/">
  Color is red, green or blue
</MTIfKeyMatches>
<MTIfKeyNotMatched key="color">
  Color is not red, green or blue
</MTIfKeyNotMatched>
</MTKeyValues>
```

MTIfKeyNotMatched

This tag enables you to output data if a given key has not been matched against using the `IfKeyMatches` tags. This attribute is allowed: `key`, which is the name of the key to test.

See the `IfKeyMatches` tag for examples.

MTKeyValue

This tag produces the value of a particular key; or if it is within an iterating `KeyValues` tag, it will print the current value. This attribute is allowed: `default`, which is an expression to use as a default in case the key does not exist. This value can contain nested MT tags in the form of [MT...].

See the `KeyValues` tag for examples.

MTKeyName

This tag produces the key name of the current key from an iterating KeyValues tag. See the KeyValues tag for examples.

<MTKeyValuesStripped>

This outputs the source of your key/value pairs without the key/value data. This enables you to retain the use of your field(s) for regular blog data and use them to store key/value data at the same time.

Here's how you'd use it:

```
<MTKeyValues>
  <MTKeyValuesStripped>
</MTKeyValues>
```

The Result

The result, as you can probably already imagine, is that Movable Type can be used as a very powerful, lightweight data input and publishing system. Anything you can dream of to put into the database, you can publish out of the database with no attention paid to the blogging-centric labels of the text fields. Given this, it's not hard to build just about anything that involves the publication of structured data.

Summary

This chapter highlighted some of our favorite plugins. However, they are by no means the only ones or the best ones for every situation. If you really want to wield the full power of Movable Type, go to `www.sixapart.com/pronet/plugins` and find your perfect set of plugins.

You won't be sorry.

Writing Plugins

So you want to write a plugin? This chapter will walk you through creating a Hello World plugin and show you how to integrate what you want into the Movable Type system.

Hello World Plugin

To provide an example, this chapter will develop a Movable Type plugin that defines the `MTHelloWorld` tag, which will take an argument, `name`, that causes the tag to output a greeting for that particular name.

Plugin Registration and Metadata

You must first create an `MT::Plugin` object. It then needs to be populated with a name (and optionally a description), a link to a configuration script, and a link to documentation.

Then, use the `add_plugin` method of the MT class to add the new plugin to the system, as laid out in Listing 10-1.

Listing 10-1: Hello World Plugin

```
package MTPlugins::HelloWorld;

use MT;
use MT::Plugin;

# Create and populate the MT::Plugin object
my $plugin = MT::Plugin->new;
$plugin->name ("Hello World");
$plugin->description ("This is my first plugin.");

# Add the plugin to the system
MT->add_plugin ($plugin);
```

Adding a Simple Tag

Simple tags are created by calling the `add_tag` method of the `MT::Template::Context` class:

```
MT::Template::Context->add_tag ( TagName => \&tag_routine );
```

- `TagName` is the tag that the template builder will recognize. All Movable Type template tags begin with MT, which will automatically be prepended to the name provided. Note that there is no requirement that the name of the tag be a fixed string; it only has to evaluate to a string when the function call is made.

- `tag_routine` is a reference to a subroutine, either anonymous or named.

The subroutine takes arguments, which we will discuss later, and it should return the text to which the tag should evaluate.

Therefore, after adding the tag to the plugin, the code looks like that shown in Listing 10-2.

Listing 10-2: Creating a HelloWorld Tag

```
package MTPlugins::HelloWorld;

use MT;
use MT::Plugin;
use MT::Template::Context;

# Create and populate the MT::Plugin object
my $plugin = MT::Plugin->new;
$plugin->name ("Hello World");
$plugin->description ("This is my first plugin.");

# Add the plugin to the system
MT->add_plugin ($plugin);

# Create the MTHelloWorld template tag
MT::Template::Context->add_tag ( HelloWorld => \&hello );

# Tag Handler Routine for MTHelloWorld
sub hello {
    return "Hello world!";
}
```

Now that a tag is defined, you can use the plugin in a template, as follows:

```
<$MTHelloWorld$>
```

When that template is built, the following will be output:

```
Hello world!
```

Handling Tag Attributes

Okay, so our plugin doesn't do much at the moment, but it's a good start. Now it's time to add attribute handling to our tag — specifically, handling an attribute named name.

Attributes are passed to the tag routines as a reference to a Perl hash, with the keys of the hash being the attribute names. This hash is passed as the second argument to the subroutine; we will explore the first attribute later. Listing 10-3 shows our code with the attribute added.

Listing 10-3: Adding a Name Attribute

```perl
package MTPlugins::HelloWorld;

use MT;
use MT::Plugin;
use MT::Template::Context;

# Create and populate the MT::Plugin object
my $plugin = MT::Plugin->new;
$plugin->name ("Hello World");
$plugin->description ("This is my first plugin.");

# Add the plugin to the system
MT->add_plugin ($plugin);

# Create the MTHelloWorld template tag
MT::Template::Context->add_tag ( HelloWorld => \&hello );

# Tag Handler Routine for MTHelloWorld
sub hello {
    my (undef, $args) = @_;

    # Get the 'name' attribute
    my $name_arg = $args->{'name'} || "world";
    return "Hello $name_arg!";
}
```

If the name attribute is provided, the name_arg variable will be set to it; otherwise, it will be set to "world." That variable is then used in the return statement that will be passed back to the template output.

Take a look at the template code thus far:

```
<$MTHelloWorld name="Brian"$>
```

Following is the Hello World template output:

```
Hello Brian!
```

Using the Context

Suppose you want to have this `name` value default to the author of the current entry. How can you get that information? By using the context. The `MT::Template::Context` object representing the current context is passed into the subroutine as the first argument. Values in the current context can be accessed via the `stash` method. Listing 10-4 shows our code with the context being passed in the first attribute.

Listing 10-4: Getting Values from the Template Context

```perl
package MTPlugins::HelloWorld;

use MT;
use MT::Plugin;
use MT::Template::Context;

# Create and populate the MT::Plugin object
my $plugin = MT::Plugin->new;
$plugin->name ("Hello World");
$plugin->description ("This is my first plugin.");

# Add the plugin to the system
MT->add_plugin ($plugin);

# Create the MTHelloWorld template tag
MT::Template::Context->add_tag ( HelloWorld => \&hello );

# Tag Handler Routine for MTHelloWorld
sub hello {
    my ($ctx, $args) = @_;

    # Get the 'name' attribute
    my $name_arg = $args->{'name'} ||
        (defined $ctx->stash ('entry') &&
         defined $ctx->stash ('entry')->author) ?
         $ctx->stash ('entry')->author->name : "world";

    # Return the text for the template
    return "Hello $name_arg!";
}
```

Now, if there is an entry in the current context, accessed via the `entry` key to the `stash` method (and if that entry's author still exists), you can get the author's name. If not, the plugin will fall back on "world."

Entries are certainly not the only objects stored in the stash. Table 10-1 lists some other commonly encountered stash keys.

Table 10-1   Common Stash Keys

Key	Description
blog	MT::Blog object for the current blog
blog_id	Blog_id for the current blog
category	MT::Category object for the current category in context (for example, if within the MTCategories container tag)
comment	MT::Comment object for the current comment in context (for example, if within the MTComments container tag)
tag	Name of the current tag being evaluated (without the MT prepended to it)
builder	MT::Builder object used to build templates
tokens	Compiled template code for the current container
uncompiled	Uncompiled template code for the current container

Expanding Hello World

A simple tag can support more sophisticated capabilities, functioning as a container tag that encloses other tags, dealing with errors, and adding to the context in which the tag exists.

Adding a Container Tag

First, let's move the Hello World plugin beyond defining a single simple tag and onto a more complex and flexible plugin.

To begin, we will convert the `MTHelloWorld` tag into a container tag. Container tags are different from simple tags in two very important ways:

- Container tags require a start and end tag, instead of just a single tag (that is, `<MTContainer> ... </MTContainer>` instead of `<MTTag>`).

- Container tags are responsible for building the template code between the start and end tags, though they still return only a text value.

To create a container tag, simply use the `add_container_tag` method of
`MT::Template::Context`, which behaves exactly the same as `add_tag` except that it will
be creating a container tag. Therefore, let's create the container tag for our expanded plugin:

```
# Create the MTHelloWorldContainer container tag
MT::Template::Context->add_container_tag
      ( HelloWorldContainer => \&helloWorldContainer );
```

Then we define the `helloWorldContainer` subroutine to handle the tag:

```
# Tag Handler Routine for MTHelloWorldContainer
sub helloWorldContainer {
    my ($ctx, $args) = @_;

    # The MT::Builder object
    my $builder = $ctx->stash ('builder');

    # The compiled tokens for the template code
    # between the opening and closing tags
    my $tokens  = $ctx->stash ('tokens');

    # Build the contained template code
    my $out = $builder->build ($ctx, $tokens);

    # Return the text for the template
    return $out;
}
```

This subroutine will get the `MT::Builder` object and the set of compiled tokens contained
within the container, build them, and then return the results. It doesn't do much yet, but it is
something that every container tag needs to do.

Handling Errors

What if the template code with the `MTHelloWorldContainer` tag contained an error? How
would you let the user know what happened?

It is the responsibility of every container tag to catch and return any errors it may encounter
(there are exceptions to that rule, but we won't be covering them here). It is an easy condition
to check for. The `build` method of `MT::Builder` will return an undefined value if an error
occurred and save the error message. Then you should call the error method of the context,
which will return the undefined value and save the error message, thus cascading the error up
the call stack. The updated subroutine to handle that condition follows:

```
# Tag Handler Routine for MTHelloWorldContainer
sub helloWorldContainer {
    my ($ctx, $args) = @_;

    # The MT::Builder object
    my $builder = $ctx->stash ('builder');
```

```perl
    # The compiled tokens for the template code
    # between the opening and closing tags
    my $tokens  = $ctx->stash ('tokens');

    # Build the contained template code
    my $out = $builder->build ($ctx, $tokens);
    if (!defined $out) {
        # build method return undefined
        # must be a build error
        return $ctx->error ($builder->errstr);
    }

    # Return the text for the template
    return $out;
}
```

The `error` method of `MT::Template::Context` is not available solely to container tags; simple tags can also return errors (for example, if a simple tag needed to be in an entry context, but no entry were available).

Adding to the Context

With our skeleton container tag handler routine completed, let's have it add a value into the context that a simple tag, which we will define, can read and display. To generate that value, we can use the argument handling code we wrote for the original MTHelloWorld plugin:

```perl
# Tag Handler Routine for MTHelloWorldContainer
sub helloWorldContainer {
    my ($ctx, $args) = @_;

    # The MT::Builder object
    my $builder = $ctx->stash ('builder');

    # The compiled tokens for the template code
    # between the opening and closing tags
    my $tokens  = $ctx->stash ('tokens');

    # Get the 'name' attribute
    my $name_arg = $args->{'name'} ||
        (defined $ctx->stash ('entry') &&
         defined $ctx->stash ('entry')->author) ?
         $ctx->stash ('entry')->author->name : "world";

    # Stash the 'name' argument
    $ctx->stash ('helloWorldGreeted', $name_arg);

    # Build the contained template code
    my $out = $builder->build ($ctx, $tokens);
    if (!defined $out) {
        # build method return undefined
```

```
            # must be a build error
            return $ctx->error ($builder->errstr);
    }

    # Return the text for the template
    return $out;
}
```

Now we simply have to define another tag to read that value out of the stash, as follows:

```
# Create the MTHelloWorldGreeted template tag
MT::Template::Context->add_tag
( HelloWorldGreeted => \&helloWorldGreeted );

# Tag Handler Routine for MTHelloWorldGreeted
sub helloWorldGreeted {
    my ($ctx, $args) = @_;

    # Get the 'name' argument from the context
    my $name = $ctx->stash ('helloWorldGreeted');
    if (!defined $name) {
        # If 'name' is not defined we must not be with
        # a MTHelloWorldContainer container
        # so return an error
        return $ctx->error ("MTHelloWorldGreeting must be used
within a MTHelloWorldContainer container tag.");
    }

    # Return the text for the template
    return $name;
}
```

Notice that the simple tag will return an error if the value does not exist in the context.

Listing 10-5 pulls the whole plugin together.

Listing 10-5: Extending the Plugin's Capabilities

```
package MTPlugins::ExpandedHelloWorld;

use MT;
use MT::Plugin;
use MT::Template::Context;

# Create and populate the MT::Plugin object
my $plugin = MT::Plugin->new;
$plugin->name ("Extended Hello World");
$plugin->description ("This is my second plugin.");

# Add the plugin to the system
MT->add_plugin ($plugin);
```

```perl
# Create the MTHelloWorldContainer container tag
MT::Template::Context->add_container_tag
     ( HelloWorldContainer => \&helloWorldContainer );

# Tag Handler Routine for MTHelloWorldContainer
sub helloWorldContainer {
    my ($ctx, $args) = @_;

    # The MT::Builder object
    my $builder = $ctx->stash ('builder');

    # The compiled tokens for the template code
    # between the opening and closing tags
    my $tokens  = $ctx->stash ('tokens');

    # Get the 'name' attribute
    my $name_arg = $args->{'name'} ||
          (defined $ctx->stash ('entry') &&
           defined $ctx->stash ('entry')->author) ?
           $ctx->stash ('entry')->author->name : "world";

    # Stash the 'name' attribute
    $ctx->stash ('helloWorldGreeted', $name_arg);

    # Build the contained template code
    my $out = $builder->build ($ctx, $tokens);
    if (!defined $out) {
         # build method return undefined
         # must be a build error
         return $ctx->error ($builder->errstr);
    }

    # Return the text for the template
    return $out;
}

# Create the MTHelloWorldGreeted template tag
MT::Template::Context->add_tag
( HelloWorldGreeted => \&helloWorldGreeted );

# Tag Handler Routine for MTHelloWorldGreeted
sub helloWorldGreeted {
    my ($ctx, $args) = @_;

    # Get the 'name' attribute from the context
    my $name = $ctx->stash ('helloWorldGreeted');
    if (!defined $name) {
         # If 'name' is not defined we must not be with
         # a MTHelloWorldContainer container
         # so return an error
```

Continued

Listing 10-5 *(continued)*

```
            return $ctx->error ("MTHelloWorldGreeted must be used
within a MTHelloWorldContainer container tag.");
    }

    # Return the text for the template
    return $name;
}
```

Here is how you could use this plugin in a template:

```
<MTHelloWorldContainer name="Fred">
Hello <MTHelloWorldGreeted>!
</MTHelloWorldContainer>
```

And that template would output the following when built:

```
Hello Fred!
```

Adding a Conditional Tag

Conditional tags are the third and final type of tag that can be created. They are handled as a special type of container tag. If the return value of the tag handler routine evaluates to true, the template code between the start and end tags is built.

Normally, any defined value will evaluate to true, *except* an empty string.

Let's now create a conditional tag to determine whether or not a name has been provided for our plugin (as opposed to the "world" default). To create a conditional tag, you use the `add_conditional_tag` method of `MT::Template::Context`:

```
# Create the MTHelloWorldIfNameProvided conditional tag
MT::Template::Context->add_conditional_tag
    ( HelloWorldIfNameProvided => \&helloWorldIfNameProvided );

# Tag Handler Routine for MTHelloWorldIfNameProvided
sub helloWorldIfNameProvided {
    my ($ctx, $args) = @_;

    # Get the 'name' attribute from the context
    my $name = $ctx->stash ('helloWorldGreeted');

    # Return true if the 'name' attribute is defined
    # and not equal to 'world'
    return (defined $name && $name ne 'world');
}
```

It is important to note that a conditional tag handler routine *cannot* return an error; it would simply be interpreted as a false value.

Listing 10-6 shows the extended HelloWorld plugin with the conditional tag added.

Listing 10-6: Adding a Conditional Tag

```perl
package MTPlugins::ExpandedHelloWorld;

use MT;
use MT::Plugin;
use MT::Template::Context;

# Create and populate the MT::Plugin object
my $plugin = MT::Plugin->new;
$plugin->name ("Extended Hello World");
$plugin->description ("This is my second plugin.");

# Add the plugin to the system
MT->add_plugin ($plugin);

# Create the MTHelloWorldContainer container tag
MT::Template::Context->add_container_tag
      ( HelloWorldContainer => \&helloWorldContainer );

# Tag Handler Routine for MTHelloWorldContainer
sub helloWorldContainer {
    my ($ctx, $args) = @_;

    # The MT::Builder object
    my $builder = $ctx->stash ('builder');

    # The compiled tokens for the template code
    # between the opening and closing tags
    my $tokens  = $ctx->stash ('tokens');

    # Get the 'name' attribute
    my $name_arg = $args->{'name'} ||
          (defined $ctx->stash ('entry') &&
           defined $ctx->stash ('entry')->author) ?
           $ctx->stash ('entry')->author->name : "world";

    # Stash the 'name' attribute
    $ctx->stash ('helloWorldGreeted', $name_arg);

    # Build the contained template code
    my $out = $builder->build ($ctx, $tokens);
    if (!defined $out) {
        # build method return undefined
        # must be a build error
        return $ctx->error ($builder->errstr);
    }

    # Return the text for the template
    return $out;
}
```

Continued

Listing 10-6 *(continued)*

```perl
# Create the MTHelloWorldGreeted template tag
MT::Template::Context->add_tag
( HelloWorldGreeted => \&helloWorldGreeted );

# Tag Handler Routine for MTHelloWorldGreeted
sub helloWorldGreeted {
    my ($ctx, $args) = @_;

    # Get the 'name' attribute from the context
    my $name = $ctx->stash ('helloWorldGreeted');
    if (!defined $name) {
        # If 'name' is not defined we must not be with
        # a MTHelloWorldContainer container
        # so return an error
        return $ctx->error ("MTHelloWorldGreeting must be used
within a MTHelloWorldContainer container tag.");
    }

    # Return the text for the template
    return $name;
}


# Create the MTHelloWorldIfNameProvided conditional tag
MT::Template::Context->add_conditional_tag
    ( HelloWorldIfNameProvided => \&helloWorldIfNameProvided );

# Tag Handler Routine for MTHelloWorldIfNameProvided
sub helloWorldIfNameProvided {
    my ($ctx, $args) = @_;

    # Get the 'name' attribute from the context
    my $name = $ctx->stash ('helloWorldGreeted');

    # Return true if the 'name' argument is defined
    # and not equal to 'world'
    return (defined $name && $name ne 'world');
}
```

The extended HelloWorld template now looks like this:

```
<MTHelloWorldContainer>
<MTHelloWorldIfNameProvided>
Hey, <MTHelloWorldGreeted>!  How are you?
<MTElse>
Hello <MTHelloWorldGreeted>.
</MTElse>
</MTHelloWorldIfNameProvided>
</MTHelloWorldContainer>
```

If this template were built within an entry context, with that entry having been written by Steven, it would output the following:

```
Hey, Steven!   How are you?
```

Or, if it were built by itself (that is, without an entry in the context), it would output the following instead:

```
Hello world.
```

Container Tag Looping

While a fairly easy implementation, it's worth demonstrating how to have a container tag loop more than once over the template code contained within its start and end tags.

Let's add a new feature to the `MTHelloWorldContainer` tag: the ability to loop through multiple names. You can do this one of two ways:

- Embed the multiple names in the name argument, separated with a text delimiter (for example, "Name 1,Name 2,Name 3").

- Write code to handle a variable number of attributes. You may have already noticed that nowhere are the attributes to a tag predefined.

Personally, I prefer the latter. It looks cleaner in the template, and it's just more fun to code. For the time being, however, to keep us from having to change the code too drastically, we will use the former.

First, we allow the users of our plugin to pass in the delimiter that they wish to use in the `glue` attribute, with a comma as the default:

```
# Get the 'glue' attribute, and default to ','
my $glue = $args->{'glue'} || ',';
```

Then we use the delimiter, along with the value we worked out for `$name_arg`, to produce the list of names over which we will be looping:

```
# Split the 'name' attribute on the 'glue' attribute
my @names = split ($glue, $name_arg);
```

Finally, the call to the `build` method of `MT::Builder`, along with the line that actually places the name to display in the stash, is placed into a `foreach` loop, with the results aggregated:

```
# Overall results
my $res = '';

# Step through each name
foreach my $name (@names) {

    # Stash the 'name' attribute
    $ctx->stash ('helloWorldGreeted', $name);

    # Build the contained template code
    my $out = $builder->build ($ctx, $tokens);
```

```
    if (!defined $out) {
        # build method return undefined
        # must be a build error
        return $ctx->error ($builder->errstr);
    }

    # Append the build results to the overall results
    $res .= $out;
}
```

Putting all of this together, the tag handler routine for `MTHelloWorldContainer` will look like what is shown in Listing 10-7.

Listing 10-7: Looping within a Container Tag

```
# Tag Handler Routine for MTHelloWorldContainer
sub helloWorldContainer {
    my ($ctx, $args) = @_;

    # The MT::Builder object
    my $builder = $ctx->stash ('builder');

    # The compiled tokens for the template code
    # between the opening and closing tags
    my $tokens  = $ctx->stash ('tokens');

    # Get the 'name' attribute
    my $name_arg = $args->{'name'} ||
        (defined $ctx->stash ('entry') &&
         defined $ctx->stash ('entry')->author) ?
         $ctx->stash ('entry')->author->name : "world";

    # Get the 'glue' attribute, and default to ','
    my $glue = $args->{'glue'} || ',';

    # Split the 'name' attribute on the 'glue' argument
    my @names = split ($glue, $name_arg);

    # Overall results
    my $res = '';

    # Step through each name
    foreach my $name (@names) {

        # Stash the 'name' attribute
        $ctx->stash ('helloWorldGreeted', $name);

        # Build the contained template code
        my $out = $builder->build ($ctx, $tokens);
        if (!defined $out) {
                # build method return undefined
                # must be a build error
```

```
                return $ctx->error ($builder->errstr);
        }

        # Append the build results to the overall results
        $res .= $out;
    }

    # Return the text for the template
    return $res;
}
```

Therefore, if you used the following template code

```
<MTHelloWorldContainer name="Thomas,Richard,Harold">
Hello <MTHelloWorldGreeted>!
</MTHelloWorldContainer>
```

you would produce the following output:

```
Hello Thomas!
Hello Richard!
Hello Harold!
```

Embedded Movable Type Tags

Often, users will want the flexibility to pass Movable Type template tags into the arguments for another tag. `MT::Builder` does *not* support this. This kind of functionality can be built into a plugin, however.

Suppose, for example, a user is making significant use of Brad Choate's wonderful KeyValues plugin throughout his site, and he wants to use it to pass the `name` argument to `MTHelloWorldContainer`. The template code could be written like the following, using the de facto standard notation for embedded Movable Type template tags:

Brad Choate's KeyValues plugin (`http://sixapart.com/pronet/plugins/plugin/keyvalues.html`) enables users to easily retrieve and embed metadata into various fields in Movable Type, most commonly the extended entry.

```
<MTHelloWorldContainer name="[MTKeyValue key='greet_names']">
Hello <MTHelloWorldGreeted>!
</MTHelloWorldContainer>
```

To support this notation, we will need to transform it into normal template code, and then use `MT::Builder` to compile and build it:

```
# Check for possible embedded Movable Type template tags
# and change them into actual template tags
if ($name_arg =~ s/\[(\/?MT[^\]]+)\]/\<$1\>/g) {

    # Compile the template tags passed in
    my $tok = $builder->compile ($ctx, $name_arg);
```

```
        # Build the tokens generated from the template tags
        defined ($name_arg = $builder->build ($ctx, $tok))
            or return $ctx->error ($builder->errstr);
}
```

Listing 10-8 shows the code that puts together the Extended HelloWorld plugin.

Listing 10-8: Embedding Template Tag Output

```perl
package MTPlugins::ExpandedHelloWorld;

use MT;
use MT::Plugin;
use MT::Template::Context;

# Create and populate the MT::Plugin object
my $plugin = MT::Plugin->new;
$plugin->name ("Extended Hello World");
$plugin->description ("This is my second plugin.");

# Add the plugin to the system
MT->add_plugin ($plugin);

# Create the MTHelloWorldContainer container tag
MT::Template::Context->add_container_tag
    ( HelloWorldContainer => \&helloWorldContainer );

# Tag Handler Routine for MTHelloWorldContainer
sub helloWorldContainer {
    my ($ctx, $args) = @_;

    # The MT::Builder object
    my $builder = $ctx->stash ('builder');

    # The compiled tokens for the template code
    # between the opening and closing tags
    my $tokens  = $ctx->stash ('tokens');

    # Get the 'name' attribute
    my $name_arg = $args->{'name'} ||
        (defined $ctx->stash ('entry') &&
         defined $ctx->stash ('entry')->author) ?
        $ctx->stash ('entry')->author->name : "world";

    # Check for possible embedded Movable Type template tags
    # and change them into actual template tags
    if ($name_arg =~ s/\[(\/?MT[^\]]+)\]/\<$1\>/g) {

        # Compile the template tags passed in
        my $tok = $builder->compile ($ctx, $name_arg);

        # Build the tokens generated from the template tags
```

```perl
            defined ($name_arg = $builder->build ($ctx, $tok))
                or return $ctx->error ($builder->errstr);
        }

        # Get the 'glue' attribute, and default to ','
        my $glue = $args->{'glue'} || ',';

        # Split the 'name' attribute on the 'glue' argument
        my @names = split ($glue, $name_arg);

        # Overall results
        my $res = '';

        # Step through each name
        foreach my $name (@names) {

                # Stash the 'name' attribute
                $ctx->stash ('helloWorldGreeted', $name);

                # Build the contained template code
                my $out = $builder->build ($ctx, $tokens);
                if (!defined $out) {
                        # build method return undefined
                        # must be a build error
                        return $ctx->error ($builder->errstr);
                }

                # Append the build results to the overall results
                $res .= $out;
        }

        # Return the text for the template
        return $res;
}

# Create the MTHelloWorldGreeted template tag
MT::Template::Context->add_tag
        ( HelloWorldGreeted => \&helloWorldGreeted );

# Tag Handler Routine for MTHelloWorldGreeted
sub helloWorldGreeted {
        my ($ctx, $args) = @_;

        # Get the 'name' attribute from the context
        my $name = $ctx->stash ('helloWorldGreeted');
        if (!defined $name) {
                # If 'name' is not defined we must not be with
                # a MTHelloWorldContainer container
                # so return an error
                return $ctx->error ("MTHelloWorldGreeting must be used
within a MTHelloWorldContainer container tag.");
        }
```

Continued

```
        # Return the text for the template
        return $name;
}


# Create the MTHelloWorldIfNameProvided conditional tag
MT::Template::Context->add_conditional_tag
    ( HelloWorldIfNameProvided => \&helloWorldIfNameProvided );

# Tag Handler Routine for MTHelloWorldIfNameProvided
sub helloWorldIfNameProvided {
        my ($ctx, $args) = @_;

        # Get the 'name' attribute from the context
        my $name = $ctx->stash ('helloWorldGreeted');

        # Return true if the 'name' attribute is defined
        # and not equal to 'world'
        return (defined $name && $name ne 'world');
}
```

Global Tag Attributes

A global tag attribute is an argument that can be given to any Movable Type template tag, which is handled by a separate routine. To create a new global tag attribute, use the `add_global_filter` method of `MT::Template::Context`.

For example, suppose that you want to write a filter to translate the output of a template tag to all uppercase, as follows:

```
# Create the global filter
MT::Template::Context->add_global_filter ( to_uppercase =>
\&to_uppercase );

# Filter Handler Routine for to_uppercase
sub to_uppercase {
        my ($text, $arg_value, $ctx) = @_;

        # Translate all lowercase characters to uppercase
        $text =~ tr/a-z/A-Z/;

        # Return the translated text
        return $text;
}
```

Notice that the filter handler routine takes different arguments than a tag handler routine:

1. The text output for the template tag

2. The value of the argument used (often "1," which is unofficial shorthand for "on")

3. The current context

An example use in a template follows:

```
<MTHelloWorldContainer name="Kyle" to_uppercase="1">
Hello <MTHelloWorldGreeted>!
</MTHelloWorldContainer>
```

The `MTHelloWorldContainer` would produce the following:

```
Hello Kyle!
```

This information would then be passed into the `to_uppercase` filter handler routine as the text argument, along with "1" for the argument to the attribute, and finally the current `MT::Template::Context` object.

After running through the filter handler routine, the final output of the template would be as follows:

```
HELLO KYLE!
```

Note While any number of global tag attributes can be applied to a given Movable Type template tag, there is no guaranteed order in which they will be called by the post process handler.

Text Formatting Plugins

Text formatting plugins are handled in a similar manner to global tag attributes. They can be added to the system with the `add_text_filter` method of MT:

```
MT->add_text_filter ( 'hello_world' => {
    label   => 'Hello World',
    docs    => 'http://www.example.com/docs/hello_world.html',
    on_format    => \&hello_world,
});

sub hello_world {
    my ($text, $ctx) = @_;

    # split the text into individual lines
    my @lines = split ("\n", $text);

    # add "Hello " and "!" to the start and end of each line
    @lines = map { "Hello $_!" } @lines;
```

```
        # Put it all back together again on separate lines
        return join ("\n", @lines);
}
```

Therefore, for an entry such as the following, with "Hello World" chosen for text formatting

```
Ben
Mena
Anil
```

when the entry is output from a template, the `MTEntryBody` tag would return the following:

```
Hello Ben!
Hello Mena!
Hello Anil!
```

Plugin Best Practices

The plugins that you create for Movable Type must be able to peacefully coexist with other plugins that may be present on a user's installation. For this and other reasons, adhering to a few best practices for your own plugins will minimize compatibility problems and improve your code in other important ways.

Avoid Plugin Collisions

- Declare a package for your plugin.

- Use a unique prefix for the keys for all of your stashed values, preferably based on the name of the plugin.

- Use a unique prefix for all of the tags you declare so that there is no confusion as to the plugin from which the tag originates.

Code Readability and Reuse

- Declare all of your tags, filters, and formatters at the beginning of your plugin code.

- While anonymous subroutines can be used for handler routines, if named subroutines are used, they can be reused by other tags. For example, if a tag handler routine is written to return a particular value, a conditional tag can use that same handler routine to determine whether or not that value is present.

Code Efficiency

Do not load any external modules at compile time (via Perl's `use` directive). Load them as needed, if possible via the `require` directive. With each invocation of Movable Type's CGI scripts, all plugins are loaded and compiled. The less that is required to build the plugin code, the less work the server will have to do with each execution of a Movable Type CGI script.

Summary

The ability to develop plugins for Movable Type should be within the capabilities of any Perl programmer. The software offers a well-planned, object-oriented design that serves as a framework upon which to design your own scripts.

Most plugin developers begin with simple noncontainer tags that collect input from one or more attributes and produce useful output. The experience of turning a Perl script into a functioning template tag can be an intoxicating hack.

By starting small and increasing the capabilities of your plugins as they become more ambitious, you can learn the ins and outs of the software's application programming interface (API).

Before you know it, you'll be completely plugged in to the mindset of a professional Movable Type developer.

Advanced Plugin Writing

While template tags seem easy enough, there is plenty more that can be done with a plugin these days.

An imaginative programmer can code plugins that expand the boundaries of Movable Type beyond the weblog and image publishing features for which the software has become known.

Two particular aspects of plugin development — data persistence and callbacks — enable a program to participate in the software's decision-making and storage processes.

A sample program drafted in this chapter shows how this is performed, filtering out comments selectively on the basis of objectionable content. These capabilities can be inserted directly into the browser-based interface of Movable Type, appearing as if they were a standard part of the software.

Data Persistence

You may recall from Chapter 4 that Movable Type's database includes `mt_plugindata`, a table that provides a place for the storage of data that plugins need to store and retrieve persistently.

All plugins share the table, so each record has an identifier associated with the plugin that created it.

Configuration Data

While configuration data can be stored in variables defined in the plugin file itself, it requires users of the plugin to edit the plugin code, and it makes upgrading plugins more difficult because the data is stored in the file. The `MT::Plugin` class has a very handy set of helper methods for the storage and retrieval of plugin configuration data in the database:

- set_config_value

- get_config_value

- get_config_hash

The name of the plugin (that is, the value passed to the `name` method) is used as the plugin name in the stored data, so do not put the version number of the plugin in there.

Both `set_config_value` and `get_config_value` operate in a manner similar to the stash method of `MT::Template::Context`.

General Data Persistence

`MT::PluginData` enables developers to store and retrieve any arbitrary bit of data they so desire. This data can be cached data from an expensive data processing routine, configuration data, or anything else you can come up with.

Callbacks

Callbacks were first introduced with Movable Type 3.0. They have given plugin developers many hooks into the Movable Type system. A callback is hooked into the system by calling the `add_callback` method of the appropriate class:

```
ClassName->add_callback ($method_name, $priority,
$plugin_object, \&callback_method);
```

Callback Priorities

Registering a callback includes specifying a priority number. For most callbacks, that number will fall somewhere in the 1–10 range, with callbacks of priority 1 being called first, and callbacks of priority 10 being called last. Special cases are priorities 0 and 11, which are exclusive. Only one callback method is allowed to be given priority 0 or 11, and if more than one request for either is made, an error will result. Callbacks of priority 0 will run before any other callbacks are handled, so they get first crack at the data, but they also may get lost in the shuffle with all the other callback methods being called. Callbacks of priority 11 will run last, after every other relevant callback has been handled. They get the absolute final chance to touch the data.

Error Handling

Callback routines are passed different arguments depending on which callback is being implemented. The first argument is always an `MT::ErrorHandler` object, from which the `error` method previously discussed originates:

```
sub callback_routine {
    my ($eh) = @_;
    ...
    if ($error_condition) {
        return $eh->error
                ("Error occurred in callback_routine.");
    }
}
```

The error is recorded in the activity log and processing will continue.

Object Callbacks

Object Callbacks can be used to inject code into the loading and saving processes. Any subclass of `MT::Object` can have callbacks applied to it in this manner. These callbacks can be applied either before or after any call to `load`, `save`, `remove`, and `remove_all`, simply by prepending either `pre_` or `post_` to the method name.

The following code will add a callback to `MT::Entry` that will run after it is saved at priority 4:

```
MT::Entry->add_callback ('post_save', 4, $plugin,
            \&post_save_callback_method);
```

A `post_save` callback method, for example, is called immediately after the object in question is saved, but before any follow-up processing is done. In the case of `MT::Entry`, this means that while the entry may have been saved, its categories that are stored with `MT::Placement` have not yet been saved. Therefore, if the entry is a completely new one, even if categories were selected in the edit entry interface, it would appear to the callback method that this entry has no categories at all.

A `pre_save` callback is called before the object is saved. If the object is new to the system, it will not have a value in the id field.

Application Callbacks

Application callbacks can be used to inject code into overall MT processes, instead of at the lower level of object callbacks.

Comment Callbacks

Several callbacks jump into the process of submitting a comment on a Movable Type site, making alterations to its content or blocking it from being stored in the database.

CommentThrottleFilter

With the increase in Internet abuse, a technique that has come into vogue is *throttling*, a software limit that determines how frequently a specific user can be allowed to make a request. Attempts to surpass the limit are rejected in some manner.

The `CommentThrottleFilter` callback supports this functionality in Movable Type. Any callback methods hooked into this callback need to return a Boolean value (that is, a `true` or a `false` value), which is then used to determine whether the incoming comment will be built and stored in the system. If any of the methods hooked into this callback return `false`, the incoming comment is discarded and the submitter receives a message about comment throttling.

This callback is passed the `MT::ErrorHandler` object, followed by the `MT::App::Comments` object and the `MT::Entry` object representing the entry on which the comment is being placed.

CommentFilter

Any callback methods hooked into this callback need to return a Boolean value, just as with `CommentThrottleFilter`. If any of the methods hooked into this callback return `false`, the comment that was built will not be saved.

This callback is passed the `MT::ErrorHandler` object, followed by the `MT::App::Comments` object and the `MT::Comment` object representing the comment that was built but has not yet been saved.

TrackBack Callbacks

Callbacks also interpose themselves in the process of submitting TrackBack pings, messages sent by a website that tie together related weblog entries on different sites.

TBPingThrottleFilter

Any callback methods hooked into this callback need to return a Boolean value. If any methods hooked into this callback return false, the incoming TrackBack ping will be ignored.

This callback is passed the `MT::ErrorHander` object, followed by the `MT::App::Trackback` object and the `MT::Trackback` object representing the destination for the incoming ping.

TBPingFilter

Any callback methods hooked into this callback need to return a Boolean value. If any methods hooked into this callback return `false`, the ping that was built will not be saved.

This callback is passed the `MT::ErrorHandler` object, followed by the `MT::App::Trackback` object and the `MT::TBPing` object representing the ping that was built but has not yet been saved.

Other Callbacks

Additional callbacks can be employed to participate in weblog entry submission, site rebuilds, and file storage.

AppPostEntrySave

Any callback methods hooked into this callback are called after an entry is saved and all of its other information is stored in related database tables, such as the assignment of categories.

This callback is passed the `MT::ErrorHandler` object, followed by the `MT::Entry` object representing the entry that was just saved.

BuildFileFilter

This is one of the more unusual callbacks in the system. It is used to determine whether a given file should be rebuilt as part of the current rebuild process. If any callback method returns `false`, the file will not be rebuilt.

This callback is passed the `MT::ErrorHandler` object, followed by a hash with the following keys:

- **Context** — The current `MT::Template::Context` object
- **ArchiveType** — The archive type of the file
- **TemplateMap** — The `MT::TemplateMap` object pertaining to the current template and the file to be written
- **Blog** — The `MT::Blog` object representing the current blog
- **Entry** — The `MT::Entry` object representing the current entry
- **PeriodStart** — The timestamp representing the start time of the included entries if this is a date-based archive
- **Category** — The `MT::Category` object representing the current category if this is a category archive

BuildFile

Similar to the `BuildFileFilter` method, this callback is called after a file has been built. It is passed the same arguments as `BuildFileFilter`, with one additional hash key, `FileInfo`, which is the `MT::FileInfo` object representing the file that was just built, with the virtual field of that object set to `true` if the file was actually created on disk, or `false` if the template is intended for dynamic building.

Putting It All Together

Suppose that you want to write a plugin that will prevent flame wars from erupting in the comments for any given entry on your blog. For simplicity's sake, we will define a flame comment as one that contains the word *jerk* in the comment body.

Jerk Filter

First you write a callback to catch comments that contain the verboten word in the comment body:

```
sub jerk_filter {
    my ($eh, $app, $comment) = @_;
    # If it is not defined, we don't care
    # Only when it is defined _and_ contains the word
    # 'jerk' do we want to return false
    return !(defined $comment->text &&
            $comment->text =~ /\bjerk\b/i);
}
```

Now, to add this into the system, call the `add_callback` method:

```
MT->add_callback ('CommentFilter', 1, $plugin, \&jerk_filter);
```

Jerk Throttle

The filter prevents comments containing the word jerk in the body from making it into the system, but that is only the first step. If a person really wants to flame somebody else, they will most likely find another way to express themselves which does not contain the word jerk any-where. In that event, writing a comment throttle callback to give them 20 minutes to cool down after they've tried to submit the initial flame comment is a good idea.

First, you will need to modify the jerk filter to record the IP of whomever is trying to leave the flame comment. Use the IP as the key column for the `MT::PluginData` record, with the timestamp stored in the data column:

```
sub jerk_filter {
    my ($eh, $app, $comment) = @_;
    # If it is not defined, we don't care
    # Only when it is defined _and_ contains the word
    # 'jerk' do we want to return false
    if (defined $comment->text &&
        $comment->text =~ /\bjerk\b/i) {
            # Create a MT::PluginData object to store
            # where the user came from and when they
            # attempted to submit a flame
            my $pd = MT::PluginData->new;
            $pd->plugin ('FlamePrevent');
            $pd->key ($app->remote_ip);

            # Get the current time
            my $ts = time;
            # Note: pass the reference to the data
            # you wish to store
            $pd->data (\$ts);
            $pd->save;
```

```
            # Return false because we got a flame comment
            return 0;
    } else {
            # Return true because the comment appears fine
            return 1;
    }
}
```

Next, you need to create a callback method to throttle the comments coming from this person:

```
sub jerk_throttle {
    my ($eh, $app, $entry) = @_;
    # Check the database to see if the current commenter
    # recently tried to submit a flame comment
    my $pd = MT::PluginData->load ({ plugin => 'FlamePrevent',
        key => $app->remote_ip });

    # If there was a record, we need to check and see
    # how long it has been
    if ($pd) {
        # When did they try to submit it
        my $then_ts = ${$pd->data};
        # What time is it now
        my $now_ts = time;
        # if it has been 20 minutes
        if ($now_ts >= $then_ts + (20 * 60)) {
                # Remove the record so that they can now
                # leave comments freely
                $pd->remove;
                # And return true
                return 1;
        } else {
                # Hasn't been long enough so return false
                return 0;
        }
    } else {
        # No record of attempted flames, return true
        return 1;
    }
}
```

Then you hook this callback method into the system:

```
MT->add_callback ('CommentThrottleFilter', 1, $plugin,
    \&jerk_throttle);
```

What if you decide to make the throttle a little less harsh? For example, what if a user has managed to calm herself down and wants to comment on another entry? The user is no longer in the original context where she attempted to leave a flame comment, and the jerk filter will catch it if she tries to leave another one, so you should give people the benefit of the doubt.

Because you are doing this based on the entry instead of globally via the user's IP address, you have to change the storage mechanism you are using, if for no other reason than you are currently not tracking the entry for which the comment was intended:

```perl
sub jerk_filter {
    my ($eh, $app, $comment) = @_;
    # If it is not defined, we don't care
    # Only when it is defined _and_ contains the word
    # 'jerk' do we want to return false
    if (defined $comment->text &&
        $comment->text =~ /\bjerk\b/i) {
            # Check to see if there is an existing
            # set of records for the relevant entry
            my $pd = MT::PluginData->load (
                    { plugin => 'FlamePrevent',
                      key => $comment->entry_id });

            # if it does not exist, create it
            if (!$pd) {
                    $pd = MT::PluginData->new;
                    $pd->plugin ('FlamePrevent');
                    $pd->key ($comment->entry_id);
            }

            # Get the current time
            my $ts = time;

            # Retrieve the current set of timestamps
            my $stamps = $pd->data;

            # Add an entry to the referenced hash
            # for the current user
            $stamps->{$app->remote_ip} = $ts;

            # Store the resulting hash reference
            # Notice that the variable is not explicitly
            # referenced (via '\') because it is already
            # a reference
            $pd->data ($stamps);
            $pd->save;

            # Return false because we got a flame comment
            return 0;
    } else {
            # Return true because the comment appears fine
            return 1;
    }
}
```

Because the storage structure has changed, the throttle callback method will need to be updated:

```perl
sub jerk_throttle {
    my ($eh, $app, $entry) = @_;
    # Check the database to see if the current entry
    # has a record defined associated with the jerk filter
    my $pd = MT::PluginData->load ({ plugin => 'FlamePrevent',
        key => $entry->id });

    # If there was a record for the entry
    # we need to check and see if there is a timestamp
    # for the current IP address
    if ($pd) {
        # Get the timestamp hash
        my $stamps = $pd->data;

        # If an entry exists for the current
        # IP address
        if (exists $stamps->{$app->remote_ip}) {
            # Get the timestamp for when the user
            # tried to submit the flame comment
            my $then_ts = $stamps->{$app->remote_ip};

            # What time is it now
            my $now_ts = time;

            # if it has been 20 minutes
            if ($now_ts >= $then_ts + (20 * 60)) {
                # Remove the record so that they
                # can now leave comments freely
                delete $stamps->{$app->remote_ip};

                # Update the MT::PluginData object
                $pd->data ($stamps);

                # Save the updated object
                $pd->save;

                # Return true
                return 1;
            } else {
                # Has not been long enough yet
                # So return false
                return 0;
            }
        } else {
            # No record of attempted flames
            # from this IP address, so return true
            return 1;
        }
```

```
        } else {
            # No record of attempted flames for this entry
            # so return true
            return 1;
        }
}
```

Now we can assemble all of the parts into a complete plugin, as shown in Listing 11-1.

Listing 11-1: Flame Prevention Plugin

```
Package MTPlugins::FlamePrevent;

use MT;
use MT::Plugin;
use MT::PluginData;

use MT::App::Comments;
use MT::Entry;
use MT::Comment;

# Create and populate the MT::Plugin object
my $plugin = MT::Plugin->new;
$plugin->name ("Flame Prevent");
$plugin->description ("A plugin that will discourage flaming and
encourage cooler heads.");

# Add the plugin to the system
MT->add_plugin ($plugin);

MT->add_callback ('CommentFilter', 1, $plugin, \&jerk_filter);
MT->add_callback ('CommentThrottleFilter', 1, $plugin,
    \&jerk_throttle);

sub jerk_filter {
    my ($eh, $app, $comment) = @_;
    # If it is not defined, we don't care
    # Only when it is defined _and_ contains the word
    # 'jerk' do we want to return false
    if (defined $comment->text &&
        $comment->text =~ /\bjerk\b/i) {
        # Check to see if there is an existing
        # set of records for the relevant entry
        my $pd = MT::PluginData->load (
                { plugin => 'FlamePrevent',
                  key => $comment->entry_id });

        # if it does not exist, create it
        if (!$pd) {
```

```perl
            $pd = MT::PluginData->new;
            $pd->plugin ('FlamePrevent');
            $pd->key ($comment->entry_id);
        }

        # Get the current time
        my $ts = time;

        # Retrieve the current set of timestamps
        my $stamps = $pd->data;

        # Add an entry to the referenced hash
        # for the current user
        $stamps->{$app->remote_ip} = $ts;

        # Store the resulting hash reference
        # Notice that the variable is not explicitly
        # referenced (via '\') because it is already
        # a reference
        $pd->data ($stamps);
        $pd->save;

        # Return false because we got a flame comment
        return 0;
    } else {
        # Return true because the comment appears fine
        return 1;
    }
}

sub jerk_throttle {
    my ($eh, $app, $entry) = @_;
    # Check the database to see if the current entry
    # has a record defined associated with the jerk filter
    my $pd = MT::PluginData->load ({ plugin => 'FlamePrevent',
        key => $entry->id });

    # If there was a record for the entry
    # we need to check and see if there is a timestamp
    # for the current IP address
    if ($pd) {
        # Get the timestamp hash
        my $stamps = $pd->data;

        # If an entry exists for the current
        # IP address
        if (exists $stamps->{$app->remote_ip}) {
            # Get the timestamp for when the user
            # tried to submit the flame comment
            my $then_ts = $stamps->{$app->remote_ip};
```

Continued

Listing 11-1 *(continued)*

```
                        # What time is it now
                        my $now_ts = time;

                        # if it has been 20 minutes
                        if ($now_ts >= $then_ts + (20 * 60)) {
                                # Remove the record so that they
                                # can now leave comments freely
                                delete $stamps->{$app->remote_ip};

                                # Update the MT::PluginData object
                                $pd->data ($stamps);

                                # Save the updated object
                                $pd->save;

                                # Return true
                                return 1;
                        } else {
                                # Has not been long enough yet
                                # So return false
                                return 0;
                        }
                } else {
                        # No record of attempted flames
                        # from this IP address, so return true
                        return 1;
                }

        } else {
                # No record of attempted flames for this entry
                # so return true
                return 1;
        }
}
```

Giving the User Some Control

This flame prevention plugin appears to work well enough on the surface, with our rather sim-
plistic view of what constitutes a flame, but what if users of the plugin want more control over
what they consider a flame? Maybe they want to discourage the use of profanity on their site.
We should give them the option to alter the prohibited word to look out for, or even to build a
list of bad words.

Configuring the Bad Word

Pull the bad word, jerk, out of the `if` statement and drop it into a configuration variable to place at the beginning of the file, where a user of the plugin can edit it easily:

```
my $bad_word = 'jerk';
```

Then incorporate it into the `if` statement for the `jerk_filter` method:

```
    if (defined $comment->text &&
        $comment->text =~ /\b$bad_word\b/i) {
```

Making It Easier for the User

Though storing configuration information within a plugin file is not difficult, asking a user to edit lines of source code in a plugin invites trouble. An inadvertent change to a line of code could render it nonfunctional. A much easier alternative is to create a configuration application.

Subclassing MT::App

The easiest way to quickly build a configuration application is to build a CGI script that makes use of a custom subclass of `MT::App`. Subclassing `MT::App` involves writing an `init` method, as well as methods for handling actions taken by the script:

```
package MTPlugins::FlamePreventCgiApp;

use MT::App;
@ISA = qw( MT::App );

sub init {
    my $app = shift;
    $app->SUPER::init (@_) or return;
    $app->add_methods (
          show_word => \&show_word,
          save_word => \&save_word,
    );
    $app->{default_mode} = 'show_word';
    $app->{template_dir} = 'cms';
    $app->{requires_login} = 1;
    $app->{user_class} = 'MT::Author';

    $app;
}
```

The first two lines of the `init` method are necessary for the subclassing to work correctly. The call to `add_methods` will tell `MT::App` which methods to call when the CGI script is passed the key in the __mode parameter. Setting the `default_mode` hash key will tell `MT::App` what the default value for the __mode parameter is. If the `requires_login` key is set to a `true` value, the application will require the user to log in before, and the `user_class` key will tell `MT::App` what class to validate the user against. The `template_dir` key tells

MT::App in which directory under the tmpl/ directory to look for templates to use to build the interface. Templates can be built by calling the build_page method of MT::App, which in turn builds the templates with HTML::Template. Details on how to write templates with the syntax used in HTML::Template are beyond the scope of this book.

The __mode handler methods simply need to return the text that is intended for the web browser. The two __mode handler methods mentioned earlier would look something like the following:

```perl
sub show_word {
    my ($app) = @_;

    # Generate HTML that will display the configured word
    return $html;
}


sub save_word {
    my ($app) = @_;

    # Save the word and generate HTML to indicate success
    return $html;
}
```

Now for the fun part: saving and retrieving the word the user has provided. The parameters passed to a CGI script are available through the query key of the MT::App object:

```perl
my $query = $app->{query};
my $param_name = $query->param ('param_name');
```

Retrieve the MT::Plugin object from the MTPlugins::FlamePrevent class, and use its set_config_value and get_config_value methods to store and retrieve the word:

```perl
sub show_word {
    my ($app) = @_;

    # Get the current bad word
    my $bad_word = $plugin->get_config_value ('bad_word');

    # If it has not yet been defined, use 'jerk'
    # as the default value
    if (!defined $bad_word) {
        $bad_word = 'jerk';
    }

    # Generate HTML that will display the configured word
    return $html;
}


sub save_word {
    my ($app) = @_;

    # Get the query object
```

```
    my $query = $app->{query};
    # Get the bad_word CGI parameter
    my $bad_word = $query->param ('bad_word');

    # Set that as the bad_word value
    $plugin->set_config_value ('bad_word', $bad_word);

    # Save the word and generate HTML to indicate success
    return $html;
}
```

Now just replace the configuration line in the plugin file to use the config value stored in the database, with the default value being `'jerk'`:

```
my $bad_word = $plugin->get_config_value ('bad_word')
    || 'jerk';
```

All that is needed now is a CGI script that will call the subclassed `MT::App` class. The quickest way to do that is simply to copy the `mt.cgi` script and replace the mentions of `MT::App::CMS` with our new `MT::App` class, `MTPlugins::FlamePreventCgiApp`.

Without too much difficulty, the plugin could be expanded to handle a list of "bad" words instead of just one single word. Give it a try on your own.

Adding to the Movable Type Interface

Any comment that contains what the user of the plugin would consider to be a bad word now triggers the cool-down period encouraged by our plugin. What if a flame comment were submitted without making use of any of the bad words? What recourse does the blog administrator have? You can give plugin users the option to mark a comment as a flame and give the user that submitted it the cool-down period.

How do you add something to the Movable Type interface? The MT class has a method named `add_plugin_action` that does exactly that:

```
MT->add_plugin_action ($where, $link_url, $link_text);
```

To add a link to the interface in the individual comment page, just use the following:

```
MT->add_plugin_action ('comment',
    'link-to-flame-prevent-cgi-app?&__mode=cool_down',
    'Let this commenter cool down.');
```

The second parameter, the `link url`, will be appended with the `where` parameter, and then the id of the individual object if the `where` is for an individual page instead of a list page. The appended text will always start with an ampersand (&), so if the `link url` does not contain any CGI parameters, be sure to end the text with a question mark (?).

Because the `__mode` parameter we are passing to the CGI script is not currently in the list of methods, it must be added.

First, change that portion of the `init` method:

```
$app->add_methods (
        show_word => \&show_word,
        save_word => \&save_word,
        cool_down => \&cool_down,
);
```

Then construct the method to handle the `cool_down` mode:

```
sub cool_down {
    my ($app) = @_;

    # The variable that will hold the result to return
    my $result_html = '';

    # Get the query object
    my $query = $app->{query};
    # Get the comment id
    my $id = $query->param ('id');

    # Load the comment
    require MT::Comment;
    my $comment = MT::Comment->load ($id);

    # If it exists, go ahead and setup the user to
    # hit the jerk throttle
    if ($comment) {
        # Check to see if there is an existing
        # set of records for the relevant entry
        my $pd = MT::PluginData->load (
                { plugin => 'FlamePrevent',
                  key => $comment->entry_id });

        # if it does not exist, create it
        if (!$pd) {
                $pd = MT::PluginData->new;
                $pd->plugin ('FlamePrevent');
                $pd->key ($comment->entry_id);
        }

        # Get the current time
        my $ts = time;

        # Retrieve the current set of timestamps
        my $stamps = $pd->data;

        # Add an entry to the referenced hash
        # for the current user
        $stamps->{$comment->ip} = $ts;

        # Store the resulting hash reference
```

```
        # Notice that the variable is not explicitly
        # referenced (via '\') because it is already
        # a reference
        $pd->data ($stamps);
        $pd->save;

        $result_html = 'User at ip '.
                $comment->ip.
                ' will be given a cool-down period.';
    } else {
        $result_html = 'Unknown comment';
    }

    $result_html;
}
```

Now, when a user views an individual comment in the Movable Type interface, a link will appear at the bottom of the page that, if clicked, will cause the person who left the comment to enter the cool-down period enforced by the jerk throttle.

Summary

As this chapter demonstrates, Six Apart isn't kidding when it bills Movable Type as a completely extensible program.

Through callbacks, data persistence, and a robust Perl API, the software has attracted a dedicated following of Perl tinkerers. After installing a few must-have plugins, even the most expert MT user will find it difficult to determine where Six Apart ends and the plugin developers begin.

The jerk throttle demonstrates how a plugin can jump into the middle of an action. After a weblog user submits a comment and before it becomes a part of a weblog, a Perl script can make decisions about what to do with it.

Greater capabilities are made possible through hooks into the software's browser interface.

Hacking Dynamic Publishing

Movable Type 3.1 introduced a new layer that enables you to publish pages dynamically instead of the traditional static publishing for which the software has become identified.

The new layer has been implemented with PHP, a popular programming language for web applications that has widespread support on several operating systems.

This chapter explores the new dynamic publishing architecture and how to use it to the fullest extent.

Dynamic Publishing Architecture

The first thing to understand is the architecture behind it all. In terms of PHP scripts, the following shows the order of invocation from request to response:

1. HTTP request

2. .htaccess rule/error document

3. mtview.php

4. `MT` class (`MT.php`)

5. `MTViewer` class, aka Smarty (`MTViewer.php`)

6. PHP

7. HTTP response with output

An examination of each stage of this process follows:

1. Requests are sent to the web server from a client (usually a web browser or an RSS/Atom client such as a newsreader). The web server attempts to resolve the request. If it can resolve the request to a physical file, it returns the appropriate file. This allows for a mix of static and dynamic publishing.

2. If the request cannot be resolved by the web server, it will adjust the request according to the active rules (.htaccess for Apache, error documents for Microsoft Internet Information Server [IIS]). The default .htaccess rule set for dynamic publishing basically instructs Apache to forward any request that cannot be resolved to a physical file or directory to the mtview.php script. The error document approach on IIS accomplishes the same thing (although less gracefully because it only logs requests of mtview.php to the log file instead of the original request).

3. If the rules point the web server to use the mtview.php script for the weblog, the request is passed to it for handling. When Apache does this, it sets the original request in a server variable named REQUEST_URI. IIS simply invokes the mtview.php script, sending the original URL as a query parameter.

4. The mtview.php script loads the primary MT class, which is responsible for the bulk of the URL resolution logic. The URL is resolved and a Smarty object is instantiated to render the page.

5. The MTViewer/Smarty object created in Step 4 is given the data it needs to build the page. Initially, this is just the active weblog ID, perhaps a start and end timestamp, and what archive type is being used (if any). The template is loaded for the active request and processed. If the template has not already been compiled by Smarty into native PHP code, this is done next (and the result of the template compilation is stored in the templates_c directory).

6. Smarty loads the compiled template (a PHP script) and executes it.

7. As the template is executed, the output is sent back to the client.

If any error occurs in this process, the MT Dynamic Pages Error Template is used to relay the error to the end user.

Smarty is a template publishing system for PHP that forms the foundation of Movable Type's dynamic rendering capabilities. Copious documentation and how-to tutorials can be read on Smarty's web site, http://smarty.php.net. You can supplement MT's template-driven features by working directly with Smarty, as you'll discover later in this chapter.

mtview.php

mtview.php is the primary script for invoking the PHP publishing engine. When you run the mtview.php script, it simply does the following (within these examples, 'MT_DIR' is a placeholder for the actual path to the Movable Type directory; please substitute this with the Movable Type directory on your server):

```
$mt = new MT(1, 'MT_DIR/mt.cfg'); # your blog id here
$mt->view();
```

The view method takes the default course of action, which is to determine the active request and attempt to serve it based on locating the URL in the Movable Type database.

The MT Class

Now, what is available in the MT class piece of the puzzle? Here are the primary methods it provides:

- `init_plugins()` — Configures for available plugins
- `context()` — Retrieves Smarty instance (actually an MT-flavored subclass of Smarty)
- `db()` — Retrieves the database instance
- `configure()` — Loads the MT configuration file
- `configure_paths()` — Establishes MT path locations
- `view()` — Mainline for dynamic publishing
- `resolve_url()` — Returns database records for a given URL
- `display()` — Utility function that displays a particular Smarty template
- `fetch()` — Utility function that returns output of a particular Smarty template
- `error_handler()` — Custom error handling method
- `doConditionalGet()` — Handles conditional GET operations

The nice thing about the MT class is that it is, in fact, a class. This means you can customize it, so if you don't like the way it does particular things, you can change it to your liking. Or, if you don't want to delve that deeply, you can do certain things from the calling script (`mtview.php`) to customize what happens between the request and serving the output.

The MTDatabase Classes

The database access layer for MT/PHP is the biggest departure from the MT/Perl architecture. It is very simple by comparison. We are utilizing the `ezSQL` package as the base class because it provides an abstraction layer between different database vendors (MySQL, PostgreSQL, SQLite). But instead of having separate objects for each table in the MT database, we are simply retrieving PHP arrays (hashes of data). Therefore, there is no "load" method at the table level for retrieving entries or other types of data. Instead, there is a method in the database class itself for fetching each type of data. This simplification was made to save precious milliseconds of CPU time, because in dynamic publishing, every millisecond counts.

There is an `MTDatabaseBase` class that is sort of an abstract class. The vendor-specific subclass is what is actually instantiated. Those classes are `MTDatabase_mysql`, `MTDatabase_postgres`, and `MTDatabase_sqlite` (the MySQL class is the only one that is functional at this time). The vendor-specific classes override or implement base class methods where there are vendor-specific differences in the SQL query syntax.

Here are some of the methods available in the database class (the `MTDatabaseBase` inherits from the `ezSQL` class):

- `resolve_url()` — Returns relevant contextual data necessary to serve a given URL.

- `load_index_template()` — Fetches `mt_template` data for a particular index template.

- `load_special_template()` — Fetches `mt_template` data for a particular class of template.

- `get_template_text()` — Returns the template source for a particular named template.

- `get_archive_list()` — This is a workhorse function for the `<MTArchiveList>` tag.

- `archive_link()` — Returns the URL for a given timestamp and archive type.

- `fetch_blog()` — Returns an individual blog record for the given blog ID.

- `blog_entry_count()` — Returns the number of entries for a given blog ID.

- `fetch_entry()` — Returns an individual entry record for the given entry ID.

- `fetch_entries()` — Returns an array of entry records that match the requested criteria.

- `entry_link()` — Returns the URL for a given entry ID and archive type.

- `entry_comment_count()` — Returns the number of comments for a given entry ID.

- `entry_ping_count()` — Returns the number of pings for a given entry ID.

- `fetch_category()` — Returns an individual category record for the given category ID.

- `fetch_categories()` — Returns an array of category records that match the requested criteria.

- `category_link()` — Returns the URL for a given category ID.

- `fetch_author()` — Returns an individual author record for the given author ID.

- `fetch_comments()` — Returns an array of comment records that match the requested criteria.

- `fetch_pings()` — Returns an array of ping records that match the requested criteria.

The fetch methods in the preceding list attempt to cache as much as possible. For example, if multiple entry records are fetched with `fetch_entries`, it will precache the comments and pings for those entries (doing a single `select` statement for all entry IDs rather than a separate query for each entry). In some cases, this gathers more data than necessary, but in most cases, it saves on execution time.

The MTViewer Class

The last major piece to cover is the `MTViewer` class. This class is a descendant of the Smarty class and has the following methods (inherited from the Smarty class):

- `add_global_filter()` — Registers a global filter, just as you would do with MT/Perl.

- `error()` — Triggers an error during runtime.

- `this_tag()` — Within plugin routines, this returns the active MT tag name.

- `stash()` — Much like the MT stash method, this lets you place/retrieve data on the stash.

- `localize()` — Saves the state of a list of elements that are in the stash.

- `restore()` — Restores the state of a list of previously localized stash elements.

- `tag()` — Invokes an MT tag handler and returns the result.

In addition to the preceding methods, this class also customizes the way templates are processed. It declares a custom Smarty prefilter called `mt_to_smarty`, which takes care of translating MT templates into Smarty-compatible syntax.

Customizing mtview.php

As previously mentioned, the main `MT` class is an object, so it lends itself to customization if you require it. For example, you may want to override the `resolve_url` method to have it try alternative search methods to find an entry based on the request. A little adjustment to the `mtview.php` script would be in order:

```php
<?php
include("MT_DIR/php/mt.php");
class MyMT extends MT {
    function &resolve_url($path) {
        $data =& parent::resolve_url($path);
        if (!$data) {
            # now try harder!
            $data =& $this->fuzzy_resolve_url($path);
        }
        return $data;
    }
    function &fuzzy_resolve_url($path) {
        # fuzzy logic to locate a given $path follows...
    }
}

$mt = new MyMT(1, "MT_DIR/mt.cfg");  # use OUR MT class
$mt->view();
?>
```

And consider this PHP snippet:

```php
<?php
  include_once("MT_DIR/php/mt.php");
  $mt = new MT(10);    # blog id 10 is my 'linkblog'
  $ctx =& $mt->context();
  $ctx->caching = 2;   # each cache file has its own lifetime
  $ctx->cache_lifetime = 60 * 30;   # cache for 30 minutes
  $output = $mt->fetch("mt:My Linkblog");
  echo $output;
?>
```

Here we have invoked the MT dynamic publishing engine to render a specific index template
(`"My Linkblog"` — the `"mt:"` prefix causes it to be pulled from the database. Smarty also
provides a `"file:"` prefix that is the default resource type if you want to load templates from
the file system), causing the output to be cached for up to 1,800 seconds (30 minutes). This can
be done from any PHP script. You could publish your entire site statically and still pull a portion of MT data this way using the PHP engine.

Within dynamic templates, you have convenient access to your data. Having a full scripting
language at your disposal may alleviate the need to create MT-specific plugins. You could just
use the wealth of functions available through PHP itself or other PHP libraries/modules that
already exist. The following example illustrates how you can access your MT content directly
from PHP, manipulate it, and then output it in whatever manner you choose:

```php
<MTEntries lastn="10">
<MTEntriesHeader><ul></MTEntriesHeader>
<?php
  $title = $this->tag('MTEntryTitle');
  $raw_body = $this->tag('MTEntryBody',
      array('convert_breaks' => '0'));
  $raw_body = preg_replace('/[^A-Za-z0-9\s]/', '',
      strip_tags($raw_body));
  $raw_words = preg_split('/\s+/', $raw_body);
  echo "<li>" . $title . " (approx. word count: " .
count($raw_words).")</li>";
?>
<MTEntriesFooter></ul></MTEntriesFooter>
</MTEntries>
```

Using MT Tags in PHP

One shortcoming (at least for now) is that you cannot mix MT tags inside PHP code blocks.
This is possible in a static publishing model, but with dynamic publishing, the MT tags are
translated into PHP code. Therefore, putting an MT tag within a PHP code block will cause
the template-to-PHP translation to output a PHP open tag within another PHP block, which
would result in a syntax error. Therefore, the preceding tag method is the recommended way to
invoke tags within PHP code blocks.

With the Smarty framework, there are even more ways to customize the rendering of your page. Another feature available through Smarty is the output filter. An *output filter* is something that runs after the template has been executed. If, for example, you want to apply a text filtering process over your entire page (not just individual entry text), you can load an output filter to do that.

I created a file in my PHP plugins directory named `outputfilter.smartypants.php` with this in it:

```php
<?php
include_once("smartypants.php");
function smarty_outputfilter_smartypants($text, &$ctx) {
    return SmartyPants($text);
}
?>
```

Then, within my `mtview.php` script, I simply load the filter:

```php
# put this above the $mt->view() step...
$ctx =& $mt->context();
$ctx->load_filter('output', 'smartypants');
```

Now I get educated quotes for the entire web page, rather than just the MT content. Fortunately, the SmartyPants parser gracefully ignores HTML, scripts, and so forth.

Smarty Templating Works Too

Because we're using Smarty as the underlying engine to process our templates, you can actually use the full Smarty template syntax if you prefer. You can even mix Smarty template code and MT template syntax together (the default delimiters for Smarty are changed from { and } to {{ and }} because the single brace delimiters cause problems if you have JavaScript within your template). You can invoke PHP script as well.

For example, Smarty has a neat little function tag called `cycle` that enables you to cycle through a list of values. Each time `cycle` is used within a loop, it will output the next one in the set. Here's how you might use it:

```
<MTEntries>
<tr bgcolor="{{cycle values="#eeeeee,#d0d0d0"}}">
  <td><$MTEntryTitle$></td>
</tr>
</MTEntries>
```

This would alternate the background color of the rows of the table for each entry output.

I encourage you to read the excellent documentation available for Smarty to discover everything that is at your disposal.

Hacking Dynamic Templates

Templates that are dynamically published are far more flexible than their static counterparts. In addition to being able to use the basic MT tags, you can do the following:

- Use any MT tags available from any MT/PHP plugins installed.
- Use `<?php ... ?>` blocks to invoke native PHP code.
- Use Smarty template code (when using {{ and }} to delimit the Smarty template code).

In fact, it is possible to write your Movable Type dynamic templates using only Smarty template syntax. For example, say you have a MT tag written like this:

```
<$MTBlogName$>
```

The Smarty way to write that follows:

```
{{MTBlogName}}
```

If you have a container tag, such as

```
<MTEntries lastn="10">
<p><$MTEntryTitle$></p>
<$MTEntryBody$>
</MTEntries>
```

you would write it in Smarty template form like this:

```
{{MTEntries lastn="10"}}
<p>{{MTEntryTitle}}</p>
{{MTEntryBody}}
{{/MTEntries}}
```

As you can see, the differences are fairly minimal. You can mix and match the syntax as well:

```
<MTEntries lastn="10">
<div class="{{cycle values="odd,even"}}">
<p><$MTEntryTitle$></p>
{{MTEntryBody}}
</div>
</MTEntries>
```

You can also refer to variables directly. For example, when processing entries, the current entry is assigned into Smarty's variable namespace as `entry`. Here is how you would refer to the title from the active entry:

```
{{$entry.entry_title}}
```

All the fields associated with the entry can be referenced like this. Note that the values you get this way are completely unprocessed — they contain the raw data taken directly from the database.

You can manipulate these variables using the variable modifiers Smarty provides:

```
{{$entry.entry_created_on|date_format:"%A, %B %e, %Y"}}
```

And there are some useful modifiers for counting things:

```
Paragraphs: {{$entry.entry_text|strip_tags|count_paragraphs}}
```

In MT template syntax, it would be as follows:

```
Paragraphs: <$MTEntryBody count_paragraphs="1"$>
```

You can even use regular expressions without having to install any additional plugins. The following will replace all tabs and newline characters with a space:

```
{{$entry.entry_text|regex_replace="/[\r\t\n]/":" "}}
```

You can do the same thing using MT template syntax (the " : " separator for multiple attribute values is only valid syntax for dynamic templates currently):

```
<$MTEntryBody regex_replace="/[\r\t\n]/":" "$>
```

One thing you can't do is embed PHP code into an MT tag and expect it to work. This syntax is currently unsupported:

```
<MTEntries lastn="<?php echo $limit ?>">
```

Instead, you would place a regular PHP variable into the Smarty variable stash where it can be accessed by Smarty tags:

```
<?php
$this->stash('limit', $limit);
?>
<MTEntries lastn="`$limit`">
```

The following is also unsupported:

```
<?php
$title = '<$MTEntryTitle encode_php="1"$>';
/* do something with $title, like transform it into an image */
?>
```

The second example is something that works in a static publishing world, where the MT tags are evaluated first and then PHP is processed later. However, with dynamic publishing, the MT tags are translated *into* PHP code. Therefore, the previous example would produce something like this:

```
<?php
$title = '<?php /* code to execute the MTEntryTitle tag */ ?>';
?>
```

Instead, you should use the `tag` method of the Smarty variable:

```
<?php
$title = $this->tag('MTEntryTitle');
?>
```

Dynamically Paging Entries

With a static publishing model, it's difficult to get paged views of your content. With a dynamic model, it becomes very easy. Let's look at how to adjust a Movable Type index template to view 10 entries at a time.

The goal is to display the last 10 entries from the weblog by default, but also provide links to navigate backward and forward by 10 more entries. These hyperlinks should display or hide themselves depending on the situation.

First, we should decide on a navigation scheme. Let's use a query parameter to identify the offset to be used when fetching the entries to display. If the `offset` parameter isn't provided, the last 10 entries will display. If an offset of 10 is specified, entries 11–20 will be shown, and so forth.

Accessing a query parameter from Smarty is quite easy. It is made available in a special Smarty variable called `$smarty.request`. To retrieve a specific parameter such as `offset`, just add that to the end of the variable name, as shown in the following example:

```
You requested:   {{$smarty.request.offset}}
```

Now we want to put that value to work. The goal is to pass it into the `<MTEntries>` tag, using it as the `offset` parameter for that tag. Here is how to do it:

```
<MTEntries offset="`$smarty.request.offset`" lastn="10">
```

If the `offset` parameter isn't given, it will default to no offset. If it is a non-numeric value, it will also default to no offset.

Next, we want to display the navigational aids, to enable users to move backward and forward through the entries:

```
{{capture assign="count"}}<$MTBlogEntryCount$>{{/capture}}

{{if $smarty.request.offset > 0}}
<a href="?offset={{math equation="max(x-10,0)"
x=$smarty.request.offset}}">Previous</a>
{{/if}}

{{if $smarty.request.offset < $count-10}}

    {{if $smarty.request.offset > 0}}
    |
    {{/if}}

<a href="?offset={{$smarty.request.offset+10}}">Next</a>
{{/if}}
```

The first statement stores the count of entries in the weblog in a Smarty variable named `count`. The next section displays a `Previous` link if the current offset is 1 or more. That presents a link with an `offset` query parameter of the current offset minus 10 entries. It will use an offset of 0 as a minimum in case the previous offset calculation is less than 0. Next, a `Next` link is conditionally displayed if the current offset is less than the count of weblog entries minus 10. This prevents the Next link from being shown if the last entry is already in view.

Now you have a functioning paged view of your weblog content with just a few additional lines of Smarty code.

Dynamically Paging an Entry

You could use a similar approach to display multiple pages of content for a single entry. If you create a marker of some kind to serve as a page delimiter, you can use it to break up a single entry into multiple pages.

Lets make <page> the marker for this example. Create an entry that has multiple pages of data in the extended entry field, as follows:

```
This is page one
<page>
This is page two
<page>
This is page three
```

Now, in your Individual Archive template, you need to add some code that breaks these up and displays them properly. You also have to create a query parameter to fetch the right page. Use page as the query parameter.

We'll use a bit of regex magic to do two things. First, we need to know how many pages are available for the entry. Second, we want to select out the proper page from the field that contains all of the pages. Add these two lines to the top of the template:

```
{{capture
assign="page_count"}}{{$entry.entry_text_more|escape:"javscript"|
regex_replace:"/<page>/":"\n\n"|count_paragraphs}}{{/capture}}
{{capture
assign="page_text"}}{{$entry.entry_text_more|regex_replace:"/^
(.*?<page>\s*){`$smarty.request.page-1`}/s":""|regex_replace:
"/<page>.*$/s":""|convert_breaks:"1"}}{{/capture}}
```

If you look closely, you can follow what's going on here. Two capture tags are being used to set a couple of variables. The first one is going to calculate the number of pages in the extended entry text field. It takes the extended text of the entry and converts all of the newline characters using the escape modifier. Next, all of the <page> markers are replaced with newline characters and that result is fed to the count_paragraphs modifier to get a count of the pages. This works because it effectively translates each page into a paragraph.

The second capture tag is going to select out the individual page to be displayed. The first regex operation deletes the number of pages requested minus 1 from the entry text. It then deletes any page markers and content from what is left. Then it runs the text through the convert_breaks text filter and formats the text into HTML. Finally, the result is stored in the Smarty variable "page_text".

We should now alter the main entry text so that it is only displayed on page 1. Here's a bit of logic to handle that. Replace the `<$MTEntryBody$>` tag in your template with the following:

```
{{if $smarty.request.page <= 1}}
<$MTEntryBody$>
{{else}}
<p>
<em>(continued from <a href="?page={{$smarty.request.page-
1}}">page {{$smarty.request.page-1}}</a>)</em>
</p>
{{/if}}
```

This will display the `<$MTEntryBody$>` tag for the first page; and for the others, it will show some text to give users some context as to the page they're looking at.

Finally, we'll display a row of page navigation so users can get to the other pages available. The following should replace the `<$MTEntryMore$>` tag:

```
{{$page_text}}

{{if $page_count > 1}}

<div>
{{section name=i loop=$page_count}}
{{if ($smarty.request.page > 0 || $smarty.section.i.iteration > 1)
&& $smarty.section.i.iteration != $smarty.request.page}}
<a href="?page={{$smarty.section.i.iteration}}">page
{{$smarty.section.i.iteration}}</a>
{{else}}
page {{$smarty.section.i.iteration}}
{{/if}}
{{/section}}
</div>

{{/if}}
```

You should now have an easy solution for composing and displaying multi-paged entries.

Creating Web Applications with Smarty

With PHP and Smarty under the hood, there's not much you can't do. You also have a live connection to the database that holds your Movable Type data. You could add some custom tables to that database and draw data from them for your templates, as shown in the following example:

```
<?php
$blog = $this->stash('blog');
# assign a selection of rows to the smarty 'rows' variable
$this->stash('rows', $this->mt->db->get_results('select distinct
comment_url from mt_comment where comment_blog_id=' .
$blog['blog_id'], ARRAY_A));
?>
```

```
{{section name=row loop=$rows}}
URL:   {{$rows[row].comment_url}}
{{/section}}
```

In this example, we're selecting all of the unique URLs from the comments table and displaying them in the order returned. You could just as easily select all of the comments that match a particular URL.

Writing to the Database

The MT dynamic publishing framework currently only reads data from the MT database. However, it is also possible to write back to the database. For example, you might update a counter on the entry currently being viewed to help identify which of your entries are more popular. To do this, a new field is required in the `mt_entry` table. We'll call it `entry_dyn_view_count`. To add it, execute the following SQL command on your MySQL database (this command will not affect MT's operation):

```
alter table mt_entry add entry_dyn_view_count integer default 0
```

Now you will need to update this field whenever a specific entry is viewed. A good place to do that is on your Individual Entry Archive template (or templates). You just need to execute a single statement to increment the counter for that entry:

```php
<?php
$entry = $this->stash('entry');
$this->mt->db->query("update mt_entry
    set entry_dyn_view_count = entry_dyn_view_count + 1
    where entry_id = " . $entry['entry_id']);
?>
```

You can also refer to this value in your Individual Entry Archive template so you can reveal how many hits it has accumulated:

```
Number of views:   {{$entry.entry_dyn_view_count}}
```

Hacking Dynamic Plugins

Just as there is a Perl API available for developing Movable Type plugins in Perl, the dynamic side of Movable Type provides a PHP API for creating custom plugins. This section delves into how to create plugins using that API.

Use the Source, Luke!

To get you started, a whole host of MT tags have been ported from Perl to PHP. These would be the core MT tag set. Both the Perl and PHP source is available with the 3.1 (and later) distribution, so that should give you a good feel for how to do a number of different types of tags. If you're comfortable with how the Perl API works, you can compare the Perl and PHP implementations for standard MT tags that are similar to your own and see how the Perl code was translated to work for PHP.

In creating the PHP implementation, we tried to preserve some concepts from the MT/Perl API. However, some things are drastically different and/or simplified, partly due to the Smarty integration and partly due to the nature of dynamic publishing — execution speed overrides everything else.

One thing that will be immediately noticeable is that the PHP API has a much simpler object model. In fact, there are just a handful of classes compared to the Perl implementation. For example, instead of having classes defined for each table, we simply use a PHP array to hold data.

Speed, Speed, Speed

Speed is critical to dynamic publishing, so it is very important that your plugin execute efficiently. Every tag used on a dynamic template will take some time to execute. If your plugin uses even 1 second of time, that will be very noticeable to someone browsing that page. And if 20 people are viewing it at once, chances are good it will take even longer per person for that page to render. This is the cost of dynamic publishing.

Creating Custom Tags

Let's start by looking at what you need to do to create a plain custom tag. In Smarty-speak, these are called *function tags:*

1. Create a PHP script named `function.MTMyTag.php`.

2. Within that script, define a PHP function named `smarty_function_MTMyTag`.

That's it! The file-naming convention is a requirement of Smarty. This is done so that Smarty can locate and load the appropriate source code at runtime to invoke the tags necessary for a given page. Unlike MT, where each individual plugin file is processed and loaded, Smarty only loads the PHP scripts that will be necessary to execute a given template. Ultimately, this winds up being a more efficient approach and a good technique to follow for the dynamic publishing model.

The Obligatory "Hello, World" Tag

Let's say you want to create a template tag that offers a greeting. Let's call it `MTHello`. The first step would be to create a PHP script named `function.MTHello.php`. This script would be stored in the `MT_DIR/php/plugins` directory (substituting your MT installation path for `MT_DIR`, of course).

Within the file, you would define the following function:

```php
<?php
function smarty_function_MTHello($args, &$ctx) {
    return "Hello, World!";
}
?>
```

This is the simplest of all tags. It merely returns a string. We can do better with the following:

```php
<?php
function smarty_function_MTHello($args, &$ctx) {
    $name = $args['name'] or 'World';
    return "Hello, $name!";
}
?>
```

We can now accept a name attribute with the `MTHello` tag. It would be used like this:

```
With name attribute: <$MTHello name="Visitor"$>
Without name attribute: <$MTHello$>
```

Producing:

```
With name attribute: Hello, Visitor!
Without name attribute: Hello, World!
```

But we can do even better. If the user has signed in using TypeKey, we should be able to personally greet her with the following:

```php
<?php
function smarty_function_MTHello($args, &$ctx) {
    $name = $_COOKIE['commenter_name'] or $args['name'] or
        'World';
    return "Hello, $name!";
}
?>
```

Now, if I am logged in, the preceding template code would produce the following:

```
Hello, Brad Choate!
```

Creating Container Tags

Let's look at what you do to create a custom container tag. We'll also create a related custom tag that is to be used within the container tag. Container tags are called `block` tags in the Smarty vocabulary.

The container tags work quite differently in PHP compared to the Perl approach. This is due to the nature of how the block functions are called from the compiled templates. Some pseudocode is in order to illustrate the process. Consider this template:

```
<MTMyContainerTag>
    I'm content being contained.
</MTMyContainerTag>
```

The preceding template would be compiled into something like the following. (This is similar to what Smarty would produce when compiling the preceding template. This is not code that you or a user has to create by any means. I've just added comments and spacing to make it more readable.)

```php
<?php
    # push the active tag onto the tag stack
    # (and any attributes it uses)...
    $this->_tag_stack[] = array('MTMyContainerTag', array());

    # call the block function once to do the initialization
    # step. it could set the $repeat parameter to false to
    # prevent *any* output.
    smarty_block_MTMyContainerTag(
        $this->_tag_stack[count($this->_tag_stack)-1][1],
        null,
        $this,
        $_block_repeat = true);

    # start a loop that ends once the $repeat parameter is
    # set to false (which it is by default-- the container
    # tag handler must explicitly set it to true to continue
    # looping)
    while ($_block_repeat) {
        # start output buffering since mixed php/plain text
        # usually follows...
        ob_start();

    # the stuff within the container tag comes next:
?>

I'm content being contained.

<?php
    # now grab the buffered content and store it so
    # we can pass it back to the container tag handler:
    $this->_block_content = ob_get_contents();
    ob_end_clean();

    # echo out whatever the container tag returns as
    # the result...
    echo smarty_block_MTMyContainerTag(
        $this->_tag_stack[count($this->_tag_stack)-1][1],
        $this->_block_content,
        $_block_repeat = false);
    }

    # our loop is complete; remove the tag from the stack
    array_pop($this->_tag_stack);
?>
```

This should help you see what is taking place when the actual `block` function is being called
and how the `block` function can control the `while` loop it lives within. The form of the
actual block handler looks like this:

```php
<?php
function smarty_block_MTMyContainerTag($args, $content, &$ctx,
&$repeat) {
    $localvars = array('one', 'two', 'three');
    if (!isset($content)) {
        # initialization and setup...
        $ctx->localize($localvars);
    } else {
        # code that executes iteratively while $repeat == true
        # optionally set $repeat to true to loop
        # manipulate the data in $content if so desired
    }
    if (!$repeat)
        $ctx->restore($localvars);
    return $content;
}
?>
```

Compare the compiled template shown previously with the code for the block handler and you
will start to see the relationship between them. In the compiled template on line 8, the block
handler is called and winds up executing the section of code on line 5 ("initialization and
setup"). Because this happens outside the loop, it's a good place to do any database fetch operations that determine whether or not the loop should execute. You can take advantage of the
`$ctx->stash()` method to store any data you want to maintain or make available for any
contained custom tags.

Preserving Stash Elements

Because PHP doesn't have a `local` statement like Perl does, a pair of routines have been
created to provide the same function. The `$ctx->localize()` method receives an array
of named stash elements whose values are to be saved for later restoration using the
`$ctx->restore()` method. It is important to pair these properly whenever they are used.

Traditional Container Tags

Now that you understand how container tags operate and are coded, let's look at a real
example:

```php
<?php
function smarty_block_MTMySuckyTag($args, $content, &$ctx,
                                   &$repeat) {
    $localvars = array('myvar');
    if (!isset($content)) {
        $ctx->localize($localvars);
        $ctx->stash('myvar', $args['string']);
    } else {
        $myvar = $ctx->stash('myvar');
        if (strlen($myvar) > 0) {
```

```
            $repeat = true;
            $myvar = substr($myvar, 0, strlen($some_var)-1);
            $ctx->stash('myvar', $myvar);
        }
    }
    if (!$repeat)
        $ctx->restore($localvars);
    return $content;
}
?>
```

Then, to complement this wonder block tag, is a tag to output the value of `'myvar'`:

```
<?php
function smarty_function_MTMySuckyVar($args, &$ctx) {
    return $ctx->stash('myvar');
}
?>
```

Then, using these tags like this

```
<MTMySuckyTag string="Testing">
  <$MTMySuckyVar$>
</MTMySuckyTag>
```

would produce the following:

```
Testing
Testin
Testi
Test
Tes
Te
T
```

Conditional Container Tags

Conditional tags operate a little differently. The `<MTElse>` tag is the issue here. We need a way to process that tag effectively:

```
<?php
function smarty_block_MTIfRandom($args, $content, &$ctx,
                                 &$repeat) {
    if (!isset($content)) {
        $condition = rand(0, 1);
        return $ctx->_hdlr_if($args, $content, $ctx, $repeat,
                              $condition);
    } else {
        return $ctx->_hdlr_if($args, $content, $ctx, $repeat);
    }
}
?>
```

Then, you can use the conditional tag like this:

```
<MTIfRandom>
  You got this message by chance.
</MTIfRandom>
```

Or you can use the `<MTElse>` tag to complement it:

```
<MTIfRandom>
  You're a winner!
<MTElse>
  You're a loser!
</MTElse>
</MTIfRandom>
```

Global Filter Plugins

Global filters are called *modifiers* in Smarty. They are very easy to create. Their filename prefix is "modifier," so an example of a modifier plugin filename would be `"modifier.my_modifier.php"`:

```
<?php
function smarty_modifier_my_modifier($text, $attr = null) {
    # do something with $text
    $text = strtoupper($text);
    return $text;
}
?>
```

If you have a third-party module you want to use, just use the `include_once` PHP statement to include the library and then call the text-processing routine in the modifier function, returning the result.

Initialization Plugins

Initialization plugins are also supported. These have an "init" prefix for plugin scripts. With MT/Perl, all `.pl` plugin files in the plugins directory are loaded at startup. Initialization scripts are the counterpart to that mechanism. To take advantage of this, you will need to name your script so that it has an "init." prefix and a ".php" suffix. Any files in the `MT_DIR/php/plugins` directory will be processed by the `$ctx->init_plugins()` method before the request is processed. The script is simply loaded with a PHP include statement.

Instructing the Template Compiler

The process that translates MT templates into Smarty templates requires some hints about particular tags and attributes in order to do that translation properly. In particular, conditional-style tags (any tags that are used in combination with the `<MTElse>` tag) are treated differently. Tags that have `"If"` in their name are recognized as such, but those that do not (such as `<MTEntriesHeader>`) must be declared as a conditional tag. In addition, global filters

(Smarty modifiers) have to be declared so they are not processed as parameters to the tag handlers (however, these will be recognized automatically because they can be discovered by scanning for files that have a "modifier" prefix in the plugins directory).

Finally, if you have a tag that recursively calls itself (the `<$MTSubCatsRecurse$>` tag fits this category), that has to be known as well. If your plugin has a tag or tags that need to be declared, you should write an `init.myplugin.php` script to do that, as shown in the following example:

```php
<?php
global $mt;
# This retrieves the Smarty instance we use to
# declare our template compilation hints...
$ctx =& $mt->context();

# Declares a conditional tag that doesn't have "If"
# already in the tag name.
$ctx->add_conditional_tag('MTMyConditionalTag');

# Declares a tag that requires a "token" function.
$ctx->add_token_tag('MTMyTokenTag');
?>
```

Summary

The PHP side of Movable Type provides a powerful way to build dynamic websites from your Movable Type database, and having the capability to mix static and dynamic publishing puts the power of both Perl and PHP at your command.

Hacking Powerful Blog Applications Together

Photo Blogs

Just as weblogs make it easy to post your writing online for the entire world to see, photo blogs help photographers share their images with an online audience.

Photo blogs rely on easy-to-use software such as Movable Type (MT) and the proliferation of high-quality, inexpensive digital cameras. Currently, however, only a few services are specially made for creating and maintaining photo blogs and they don't offer much flexibility or customizability.

With MT's template-driven publishing system, you can build a powerful photo blog manager that is custom tailored to exactly how you want your photos to be shown. Along with MT's plugin system, you will be able to produce thumbnails, send photos from your phone, and display photo information in ways no other photo hosting service provides.

While MT was originally designed for text with an occasional image, photo blogs are typically image driven, with a little bit of text. You should set up your photo blog based on its use and how you want the output to display. Most photo blogs are MT blogs that stick to individual entry archives, with an index page showing the most recent photo entry. Using the built-in tools that MT provides, you'll be able to upload photos directly from MT, and post on the go just as if you were writing.

Creating a Simple Photo Blog

When you create a photo blog, it's important to plan how you want the output to look and behave.

Planning

If you've already got a standard weblog that features text and links and want to add a companion photo blog, there are several ways to do that. You might want to display just the latest photo along the side of your weblog, with a link to the full-sized image. You might want to list the past five photo titles with links to view them. Or, you might want to do something ingenious like have the header of your weblog be your latest photo of the day. All of these options will require tweaking the Main Index (or a custom index you create). If you want to start a new standalone photo blog, how you want to display photos, indexes, and archives will also determine how you go about creating templates.

Another important point to think about up front is how you will organize your photos. Photo management software (both online and on your desktop) typically offers some options to organize your photos into galleries. Because Movable Type isn't a photo manager per se, by organizing your photos into a MT weblog, you are essentially creating a single gallery, with each entry being part of the gallery. This is worth noting because many photographers are accustomed to having several galleries arranged around locations, time periods, and/or subject matter, and the typical way MT is used for photo blogs is to limit items to one big gallery.

Although MT version 3.1 doesn't offer specific photo management capabilities out of the box, it is worth noting that the Movable Type hosting service Typepad currently offers photo galleries that add a variety of upload tools and template output in addition to multiple galleries. These galleries appear to be separate weblogs in a programmatic sense, so every new gallery in Typepad is a streamlined process of creating a new blog. The layout and output of Typepad photo galleries can certainly be reproduced with MT and a couple of plugins described in this chapter. Future versions of MT may include photo gallery functionality, but for now these simple hacks will help you create the ultimate photo blog.

Setting Up an Example Photo Blog

Imagine you'd like to create a photo blog that displays the most recent photo on the index page, with individual archives. To make things simple, limit your photo blog to navigation by Next and Back links. For now, there will not be an archives page listing every photo; visitors will have to page through photos one by one, from the most recent to the oldest.

Your Index template will be fairly simple to set up. Listing 13-1 shows the code that would be used.

Listing 13-1: Index Template

```
<MTEntries lastn="1">
<$MTEntryTrackbackData$>
<a name="<$MTEntryID pad="1"$>"></a>

<h1><$MTEntryTitle$></h1>

<h2><$MTEntryDate format="%x"$></h2>

<$MTEntryBody$>

<p>Posted by <$MTEntryAuthor$> at <a
href="<$MTEntryPermalink$>"><$MTEntryDate format="%X"$></a></p>

</MTEntries>

<MTEntryPrevious>
<a href="<$MTEntryPermalink$>">&laquo; <$MTEntryTitle$></a> |
</MTEntryPrevious>
```

Your Individual Entry Archive will look fairly similar to what is shown in Listing 13-2.

Listing 13-2: Individual Entry Archive Template

```
<p><MTEntryPrevious>
<a href="<$MTEntryPermalink$>">&laquo; <$MTEntryTitle$></a> |
</MTEntryPrevious>
<a href="<$MTBlogURL$>">Main</a>
<MTEntryNext>
| <a href="<$MTEntryPermalink$>"><$MTEntryTitle$> &raquo;</a>
</MTEntryNext></p>


<h1><$MTEntryTitle$></h1>

<h2><$MTEntryDate format="%x"$></h2>

<$MTEntryBody$>

<p>Posted by <$MTEntryAuthor$> at <$MTEntryDate$></p>
```

If you've got MT installed on your server along with the ImageMagick Perl module, you can use MT's existing feature set to add new entries to your photo blog. The Upload File option in the main administration navigation can be used for adding a new photo, and if you choose the Embedded Image option and create a new post, MT will write the image display code for you.

Managing Photos

You can either embed image tags (for uploaded, uniquely named images) within posts using MT's upload file menu shortcut, use a separate, unused field for tracking images, or use the filesystem to manage your photos.

The first method is easiest, but aside from making blog posts containing photos, reusing photos once they are coded into posts is difficult to do.

Although you would limit your blog to exactly one photo per post, using a separate field would enable you to call up that image to do other things or use it in other ways (as you will see in the next section).

If you'd like to build a daily photo blog, you can name your images ahead of time, based on the date, and then upload those before making new posts, though this limits you to one photo posted per day.

Both the unused field method and the date/filesystem naming method enable you to predict what an image URL will be for each post, letting you create various templates based on it.

Using EmbedImage to Hack Images

MT uses the ImageMagick module to determine the height and width of uploaded images and perform some rudimentary thumbnailing, but ImageMagick is capable of much more in terms of photo manipulation functionality. The MT plugin EmbedImage exploits some of the image manipulation features in ImageMagick and builds upon what MT ships with.

Among the features available to your MT templates, EmbedImage enables you to figure out the file properties and dimensions of the original image and enables the creation of thumbnail images (and provides all the file properties and dimensions of those too). As an example, we'll create an archive template for an example photo blog that uses the date to name images. MT EmbedImage is available for download at `http://bradchoate.com/weblog/2002/08/07/mtembedimage`.

After installing the plugin contents into your `/plugins/` and `/extlib/bradchoate/` directories, you will have the following properties available in your MT templates:

- `<MTEmbedImageHeight>`: Provides the height of the given image in pixels.

- `<MTEmbedImageWidth>`: Provides the width of the given image in pixels.

- `<MTEmbedImageScaleHeight>`: Provides the scaled height of the given image in pixels.

- `<MTEmbedImageScaleWidth>`: Provides the scaled width of the given image in pixels.

- `<MTEmbedImageSize>`: Provides the size of the given image.

- `<MTEmbedImageFilename>`: Provides the filename of the given image.

- `<MTEmbedImageFullFilename>`: Provides the full filepath and name of the given image.

- `<MTEmbedImageThumbHeight>`: Provides the thumbnail image height.

- `<MTEmbedImageThumbWidth>`: Provides the thumbnail image width.

- `<MTEmbedImageThumbSize>`: Provides the size of the thumbnail image.

- `<MTEmbedImageThumbFilename>`: Provides the filename of the thumbnail image.

- `<MTEmbedImageThumbFullFilename>`: Provides the full filepath and name of the thumbnail image.

The base tag for this plugin, `<MTEmbedImage>`, carries the following attributes:

- `basename`: Defines the prefix of the image you want to embed. If you specify a file without an extension, EmbedImage will hunt for that file with a .gif, .jpg, or .jpeg extension (in that order).

- `thumbsuffix`: Defines the suffix to use for creating a thumbnail version of the image. This is useful only if the height or width attributes are used as well. MT must have write access to the directory in which your original image is stored in order to create the thumbnail image.

- `height`: Enables you to specify an alternate height for the image. If `width` is unspecified, the width will be set proportionate to the height you've given.

- `width`: Enables you to specify an alternate width for the image. If `height` is unspecified, the height will be set proportionate to the width you've given.

- `fit`: You can specify either crop, scale, or fit (the default is scale). This option is for creating scaled thumbnails only.

- `default`: An expression (which can use embedded MT tags, escaped with [and] instead of < and >) that is returned in case the image could not be found.

Suppose you have a photo blog posting daily photos, all named using the YYYYMMDD.jpg convention and relying on the filesystem to predict image locations. A standard archive might look something like this:

```
<MTArchiveList>
<$MTArchiveDate format="%x"$> <a
href="<$MTArchiveLink$>"><MTEntries><$MTEntryTitle$></MTEntries>
</a><br />
</MTArchiveList>
```

This type of archive would produce a list like the one shown in Figure 13-1.

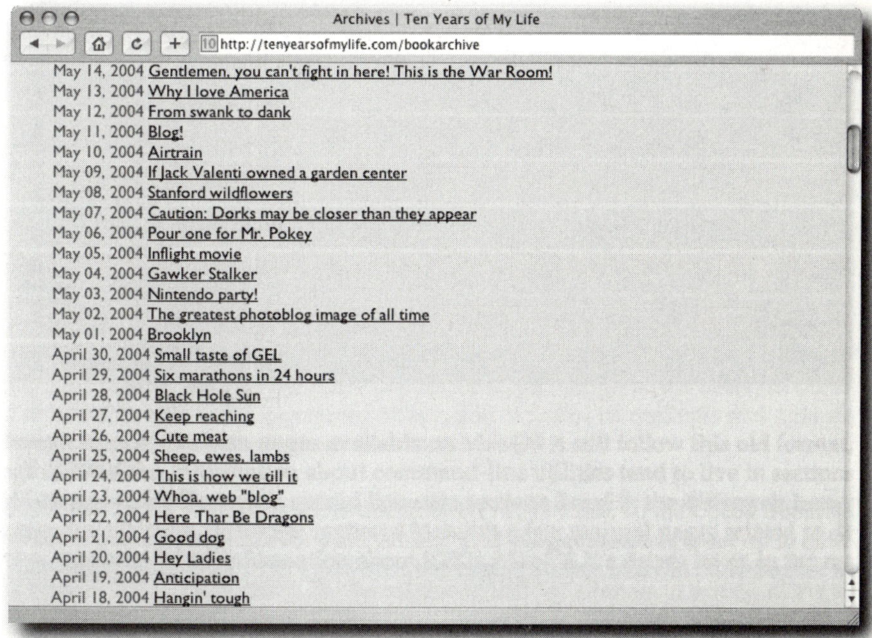

FIGURE 13-1: Presenting links to photo archives

Adding MT EmbedImage into the template, you could create a small thumbnail of the daily photograph at any size you like. If daily images are posted to the `/images` directory on the server, the code to add 60px by 60px thumbnails to the archive list would be as follows:

```
<MTArchiveList>
<MTEmbedImage basename="images/[MTEntryDate format='%Y%m%d'].jpg"
    height="60" width="60" thumbsuffix="-60">
<MTEntries lastn="1">
<img src="<MTEmbedImageThumbFilename>"
        width="<MTEmbedImageThumbWidth>"
        height="<MTEmbedImageThumbHeight>"
        alt="<$MTEntryTitle$> | <$MTEntryDate format='%Y/%m/%d'$>"
        title="<$MTEntryTitle$> | <$MTEntryDate
format='%Y/%m/%d'$>"
hspace="5" vspace="5" /></a> <$MTArchiveDate format="%x"$> <a
href="<$MTArchiveLink$>"><$MTEntryTitle$></a><br />
</MTEntries></MTEmbedImage>
</MTArchiveList>
```

The preceding code will look something like the image shown in Figure 13-2.

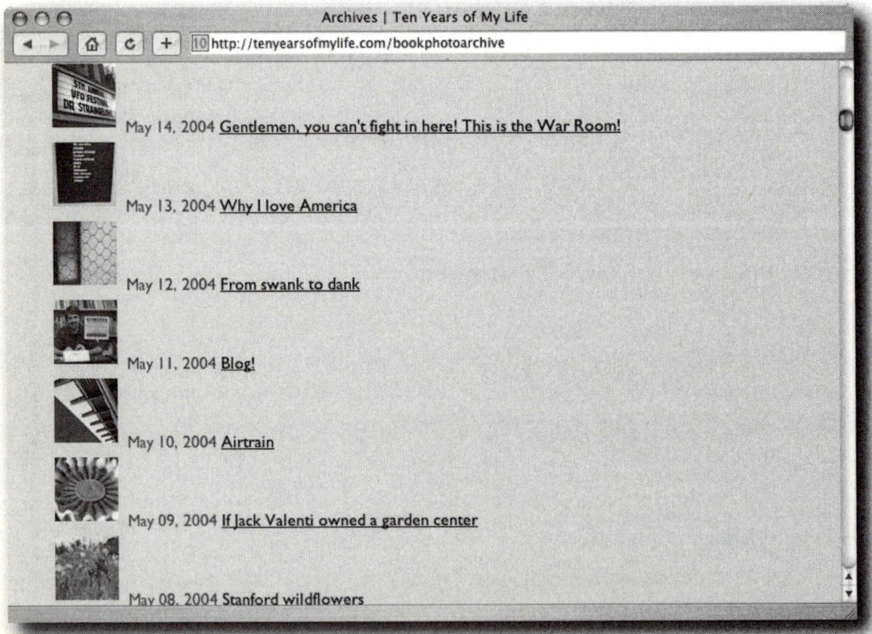

FIGURE 13-2: Presenting links and thumbnails

Keep a few things in mind here. All MT tags that show up within MT EmbedImage tags are escaped with [and] in place of < and >. In addition, attributes within those escaped MT tags are set with single quotation marks.

When this template is rebuilt, it will create 60px by 60px thumbnails with the suffix -60. This would mean that the image `20040927.jpg` (the daily photo for September 27, 2004) would have a thumbnail within the images directory called `20040927-60.jpg`. Next, that new filename is passed to the image tag along with the height and width of the thumbnail image. You could hardcode 60 and 60 here, but with the code like this, you can adjust the size of thumbnails later and the template will still work. The great thing about MT EmbedImage is that your thumbnails will be created only once, after which the cached image will be called up, instead of the script having to recreate all your thumbnail images.

This is one possible use of MT EmbedImage, but there are many other possible uses. If you have unpredictable image sizes in your blog, you can use MT EmbedImage to determine the height and width, often useful for specialized HTML layouts. You can use the plugin to extract the file size of an image, so if you want to warn users ahead of time how large your images are, perhaps in a RSS feed, you can do that. In photo blogs of any stripe, MT EmbedImage is a helpful power-user tool that enables you to manipulate images, and it is often a solution to many custom photo blog problems.

Setting Up a Mobile Phone Photo Blog

Over the past couple of years, the availability of cameras within cell phones has exploded, providing a new way for people to take and share photos with family and friends.

Most camera phones and cellular plans offer the capability to e-mail images either for a set rate or based on the number of images or total monthly bandwidth. However, most phones do not offer the capability to easily upload images to the web. With a bit of software tinkering, MT can be used as a photo blog for your camera phone, enabling you to post photos on the go for the world to see, in just a few presses of buttons thanks to the magic of Perl and XML-RPC.

Using pop2blog

The easiest way to get photos off your phone and onto the web is to use an e-mail-to-weblog gateway program such as pop2blog. It is available for free download at `http://bixworld.com/pop2blog` and is licensed under the GPL open source license. pop2blog will check an e-mail account and then process messages on the server for inclusion in an MT weblog. Depending on your carrier's message format, pop2blog can post and format images, titles, and text entries directly from your phone.

pop2blog carries with it a few requirements in order to function properly. First, you'll need to have the following Perl modules installed on your server: `Net::Blogger`, `Mail::Box`, `File::Temp`, and `File::Basename`. These packages (especially `Mail::Box`) may require additional packages in order to function.

Next, you will need a special e-mail account set aside for your mobile phone blog. Because pop2blog checks an account and processes unread messages, it's good to set up a secret, specific account like `photoblog@example.com` (where example.com is your e-mail host). You can also set the security of pop2blog to only post messages with a specific e-mail in the From: field, so even free e-mail providers will suffice in this case. Be sure to make an entry in your phone's address book with this e-mail in it, to make sending photos to the e-mail address as easy as possible.

On the MT side of things, you will likely want to set up a new blog specifically for this purpose, following earlier instructions about how to set up a photo blog. You will also want to create an images directory off your archive directory into which pop2blog can place photos.

Configuring pop2blog

With everything set, you need to edit the following configuration into `pop2blog.pl`, the main script, customizing it for your specific settings:

- $imgdir = "file path to image/" — This is the filesystem location of the images folder created. If you put it within your archive directory, just add '/images' to the "Local Archive Path" as defined under your blog config in MovableType.

- $imgpath = "web path to image/" — This is the actual path to the images on your web server. If you put the images within your archive directory, just add '/images' to the "Archive URL" as defined under your blog config in MovableType.

- $blogsite = `http://example.com/mt/mt-xmlrpc.cgi` — This is the URL of your `mt-xmlrpc.cgi` script.

- $blogid = "1" — This is the blog ID to which you wish to post entries. To figure this out, log into MT, click the Manage Blog link under the blog to which you wish to post entries, and read the URL of the page that loads. It will be something like `http://example.com/mt/mt.cgi?__mode=menu&blog_id=1`. Copy the `blog_id` from the URL to this setting.

- $bloguser = "username" — Your MT username under which entries will be posted

- $blogpass = "password" — The password that goes with the account

- $popsite = "mail.example.com" — The pop3 mail server the script will be checking

- $popuser = "username" — Username of the pop3 account created for photo blogging

- $poppass = "password" — Password for the pop3 account

- %allowed = ('myphone',1) — This is a list of usernames of e-mail accounts you would like to allow to post to your blog. If your phone's From: address in e-mail were `myphone@example.com,` the previous example would only allow e-mail from that address to be posted to the blog.

The pop2blog code itself is a Perl script that is meant to be run from the command line, not from your plugins directory, so you will likely want to run the script periodically with a regularly executed cron job command, as described in Chapter 5. Depending on how often you post photos from your mobile phone, you might want to set it to check the account every 10 to 15 minutes.

Depending on how your cell phone carrier formats your e-mail, you may want to tweak the `pop2blog.pl` script further. Some carriers append photos from your phone as attachments. In that case, you'll likely want to set blog post titles as the subject of your e-mails, with the attachment as the image, ignoring the message body entirely. If your carrier puts images inline within e-mail messages, some regular expressions may need to be employed. Either customization technique can be achieved by commenting out and modifying lines of the `pop2blog.pl` script as appropriate.

With pop2blog and a bit of server hacking, you'll soon find out how incredibly useful camera phones can be, and you will enjoy the freedom of blogging on the road, far away from computers and using only your phone.

Using ImageInfo to Display Extra Photo Data

The vast majority of photographs uploaded to weblogs are taken with digital cameras. These cameras, almost without exception, embed a considerable amount of additional data into the picture file: the date and time the shot was taken, the focus and aperture settings, the make and model of the camera, and so on. This data conforms to the *Exchangeable Image File Format standard*, commonly called *Exif*.

Professional photographic databases use the Exif data to index their collections; and happily, MT is also capable of getting at the data and doing things with it. You won't be using it to index the photographs per se, although displaying the contents of the Exif data will enable regular search engines to do this for you, but you will be able to use the Exif information to provide information to the reader, and, very importantly, loosely link your MT site to other web services.

Exif has evolved quite rapidly over the past few years as more and more digital devices are brought to the market; the number of possible data fields grows ever larger; and work continues to include quite considerable amounts of information within a file. A single Jpeg can carry many kilobytes of text data, plus audio. Here's an example of some Exif data:

```
BitsPerSample => (8, 8, 8)
color_type => YCbCr
 ComponentsConfiguration => YCbCr
 CompressedBitsPerPixel => 2/1
 CustomRendered => Normal process
 DateTime => 2003:08:02 12:17:27
 DateTimeDigitized => 2003:08:02 12:17:27
 DateTimeOriginal => 2003:08:02 12:17:27
 ExifImageLength => 1200
 ExifImageWidth => 1600
 ExifVersion => 0220
 ExposureBiasValue => 0/10
 ExposureMode => Auto exposure
 ExposureProgram => Program
 ExposureTime => 10/500
 filename => cute_kitten.jpg
 FileSource => (DSC) Digital Still Camera
 file_ext => jpg
 file_media_type => image/jpeg
 Flash => Flash fired, compulsory flash mode, red-eye reduction
mode, return light detected
 FlashPixVersion => 0100
 FNumber => 38/10
 FocalLength => 63/10
 height => 320
 ImageDescription =>
 InteroperabilityIndex => R98
```

```
InteroperabilityVersion => 0100
ISOSpeedRatings => 400
JFIF_Version => 1.01
JPEG_Type => Baseline
LightSource => unknown
Make => SONY
MakerNote =>
MaxApertureValue => 62/16
MeteringMode => Spot
Model => CYBERSHOT
Orientation => top_left
resolution => (72 dpi, 72 dpi)
SamplesPerPixel => 3
SceneCaptureType => Standard
SceneType => Directly Photographed Image
WhiteBalance => Auto white balance
width => 240
YCbCrPositioning => 2
```

You won't be dealing with the audio, but it can be very useful to pull out this sort of text. To do this, as ever, there is an MT plugin — ImageInfo.

Introducing ImageInfo

ImageInfo can be downloaded from the website of its author, David Phillips, at `http://tweezersedge.com/archives/stories/mtimageinfo_plugin.html`.

It consists of a container tag and a single tag to represent the properties of the image. The container tag, `<MTImageInfo>`, takes up to four attributes:

- `img`, which is the only required attribute, specifies the local path of the image file. The file must be on the local filesystem, so this cannot be a URL.

- `leading_text`, which defines text and markup to display before image information.

- `trailing text`, which defines text and markup to display afterward.

- `show_empty`, which can equal 1 or 0, chooses whether to display image information for empty fields.

Here's a simple use of the plugin to display a fetching feline:

```
<MTImageInfo image="images/cute_kitten.jpg">
```

This tag uses a relative path reference to the kitten photo. For more control, the tag could take advantage of MTImageInfo's support for other template tags. To include tag output in an attribute, place the tag within square brackets instead of angle brackets, like so:

```
<MTImageInfo img="[MTBlogSitePath]images/cute_kitten.jpg">
```

However, note that if the embedded tag requires one or more arguments, you need to enclose the value of the argument(s) in single quotes:

```
<MTImageInfo img="[MTBlogSitePath][MTEntryCategory
dirify='1']/cute_kitten.jpg">
```

To include XHTML tags, replace the angle brackets with square ones, as shown in the following example:

```
<MTImageInfo img="../cute_kitten.jpg" leading_text="[li]"
trailing_text="[/li]">
```

The leading and trailing text settings are not displayed if the field is empty in the image's Exif data, so you might not be clear as to what would happen in the following template code when no width variable is set in the Exif data of the image:

```
<MTImageInfo img="../cute_kitten.jpg" leading_text="[li]"
trailing_text="[/li]">
<p>Width = <$MTImageInfoField name="width"$></p>
</MTImageInfo>
```

The following output results (unless, that is, you set the final parameter as show_empty):

```
<p></p>
```

This attribute defaults to 0, in which case the leading text, trailing text, and labels of empty fields are not shown. If set to 1, the little bits of text will be shown, but the value will not. The <MTImageInfoField> tag displays the different fields within the Exif data. It takes the following three parameters:

- name takes the name of the variable in the Exif data, or it can take "all" which will print out all of the data within the picture.

- label, which is optional, takes the string with which you want to label the data. If the field is empty, the label isn't printed (unless the show_empty attribute is set, as above).

- format takes the standard Movable Type date formatting codes, and will come into effect if the field you are querying contains a date.

Regarding the final attribute, the Exif standard represents dates in the format *yyyy:mm:dd hh:mm:ss,* so this comes in handy when you want things to look a lot neater. For example:

```
<MTImageInfoField name="DateTime" format="%a %d %b %Y">
```

Continuing the Example

To continue the example started earlier, to start to look at the data contained within a daily photograph, you open the block with this:

```
<MTImageInfo img="images/[MTEntryDate format='%Y%m%d'].jpg">
```

You then insert the <MTImageInfoField> tags you need to show the information you want. If you are always using the same camera, it's a good idea to first build a template with <MTImageInfoField name="all"> and check what information your camera is giving you. Assume you're getting the date and time the picture's taken, the ISO speed of the shot, and the exposure time. You can build this into the template with these lines:

```
<MTImageInfoField label="Taken: " name="DateTime" format="%a %d %b
%Y">
<MTImageInfoField label="ISO: " name="ISOSpeedRatings" >
<MTImageInfoField label="Exposure: " name="ExposureTime" >
```

Embedding Additional Information

Japanese mobile phones habitually come with cameras, and some of these are being introduced to the market with GPS units included as well. The Exif data in the pictures these phones can take does contain the GPS location of the photograph, but currently there is no standard for this data, which affords many intriguing possibilities.

In addition, at the time of writing, interesting uses for the embedding of RDF data within images are emerging, which will enable different sections of an image to be isolated and labeled. See the proposed Fotonotes specification site at www.fotonotes.net for more information on these developments.

The <MTImageInfo> tag is closed up, as follows:

```
</MTImageInfo>
```

Of course, this isn't very nicely formatted, so you can make it a bit more stylable and XHTML compliant:

```
<div id="ExifDetails">
<ul>
<MTImageInfo img="images/[MTEntryDate format='%Y%m%d'].jpg"
leading_text="[li]" trailing_text="[/li]">
<MTImageInfoField label="Taken: " name="DateTime" format="%a %d
%b %Y">
<MTImageInfoField label="ISO: " name="ISOSpeedRatings" >
<MTImageInfoField label="Exposure: " name="ExposureTime" >
</MTImageInfo>
</ul>
</div>
```

You can now put this into your template and add the necessary styling to your CSS file.

Summary

In this chapter, you learned how to set up a basic photo blog using MT EmbedImage to create rich thumbnails of your archives. You also learned how to create a photo blog for your mobile phone camera using pop2blog. Finally, you learned how to display Exif photo metadata for your readers.

Thanks to MT's flexibility and extensibility, you'll find that with some simple hacking, you can create a photo blog custom-tailored to exactly how, when, and where you take photos to share with the world.

Linklogs

As weblogging evolved, many of the original weblogs evolved from logs of interesting and wacky links to more journal-type entries. However, the more compulsive bloggers found that their need to post interesting stuff was limited by the time they had to write about it, and things came full circle. In the past couple of years, linklogs, or link-driven blogs, have grown in popularity.

Often seen on the sidebars of regular blogs, these links are easy to post and are a way of keeping track of interesting bookmarks in a public manner.

They usually contain entries with a fairly specific format: a single link to an offsite destination, with a short description. Sometimes linklog authors include some pithy commentary in a title tag on the link or companion text, and often authors will credit other blogs where they found the links with a via link.

This chapter describes how to design a Movable Type template for linklogs, explains ways to further enhance the storage and output, and shows you how to link your MT weblog into the most popular external linklogging service, Del.icio.us.

Templating Your Linklog

Structurally, linklogs are simple creatures, making them much easier to format within Movable Type, as you can reuse existing fields within the MT database for storing the entries, in much the same way as you do with blogrolls.

Let's look at an example linklog entry, break it down into each part, and then examine how you can store the information within MT.

A linklog entry consists of the following:

- The URL of the website
- The title of the website
- The description text

in this chapter

☑ Introducing linklogs

☑ Templates for linklogs

☑ Using linklog services

☑ Integrating Del.icio.us

Put together, these elements create some HTML that looks like this:

```
<p><a href="The URL of the website" title="The title of the
website">The Title of the Website</a> - The Description Text</p>
```

This translates to an MT template rather like this one:

```
<MTEntries><a href="<$MTEntryExcerpt$>"
title="<$MTEntryTitle$>"><$MTEntryTitle$></a>
<$MTEntryBody$></MTEntries>
```

All you need to do is set up another weblog within your own installation, and use it to store your linklog. Place the link in the Entry Excerpt component, its title in the Entry Title, and the accompanying witticisms in the Body, as usual.

Then it's an easy matter to add code to your blog. Using the Plugin Manager, or manually, install David Raynes' OtherBlog plugin, which you can find at the following URL: `www.sixapart.com/pronet/plugins/plugin/otherblog.html`.

Once the plugin has been downloaded and installed in MT's `plugins` directory, you can create the template for a linklog: Add this code to your main blog's template — changing, of course, the `blog_id` attribute at the top to reflect the `id` of the linklog you have set up:

```
<div id="linklog">
<MTOtherBlog blog_id="6">
<ul>
<MTEntries>
<li>
<a href="<$MTEntryExcerpt$>"
title="<$MTEntryTitle$>"><$MTEntryTitle$></a><$MTEntryBody$>
</li>
</MTEntries>
</ul>
</MTOtherBlog>
</div>
```

Using this method, it's easy to set up RSS and Atom feeds of your links, and even offer the capability to comment or TrackBack to the postings. This is rarely done among existing linklogs but easy to implement if you'd like to buck the trend by using an MT weblog as the storage place for your links.

Using Linklog Services

Along with the growing popularity of linklogs, third-party web applications have appeared for creating these sites. Del.icio.us, found at `http://del.icio.us`, is perhaps the most well known, and certainly the most hackable.

Del.icio.us enables entries to be assigned the usual link title and description, and a set of keywords to categorize it. We'll touch on those in a moment. Figure 14-1 shows what Del.icio.us looks like as I write this.

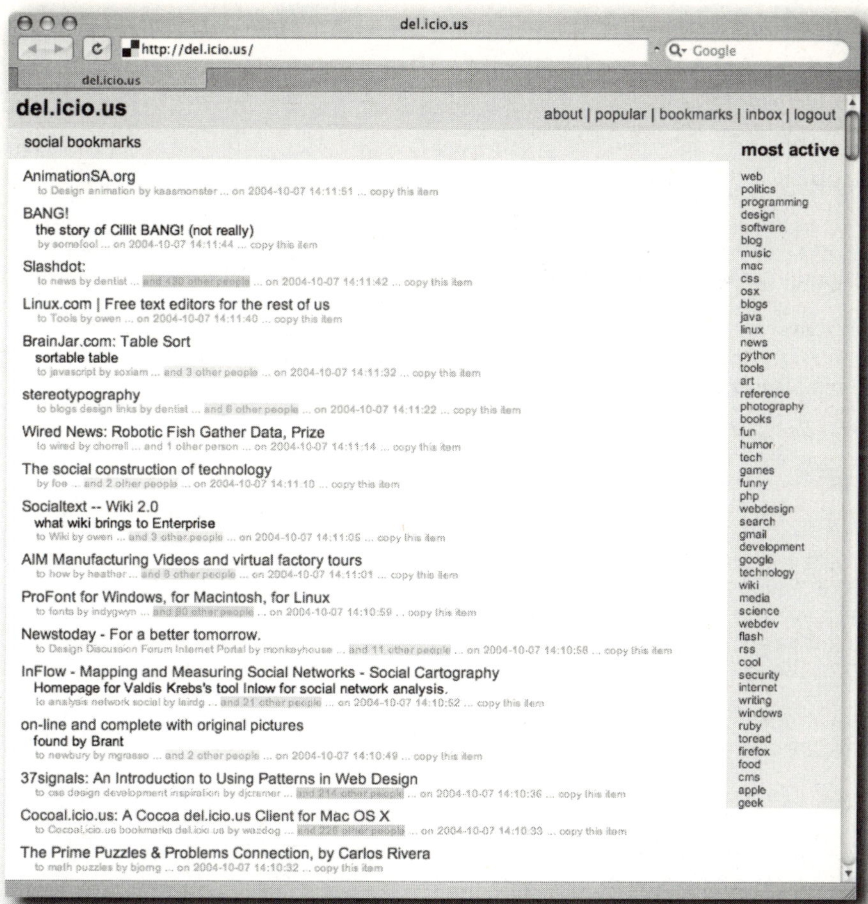

FIGURE **14-1: The Del.icio.us application**

Posting links to the Del.icio.us application is easy. Most people use a JavaScript bookmarklet that, when clicked, loads a form on Del.icio.us and populates the fields of the submission form. You fill in the description and the keywords, hit the Submit button, and you're returned back to the page you were reading.

Altogether it takes only a few seconds to post a new link, and it's much simpler than posting a new entry to your blog. Furthermore, various social aspects of Del.icio.us make it worth using in its own right.

Integrating Del.icio.us and Movable Type

That's all very well, but this is a book about MT. How do you combine the two? There are two straightforward ways of doing it, each with its own advantages and disadvantages. First, there's the RSS method.

Using RSS

Del.icio.us automatically produces an RSS feed of your links at a URL matched to your username, `http://del.icio.us/rss/`*username*, so it's an obvious move to use this feed to display your linklog in your main template.

Doing that is easy. Tim Appnel's RSS Feed plugin, available at `www.sixapart.com/pronet/plugins/plugin/rss_feed.html` will help. Install that, and then add this code to your main template and style as necessary with your CSS:

```
<div id="linklog">

<MTRSSFeed file="http://del.icio.us/rss/username">
<ul>

<MTRSSFeedItems lastn="5">
<li><a href="<$MTRSSFeedItemLink$>"><$MTRSSFeedItemTitle$></a>
<MTRSSFeedItemDescriptionExists> -
<$MTRSSFeedItemDescription$></MTRSSFeedItemDescriptionExists></li>
</MTRSSFeedItems>

</ul>
</MTRSSFeed>

</div>
```

Don't forget to change the RSS feed URL to reflect your own Del.icio.us username.

This method has one small disadvantage in that you need to rebuild the front page manually for new links to appear. This can be done with the `mt-rebuild.pl` script included with the RSS plugin. Set up a cronjob to run it, say, every hour, and your site will never be entirely out of date.

This method will be improved greatly once a PHP version of the RSS plugin has been written and you can use dynamic pages with it. Until then, however, a cron-processed rebuild will do.

You could use the RSS Digest service at `www.bigbold.com/rssdigest/` and have it create a snippet of JavaScript that will display the RSS as well; but that doesn't solve the refresh problem, as it would be very bad manners indeed to ask a third-party service to refresh itself from the feed more than once an hour.

Using a Scheduled Post

There is an alternative. If you would rather not run a separate linklog within your template, you can automatically post your day's collected links en masse, as a normal entry. This, to my mind, is more elegant anyway. The simplest way to do it is with a Perl script to query Del.icio.us and post the result using the MT Perl API. Happily, Jeffrey Veen wrote just this sort of script and released it under a Creative Commons license. From `www.veen.com/jeff/archives/000424.html`, here it is:

```perl
#!/usr/bin/perl
#
# Post Delicious Links to MovableType with XPath
# (MT installed on local machine)
#
# Jeffrey Veen
# jeff at veen dot com
#
# 10 December 2003
#
# Distributed under the Creative Commons "Share Alike" license.
# http://creativecommons.org/licenses/sa/1.0/
#
###

# load modules

use POSIX;
use lib "/path/to/your/mt/lib"; # change to your installation
use MT;
use MT::Entry;
use XML::XPath;


# set up local variables - change to suit your needs

my $MTauthor = "1";
my $MTblogID = "2";
my $MTconfig = "/path/to/your/mt/mt.cfg";
my $delUser  = "veen";
my $delPW    = "****";

# get today's date and format it

my $date=strftime( "%Y-%m-%d", localtime());


# go get the xml file

my $xml = `curl -s -u $delUser:$delPW
http://del.icio.us/api/posts/get?dt=$date`;

# get a new XPath object

my $xp = XML::XPath->new(xml => $xml);
```

```perl
# see if anything was posted to day

if ($xp->exists('/posts/post')) {

my $title = "Links: $date";
my $guts  = "<ul>\n";

# grab XML values and write HTML

    foreach my $posts ($xp->find('//post')->get_nodelist){

        $guts .= "    <li><a href=\"" . $posts->find('@href') .
"\">";
        $guts .= $posts->find('@description')  . "</a><br />";
        $guts .= "<em>Posted: "   . $posts->find('@time');
        $guts .= ' (categories: ';

# loop through category tags and build a link for each

        foreach my $tag (split(/ /, $posts->find('@tag'))){
            $guts .= "<a
href=\"http://del.icio.us/$delUser/$tag\">$tag</a> "
        }
        $guts .= ")</em></li>\n";
    }
    $guts .= "  </ul>\n";

# post to MT

    my $mt = MT->new( Config=>$MTconfig) or die MT->errstr;
    my $entry = MT::Entry->new;

    $entry->blog_id($MTblogID);
    $entry->status(MT::Entry::RELEASE());
    $entry->author_id($MTauthor);
    $entry->title($title);
    $entry->text($guts);
    $entry->convert_breaks(0);
    $entry->save
       or die $entry->errstr;

# rebuild the site

    $mt->rebuild(BlogID => $MTblogID )
      or die "Rebuild error: " . $mt->errstr;

# ping aggregators

    $mt->ping($MTblogID);

} # end of "check if there are posts"
```

You should have all of the required modules already installed, as XML::Xpath comes with MT. Copy this script over to your MT directory, changing the variables at the top to reflect your own setup. Set up a cronjob to run the script once a day, or at your preferred interval.

Other Uses for Del.icio.us

A minor digression to close this chapter: The keyword tagging used at Del.icio.us is quite addictive. I've started to use it to categorize my own main blog postings, too, using the Keywords field.

The first thing to do, therefore, is to show these tags and provide links to the related tag directories within Del.icio.us. To do this, I'm using a bit of PerlScript in the template, which requires the MT-PerlScript plugin.

This plugin can be viewed and downloaded from Six Apart's plugins directory at www.six apart.com/pronet/plugins/plugin/perlscript.html. Here's the template code, which embeds a Perl script in a template by enclosing it within an MTPerlScript tag:

```
<MTPerlScript package="delicious_links">
# MT PerlScript to split keywords into Del.icio.us tags, and then
append the links
my $keywords="<MTEntryKeywords>";

if ($keywords eq "") {
print "<!-- No Del.icio.us Tags to print out //-->";
} else {

my @split_keywords = split(/ /, $keywords);
my $split_keyword;
print '<br/><br/><h2>Related Posts Elsewhere</h2>';
print '<br/><a href="'.'http://del.icio.us/"
title="del.icio.us">del.icio.us</a> ';

foreach $split_keyword (@split_keywords) {
print ' / <a
href="'."http://del.icio.us/tag/$split_keyword".'">'."$split_keywo
rd".'</a> ';
}
}
</MTPerlScript>
```

Place this template code on an index or archive template that displays one or more weblog entries, positioning it within an MTEntries container tag if you're editing an index template.

Entry keywords will be presented as a list of tags, each tag linking to related entries from other sites on De.licio.us.

Summary

The World Wide Web has been described as an attention economy, a place where the primary unit of exchange is the link. Providing a link to an interesting site attracts more attention to it, and you can probably imagine many different ways that such attention would be valued by a web publisher.

Linklogs can be implemented quickly with Movable Type using the Otherblog plugin. Devote an MT weblog to the links and you can incorporate its entries into another weblog, presenting them in a distinct sidebar, syndicated RSS or Atom feed, or in some other fashion.

By providing more links on your weblog, you bestow more attention on the sites and writers who draw your interest. There aren't many better ways than that to pay a compliment on the Internet.

Blogroll

One traditional feature of a weblog is the blogroll: a list of Web sites, usually other weblogs, that the author regularly visits. There are online tools to build these things — Blogrolling.com being the best known — but with some MT wizardry you can go a few steps further.

In this chapter, you'll learn how to set up a simple blogroll using Movable Type, and then how to tie Movable Type into a web service to provide other information. You'll be using a variety of plugins to demonstrate different ways of doing this, and considering the various choices you need to make regarding your site's coding in relation to loosely joined web services.

Setting Up Your Blogroll

Create a new weblog within your MT installation. From now on, we'll refer to this as the blogroll blog. Don't worry. No matter which license you have MT under, this additional weblog will not count against your per-weblog limits, as its contents are only going to be displayed inside your main site, albeit in a variety of ways.

In this new blog, you can delete all of the templates except for the Individual Entry Archive — you don't need them. Make sure weblogs.com and blo.gs pinging is turned off, and that archiving is set to Individual Only. Basically, turn everything off. What you're going to do is store each URL as an individual entry within this blog and then use various plugins on your main site to pull that data out and display it. Therefore, you don't need any of MT's cool features turned on and wasting disk space.

Now, create entries within your blogroll blog, one for every URL, with the URL as the entry body, and the title you want to give it as the entry title. Note that the title you give it and the site's actual title need not be the same. Through the power of the Internet you can display both. Right now, however, you only need to enter the name you want it to have.

When you're done, scoot over to your main blog and decide where you want to put this blogroll: on every page, on one page only, or on its own page. If you're going to have it in more than one place, create a template module. If you're giving it its own page, create a new index template. Not sure? Err on the side of the template module. That way, it's easily reusable around your site.

Before getting into this, you need to install a few plugins. Using the Plugin Manager (or manually), install David Raynes' OtherBlog plugin from Six Apart's website at `www.sixapart.com/pronet/plugins/plugin/otherblog.html`.

You'll also need Brad Choate's PerlScript plugin from `www.sixapart.com/pronet/plugins/plugin/perlscript.html`.

That done, you can start building your template. Consider what you have: another weblog with a link URL and a link title, one per entry. Using the OtherBlog plugin, you can do this:

```
<MTOtherBlog blog_id="6">
<ul>
<MTEntries sort_by="title" sort_order="ascend">
<li>
<a href="<$MTEntryBody convert_breaks="0"$>">
<$MTEntryTitle$></a>
</li>
</MTEntries>
</ul>
</MTOtherBlog>
```

Make sure that you change the `blog_id="6"` to reflect the real id number of the blogroll blog. Save that into the template module and place a `<MTInclude module="blogroll">` within the template in which you want the blogroll to appear, and you're done.

Going Deeper with Technorati

A static blogroll is handy to have around, but it doesn't reflect the dynamic nature of the web: how things change, how weblogs move on, how stale a blogroll can become.

You only have two bits of information, but either of them can go astray without you knowing it. Plus, and this is really nice, there is a lot of other information available about the sites in your blogroll that other people, not to mention yourself, might like to see. The place to get this information is via Technorati.com, and happily enough, that fine site provides an API for programmers to get to it. At first you'll be doing this with the PerlScript plugin.

For now, however, get yourself over to `www.technorati.com/developers/index.html` and register for an API key. You need one to use the service, and you're not having mine.

Okay, let's recap. Here's the key bit of the code that you want to augment:

```
<MTEntries sort_by="title" sort_order="ascend">
<li>
<a href="<$MTEntryBody convert_breaks="0"$>">
<$MTEntryTitle$></a>
</li>
</MTEntries>
```

In this code, `<$MTEntryBody convert_breaks="0"$>` represents the URL. Here's the code with a PerlScript plugin–enabled block of Perl, which takes this URL and runs it through Technorati's `bloginfo` query, and uses what it retrieves to replace the `<$MTEntryTitle$>` part of the link:

```
<MTEntries sort_by="title" sort_order="ascend">
<li>


<MTPerlScript package="BlogrollTechnorati">
use warnings;
use strict;
use XML::Simple;
use LWP::Simple;

my $technorati_api_key = "PUT YOUR KEY HERE";
my $blogroll_url = "<$MTEntryBody convert_breaks="0"$>";

my $technorati_result =
get("http://api.technorati.com/bloginfo?url=$quotation-
>{url}&key=$technorati_dev_token") or die "Could not connect to
Technorati";

my $technorati_result_xml = XMLin($technorati_result);

print '<a href="'."$blogroll_url".'">'.$technorati_result_xml-
>{document}->{result}->{weblog}->{name}.'</a>';

</MTPerlScript>


</li>
</MTEntries>
```

This is nice, but not as far as you can go. Technorati returns a great deal of information about the URL you give it. This is the XML returned by an example query:

```
<?xml version="1.0" encoding="utf-8"?>
<!-- generator="Technorati API version 1.0 /bloginfo" -->
<!DOCTYPE tapi PUBLIC "-//Technorati, Inc.//DTD TAPI 0.01//EN"
"http://api.technorati.com/dtd/tapi-001.xml">
<tapi version="1.0">
<document>
<result>
  <url>http://www.benhammersley.com</url>
  <weblog>
    <name>Ben Hammersley</name>
    <url>http://www.benhammersley.com</url>
    <rssurl>http://www.benhammersley.com/index.rdf</rssurl>
```

```
        <inboundblogs>709</inboundblogs>
        <inboundlinks>834</inboundlinks>
        <lastupdate>20040517T10:05:02Z</lastupdate>
        <rank>180</rank>
    </weblog>
    <inboundblogs>709</inboundblogs>
    <inboundlinks>834</inboundlinks>
</result>
</document>
</tapi>
```

As you can see, you can fish out other data: the URL to the RSS feed, the numbers of inbound links, the ranking in the Technorati popularity league, last update date and time, and so on. You can change the PerlScript to use this data with little difficulty.

Better Living Through Plugins

The previous system is very simple and direct and shows you how the Technorati service can be loosely tied to Movable Type with a PerlScript. Indeed, any REST-based web service that can be controlled with URLs can be used in the same way. There are, however, serious flaws with this method.

One problem with this system is that it is quite fragile if Technorati is down when you attempt to rebuild your pages. As it stands, in fact, the script will die, and take your rebuild with it. Therefore, you need to add in some fault tolerance to the script, and drop back to the `<MTEntryTitle>` when you can't get the data you want. Plus, if you're including this as a template module in your individual entry archives, the first time you rebuild your entire site you'll probably be trying to pass a few thousand queries to Technorati in a row, with all but the very first few totally pointless. You need to deal with both of these issues, and to do so with the PerlScript method would mean writing your own caching and fault tolerance code. It's far too nice a day to be stuck inside doing that, so let's cheat.

The way to accomplish both of these fixes is to use another plugin — Kevin Shay's GetXML from `www.staggernation.com/mtplugins/GetXMLReadMe.html`.

GetXML can replace the entire PerlScript code shown previously, taking care of retrieving the query, parsing the result, caching the result, and fault-tolerance. Here's the template with GetXML instead of MTPerlScript:

```
<MTOtherBlog blog_id="6">
<MTEntries sort_by="title" sort_order="ascend">
<MTGetXML location="http://api.technorati.com/bloginfo"
url="<$MTEntryBody convert_breaks="0"$>" key="PUT YOUR KEY HERE"
cache="10800" suppressempty="1" errors="ignore">

<MTGetXMLElement name="document">
<MTGetXMLElement name="result">
<MTGetXMLElement name="weblog">
```

```
<li><a href="<$MTEntryBody convert_breaks="0"$>"
title="<MTIfXMLElementExists name="name"><$MTGetXMLValue
name="name"$></MTIfXMLElementExists><MTIfXMLElementNotExists
name="name"><MTEntryTitle></MTIfXMLElementNotExists>">
<MTIfXMLElementExists name="name"><$MTGetXMLValue name="name"$>
</MTIfXMLElementExists><MTIfXMLElementNotExists
name="name"><MTEntryTitle></MTIfXMLElementNotExists></a>
<MTIfXMLElementExists name="rssurl"> - <a href="<$MTGetXMLValue
name="rssurl">">RSS Feed</a></MTIfXMLElementExists></li>

</MTGetXMLElement>
</MTGetXMLElement>
</MTGetXMLElement>
</MTGetXML>
</MTEntries>
</MTOtherBlog>
```

GetXML offers two major improvements to the hand-rolled PerlScript code. First, it caches the results. The `cache="10800"` attribute to the `<MTGetXML>` line means that it will cache the results for 10,800 minutes — one week. You can change this, however.

Second, as you can see from the code, it allows for fallbacks if certain information is not there. In the example shown, you're not printing anything about an RSS feed if Technorati doesn't know about one.

Styling and Accessibility

The final thing to do to the code is to enable yourself to make it look pretty but also retain accessibility. This means assigning class attributes to the list and titles to the links themselves:

```
<div class="blogroll">
<MTOtherBlog blog_id="6">
<MTEntries sort_by="title" sort_order="ascend">
<MTGetXML location="http://api.technorati.com/bloginfo"
url="<$MTEntryBody convert_breaks="0"$>" key="PUT YOUR KEY HERE"
cache="60" suppressempty="1" errors="ignore">

<MTGetXMLElement name="document">
<MTGetXMLElement name="result">
<MTGetXMLElement name="weblog">

<li><a href="<$MTEntryBody convert_breaks="0"$>"
title="<MTIfXMLElementExists name="name"><$MTGetXMLValue
name="name"$></MTIfXMLElementExists><MTIfXMLElementNotExists
name="name"><MTEntryTitle></MTIfXMLElementNotExists>"><MTIfXMLElem
entExists name="name"><$MTGetXMLValue
name="name"$></MTIfXMLElementExists><MTIfXMLElementNotExists
name="name"><MTEntryTitle></MTIfXMLElementNotExists></a>
```

```
<MTIfXMLElementExists name="rssurl"> - <a href="<$MTGetXMLValue
name="rssurl">">RSS Feed</a></MTIfXMLElementExists></li>

</MTGetXMLElement>
</MTGetXMLElement>
</MTGetXMLElement>
</MTGetXML>
</MTEntries>
</MTOtherBlog>
</div>
```

As you have no doubt realized by now, the blogroll template does a lot of work. It pulls an entry from the other blog, checks inside a cache, perhaps runs a query on a remote source, and checks the site itself, before carrying on to the next entry. With a very large blogroll, this might take quite a while the first time it is run.

Publishing the Blogroll as OPML

Many applications are capable of importing and exporting blogrolls formatted as OPML, an XML dialect for representing outlines and other list-based information.

These OPML-capable applications range from RSS readers to social network analysis tools. You can learn more about the format and supporting software by visiting the official OPML website at www.opml.org.

Or perhaps you just want to back up your blogroll for your own amusement. Either way, OPML is the way to do it.

Listing 15-1 contains a simple OPML file with only one site in it.

Listing 15-1: A Simple OPML Blogroll

```
<?xml version="1.0" encoding="ISO-8859-1"?>
<opml version="1.1">
    <head>
        <title>mySubscriptions</title>
    </head>
    <body>
        <outline text="Ben Hammersley" description="Ben
Hammersley's Dangerous Precedent"
title="Ben Hammersley" type="rss" version="RSS"
htmlUrl="http://www.benhammersley.com"
xmlUrl="http://www.benhammersley.com/index.rdf"/>
    </body>
</opml>
```

Because OPML is an XML dialect, producing such output from techniques you're using in this chapter will be simple. Create a new Index template containing the text of Listing 15-2.

Listing 15-2: An OPML Blogroll Template

```
<MTOtherBlog blog_id="6">
<?xml version="1.0" encoding="<MTPublishCharset>"?>
<opml version="1.1">
<head>
<title>mySubscriptions</title>
</head>
<body>

<MTEntries sort_by="title" sort_order="ascend">

<MTGetXML location="http://api.technorati.com/bloginfo"
url="<$MTEntryBody convert_breaks="0"$>" key="PUT YOUR KEY HERE"
cache="60" suppressempty="1" errors="ignore">


<MTGetXMLElement name="document">
<MTGetXMLElement name="result">
<MTGetXMLElement name="weblog">

<outline text="<MTIfXMLElementExists name="name"><$MTGetXMLValue
name="name"$></MTIfXMLElementExists><MTIfXMLElementNotExists
name="name"><MTEntryTitle></MTIfXMLElementNotExists>"
description="<MTIfXMLElementExists name="name"><$MTGetXMLValue
name="name"$></MTIfXMLElementExists><MTIfXMLElementNotExists
name="name"><MTEntryTitle></MTIfXMLElementNotExists>"
title="<MTIfXMLElementExists name="name"><$MTGetXMLValue
name="name"$></MTIfXMLElementExists><MTIfXMLElementNotExists
name="name"><MTEntryTitle></MTIfXMLElementNotExists>" type="rss"
version="RSS" htmlUrl="<$MTEntryBody convert_breaks="0"$>"
<MTIfXMLElementExists name="rssurl"> - xmlUrl="<$MTGetXMLValue
name="rssurl"></MTIfXMLElementExists>/>

</MTGetXMLElement>
</MTGetXMLElement>
</MTGetXMLElement>
</MTGetXML>
</MTEntries>
</body>
</opml>
</MTOtherBlog>
```

Use the Output File field to give the template's output a filename that ends in `.opml`, to indicate its format.

When you render the template, it produces an OPML file containing all of the links in your blogroll blog, which you can load with other programs and share for other purposes.

Summary

A weblog can be more strongly connected to other blogs through the use of one or more blogrolls. The links between sites are analyzed and counted by services such as Technorati to rate the relative prominence of different blogs. Some of the most widely read bloggers show up on more than 1,000 blogrolls.

By organizing a blogroll as a separate weblog and reading the data with the OtherBlog plugin, you can present a site list as easily as you present weblog entries.

Events, Reminders, To-Dos

In its simplest form, a day planner is just a collection of two kinds of information: dates and notes. Movable Type is very good at managing this kind of information. The goal of this chapter is to restructure that content into a functioning day planner. It's just a matter of some clever tag and template work.

Without any help, Movable Type enables you to enter dated entries into a weblog that can be output into monthly, weekly, and daily archives. This gets you a long way toward your day planner functionality, but MT needs help in a few areas. First, MT doesn't have a way to handle recurring events. Second, one of the views that you want to produce is a daily view showing all of the hours of the day, with the day's events properly interspersed. MT can't produce a view like that by itself. You'll need to utilize a plugin to produce this view as well as to handle recurring entries.

Why would you want to use Movable Type to create a day planner or calendar? There are certainly better and more natural ways to go about maintaining a calendar. Isn't this better left to an application written specifically for this purpose? Perhaps, but there are advantages to having a MT-powered calendar:

➤ **It's web-based and web-hosted.** Because it is hosted on the web, your calendar is accessible to everyone and from anywhere. You can control who has access to it or leave it wide open for all to see.

➤ **Multiple authors provide collaboration.** If you set it up for multiple users, your planner weblog can include the event information for everyone in your family, or your department at work, or your softball teammates.

➤ **The power of publish and subscribe.** You can publish your calendar information in a variety of ways — for example, an Atom, RSS, and/or vCalendar/iCalendar feed that keeps everyone in sync.

Creating the Day Planner Weblog

First you will want to create a new, separate weblog. Name it My Planner or whatever you prefer. This weblog will be configured to be viewed dynamically, so the local site path and local archive path settings are not necessary. The process of configuring the weblog to be dynamic will be explained shortly.

Template Configuration

Create the following templates in your new planner weblog:

- Daily Archive
- Monthly Archive

You may also want individual archives so you can see the details of your event. You should edit your Stylesheet template to append the additional stylesheet rules found on the companion website.

Archiving Configuration

For archiving (the Archiving panel of the Weblog Configuration options), configure the weblog for Individual, Monthly, and Daily archives at a minimum. You'll also be creating a yearly archive, but you'll need to do that separately (see the "Yearly Archives" section later in this chapter).

By default, the Daily and Monthly archives are linked to the same template, named Date-Based Archive. But you want to use a different archive template for each of these. To fix this, delete the existing Daily and Monthly archive options and create new Daily and Monthly archives, linking them to the Daily Archive and Monthly Archive templates, respectively (these were created in the preceding "Template Configuration" section). The result of this will be more apparent once you've entered a few items.

Category Configuration

Create a few categories for the different types of entries that will be used in the planner. At a minimum, you'll want to create the categories shown in Table 16-1.

Table 16-1   Categories

Category Name	Purpose
Event	Dated event entry
Reminder	Reminder entry
To-Do	To-Do entry
Every Day	Daily recurring events
Every Sunday	Events repeating on Sunday
Every Monday	Events repeating on Monday

Category Name	Purpose
Every Tuesday	Events repeating on Tuesday
Every Wednesday	Events repeating on Wednesday
Every Thursday	Events repeating on Thursday
Every Friday	Events repeating on Friday
Every Saturday	Events repeating on Saturday
Every Week	Weekly recurring events
Every Month	Monthly recurring events
Every Year	Yearly recurring events

The Every categories will be used to establish basic recurring entries.

Whenever you create an entry that is to appear in your calendar views, assign it an Event category. For reminder and to-do entries, assign them with those categories. You can define additional categories to further classify your planner entries. For example, Anniversary, Birthday, Holiday, Movie, and Vacation might be useful to start with.

Creating Entries for Your Planner

Creating entries is the easy part. You use Movable Type as you normally would. Just take care to assign the categories that are appropriate to the entry. For recurring entries, assign them into the Every Year, Every Month, Every Week, Every Day, and so on categories as appropriate. The recurring date will depend upon the creation date assigned to the entry. You can alter the creation date for a particular recurring entry so that it begins at the proper date.

Template Design

You've already created the templates by using the examples that are provided with this book, but it's important to take a look at how they work. That way you can feel more comfortable customizing them to your liking.

The templates use a plugin named MT-Planner, which can be downloaded from the website for this book at www.hackingmt.com.

Introducing MT-Planner

The custom tags provided by the MT-Planner plugin provide similar functionality to MT's own Calendar tag. However, instead of being limited to producing a single month, the MT-Planner tags can also produce output for an entire year, a single week, or a day. Almost any sort of calendar view you can image can be reproduced using these tags.

Installing the MT-Planner Plugin

To install MT-Planner, store the `planner.pl` Perl script and copy it into your `plugins` sub-directory for Movable Type. That's all you have to do to install the new tags that are necessary to run your planner.

MT-Planner Tag Overview

To gather the entries to publish the web pages for your planner, you'll be using some tags provided by the MT-Planner plugin. The primary tags provided by this plugin are as follows:

- `<MTPlanner>`

- `<MTPlannerYears>`

- `<MTPlannerMonths>`

- `<MTPlannerWeeks>`

- `<MTPlannerDays>`

- `<MTPlannerHours>`

- `<MTPlannerEntries>`

- `<MTPlannerIfBlank>`

- `<MTPlannerIfEntries>`

- `<MTPlannerIfNoEntries>`

- `<$MTPlannerDay$>`

- `<$MTPlannerMonth$>`

- `<$MTPlannerYear$>`

- `<MTPlannerNext>`

- `<MTPlannerPrevious>`

- `<$MTPlannerTitle$>`

- `<$MTPlannerLink$>`

The main `<MTPlanner>` tag is a controller for the others. It preloads the recurring entries, so you should use it once in your template, placing it so that it surrounds all the other MT-Planner tags. It also enables you to define what categories are to be considered for recurring entries.

The `<MTPlannerYears>`, `<MTPlannerMonths>`, `<MTPlannerWeeks>`, `<MTPlannerDays>`, and `<MTPlannerHours>` tags will produce a list of years, months, weeks, days, and hours, respectively. For example, if you were to create a daily archive template for your planner, you would utilize the `<MTPlanner>` and `<MTPlannerHours>` tags. The `<MTPlannerHours>` tag would produce the hours for that day. You can even limit the range that is produced — for example, to be 8:00 A.M. to 6:00 P.M. (or whatever range you would prefer). By placing a `<MTPlannerEntries>` tag inside any of these timely tags, you are given the relevant entries available for that period of time.

Implementing Month Views

The Monthly Archives template is a full-page calendar view of a particular month (see Figure 16-1). Each day within the calendar lists any of the events scheduled for that day. The day itself is hyperlinked to the daily archive, which reveals more detail about the events of the day. Of course, the presentation of the calendar view is driven by CSS, so you have a lot of flexibility with respect to how the calendar is formatted.

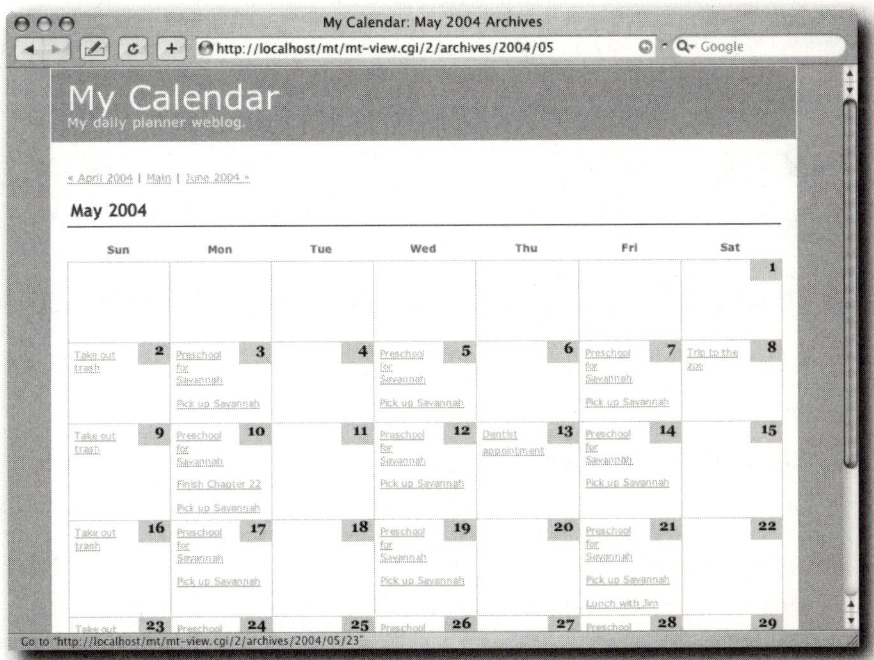

FIGURE 16-1: Planner monthly view

Implementing Day Views

The Daily Archives template produces a single day's events (see Figure 16-2). It is a familiar view, mimicking what you might see in Outlook's calendar. The calendar displays events for the day divided by hour. The familiar Previous and Next navigation links at the top enable you to browse to adjacent days.

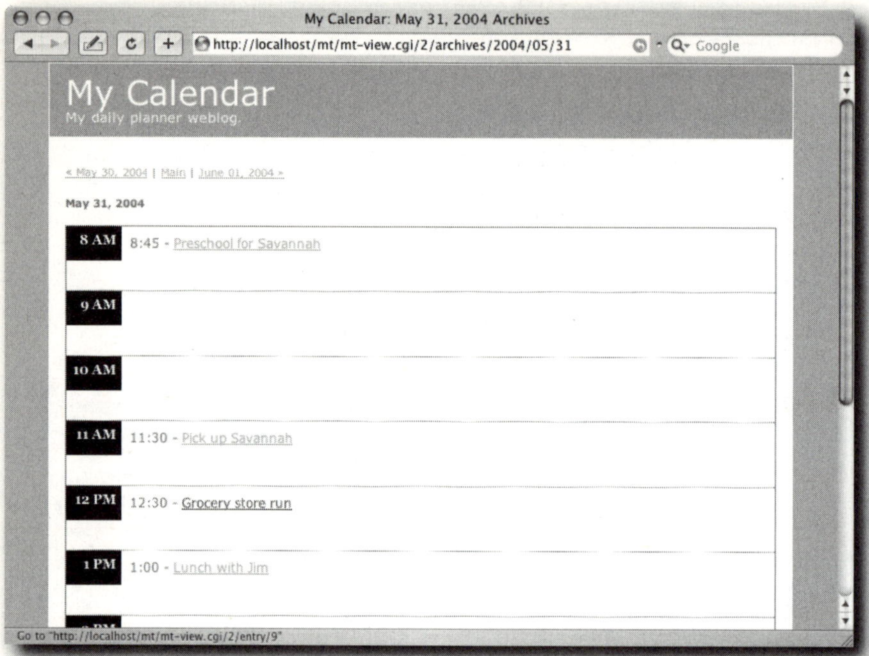

FIGURE 16-2: Planner daily view

The Main Index Template

The Main Index template can be configured to your liking (see Figure 16-3). What would you prefer to display on the home page of your planner? The current events for today? Or for the month? The one provided with this chapter is a combination of both.

Now comes the main problem with Movable Type and implementing a day planner application. Movable Type produces static Web pages by default. You don't want that. You want to view things dynamically, for the following reasons:

- Static page publication produces a lot of pages.

- MT doesn't know to build the static pages for any of our recurring entries.

- Static pages will not update when new recurring entries are added (you'd have to do a Rebuild All operation in MT for most entries you add to keep things in sync).

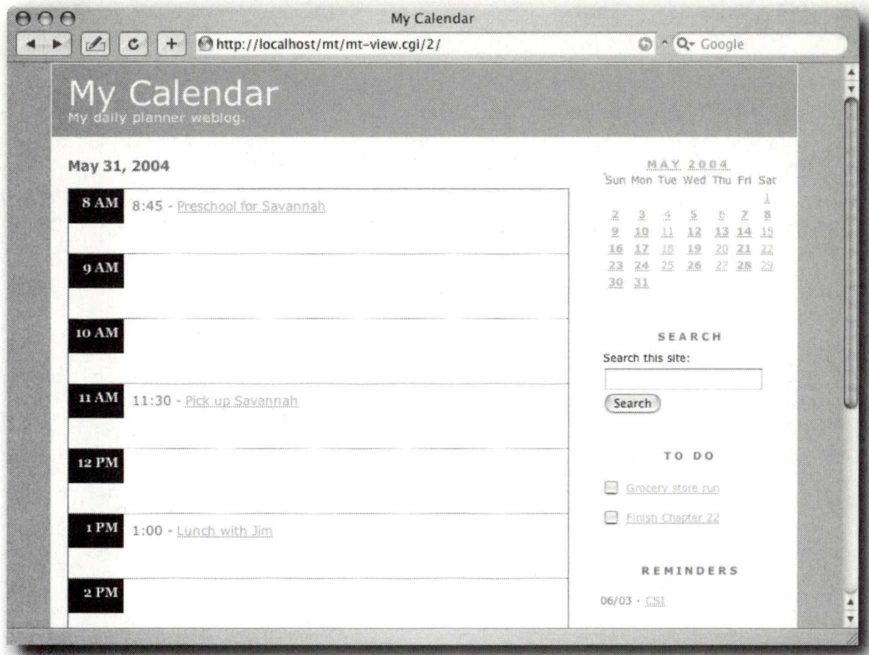

FIGURE 16-3: Planner main index view

Movable Type has a way to provide a dynamic view of your weblog. It isn't enabled by default and is still considered as an experimental feature, but it is working well enough for our purposes. Here's how you can enable dynamic rendering for your Planner weblog:

1. Edit your `mt.cfg` file and add SafeMode 0 to it (or change SafeMode 1 to SafeMode 0 if it is present). This is necessary to use the `mt-view.cgi` script that comes with Movable Type.

2. Create a new index template named Make Dynamic and add this to it: `<$MTPlannerDynamic$>`. Build that page once, and then you can delete it. This tag will reconfigure the current weblog to operate as a dynamic weblog.

If you ever wish to reverse this and make your Planner weblog run as a static weblog again, do the second step listed, substituting `<$MTPlannerStatic$>` for the `<$MTPlannerDynamic$>` tag. If you do this, remember that Movable Type will only produce the archive pages that are relevant to the entries in your Planner weblog.

Yearly Archives

You may also want to display your planner data in a yearly view (see Figure 16-4). Unfortunately, Movable Type doesn't offer a yearly archive option just yet, so we have to do a little bit of manual labor. We have supplied a Yearly Archives template to be added to your weblog as a template module (this is the bottom-most group of templates on the Movable Type Templates configuration page). Once this template has been added, you will need to create a single main index template. Name this template Yearly Archives and set the output filename to be Years.

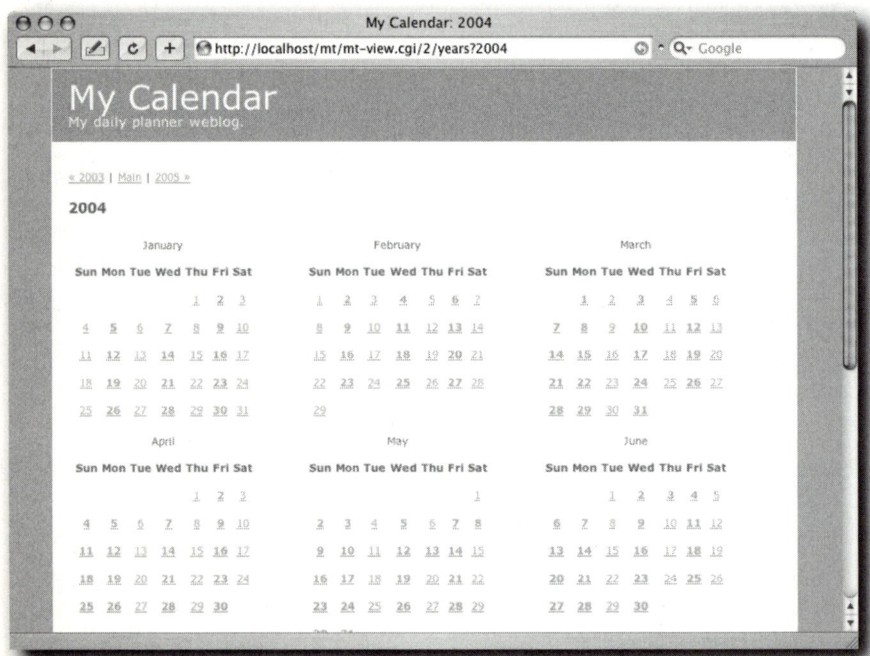

FIGURE 16-4: Planner yearly archive view

With this in place, you can browse to your yearly archive views using links like this:

```
http://myblog.com/mt/mt-view.cgi/1234/years?2004
```

Again, replace 1234 with the blog ID of your Planner weblog, and substitute the domain name for your website and the proper path to the `mt-view.cgi` script.

CSS Design

Through the use of additional categories and CSS rules, you can further enhance the view of your planner. You can add graphic icons for birthdays, anniversaries, holidays, and other events. All categories assigned to the entry are added to the CSS class for the containing `<div>` or `<span>` tag for the item in the planner views. Here's a CSS rule for a Birthday category:

```
.birthday {
    background-image: url(/images/icons/birthday.gif);
    background-repeat: no-repeat;
    background-position: top left;
    padding-left:20px;
}
```

This rule would add a small birthday icon to the left of the event wherever it was shown.

In the templates provided, each assigned category is added to the `class` attribute of the span that surrounds a particular event item. Therefore, if you assign an item to the Birthday and Special Events categories, the CSS selectors `.birthday` and `.special_events` would both be applied.

Exporting Your Planner

The iCalendar format is to calendar applications as RSS and Atom are to newsreaders. For example, you can use iCal on the Macintosh or Mozilla's Calendar on other platforms to subscribe to an iCalendar formatted feed to import all the appointments it contains. The iCalendar template included with the files for this chapter can be added to your weblog to produce such a feed. Simply add it to your list of index templates. Make the output filename `calendar.ics`. The URL for the feed would be as follows (replacing the number 123 with the blog ID for your Planner weblog and using the proper domain and path to your Movable Type CGI directory):

```
http://myblog.com/mt/mt-view.cgi/123/calendar.ics
```

You would use that URL to subscribe to the calendar produced by your Planner weblog. In addition, upon adding or updating your MT planner, your subscription will keep your local calendar application up-to-date.

Extending Your Planner

A daily planner can be enhanced by weekly archives and recurring entries based on complex rules.

Implementing Weekly Views

We haven't included a Weekly archive template, but using the examples for the Monthly and Daily archives, you should be able to produce a Weekly archive template without much trouble; and with the dynamic rendering support in Movable Type, you can create any number of views of your planner using alternate templates. Because everything is dynamic, there is no penalty of disk space usage or extra rebuild time for having these extra templates.

More complex recurring entries

The current implementation of recurring entries will handle most common recurring entries, but it isn't elaborate enough to handle all possible situations. Scenarios such as "every third week" or "the second Tuesday of the month" aren't currently possible with MT-Planner. You could, however, extend the plugin to handle more complicated recurring rules. If you are interested in extending the Planner plugin in this way, we would recommend using the Keywords field of the entry to enable users to supply a textual repeating rule. There is a free Perl package called `Date::Manip` (available on CPAN) that includes a powerful language-parsing function that will translate English phrases into a recurring rule. For example, it can understand phrases like "last Tuesday of every month." With a little work, you can use `Date::Manip` to extend the capabilities of the MT-Planner plugin to handle most any recurring rule.

Summary

Movable Type was built for blogging, but as an extensible web-based application, it can be manipulated to do much, much more. In this chapter, you've looked at how to transform it to power a web-based day planner that can produce any number of dynamic, data-rich views.

The planner project serves as an apt demonstration that the software can manage any kind of web content, with a little help from plugins and a hacker's mindset.

Polls

This chapter demonstrates how to implement a simple polling system using Movable Type and the PerlScript plugin.

Polls are a great complement to a weblog site and can be an excellent way to solicit feedback or input from your visitors.

Creating the Polls Weblog

First, create a new weblog that will hold the poll data. Don't worry, you will only need one, even if you create thousands of polls. Each entry in this blog will be a separate poll. For each entry, the entry body text is the description or question being posed. The extended entry text will hold the poll options. Each poll option should be on a separate line. Figure 17-1 shows an example poll entry.

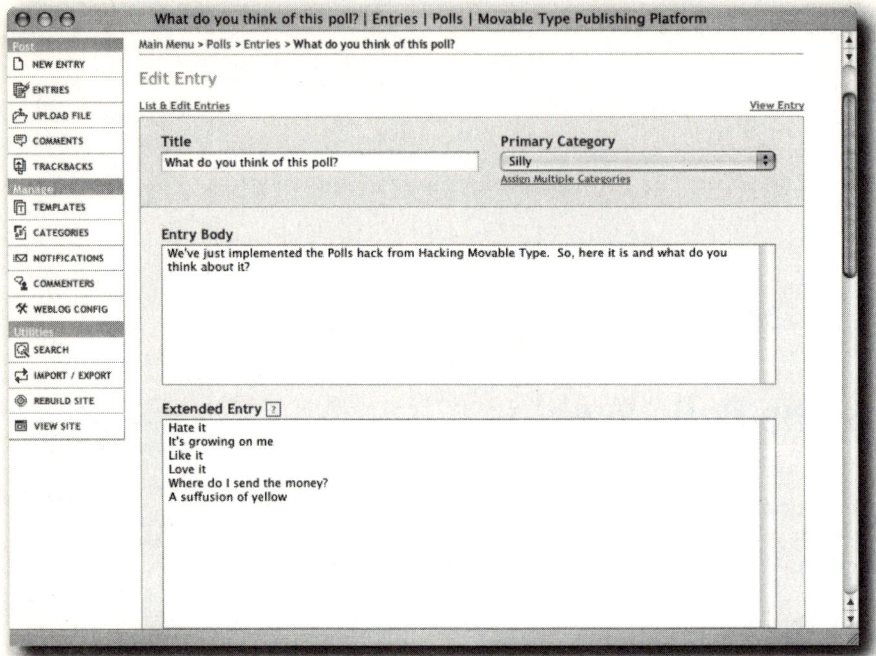

FIGURE 17-1: An example poll entry

Template Configuration

Some template changes will be necessary. Start by creating a template module named "Polls." You'll be hacking poll support into MT using the PerlScript plugin.

If you haven't downloaded it already for a previous chapter, you can find this add-on from the Six Apart plugins directory at `www.sixapart.com/pronet/plugins/plugin/perlscript.html`. Download the archive file containing the software, and then follow its directions regarding where to install the `perlscript.pl` script and the `perlscript.pm` module.

The Polls template will hold the code necessary to process the extended entry text to retrieve the poll options and tabulated votes. Listing 17-1 contains the code for the Polls template.

Listing 17-1: A Polling Template

```
<MTPerlScript package="polls" cache="1" once="1">
sub list {
  my ($tmpl) = @_;
  my $blog = $ctx->stash('blog');
```

```perl
  my $entry = $ctx->stash('entry');
  my $out = '';

  # load the MT template we use to print a single day
  my $template = MT::Template->load({blog_id=>$blog->id,
    name => $tmpl});

  my (%counts, $count);
  $count = 0;
  # if the "poll_option_votes" variable is referenced
  # in the template, go to the extra step of counting
  # votes...
  if ($template->text =~ /poll_option_votes/) {
    my %votes;
    foreach my $comment (@{$entry->comments}) {
      my ($vote) = $comment->text =~ m/(\d+)/;
      next unless $vote;
      my $vote_key = $comment->commenter_id || $comment->ip;
      # remove the following line if you allow
      # users to change their vote...
      next if exists $votes{$vote_key};
      $votes{$vote_key} = $vote;
    }
    $counts{$votes{$_}}++ foreach (keys %votes);
    $count = scalar(keys %votes);
  }

  my @options = split /\r?\n/, $entry->text_more;

  my $ln = 0;
  my $vars = $ctx->{stash}{vars};
  $vars->{poll_vote_count} = $count;
  foreach my $option (@options) {
    $ln++;
    $vars->{poll_option_value} = $ln;
    $vars->{poll_option_label} = $option;
    if (exists $counts{$ln}) {
      $vars->{poll_option_votes} = $counts{$ln};
    } else {
      $vars->{poll_option_votes} = 0;
    }
    # this builds the output for a single day
    my $row = $template->build($ctx);
    # display any error that might have occurred
    warn $ctx->errstr unless defined $row;
    $out .= $row if defined $row;
  }

  print $out;
}
</MTPerlScript>
```

Now add the following to the top of your Main Index and Individual Archive templates (and any other MT templates that will be listing polls):

```
<$MTInclude module="Polls"$>
```

The Polls template code assumes that there is an entry in context whenever it runs. The weblog entry is the poll definition, so you need one of those for this routine in order to do anything. When the list routine is called, you pass to it the name of a Movable Type template module to process. It will iterate over each poll option and process the template, printing the result. Here's a template for listing the poll options as radio buttons. Name this template "Poll Radio Option":

```
<input type="radio" name="text"
  value="<$MTGetVar name="poll_option_value"$>"
  id="poll_option_<$MTGetVar name="poll_option_value"$>" />
<label for="poll_<$MTEntryID$>_option_<$MTGetVar
  name="poll_option_value"$>">
  <$MTGetVar name="poll_option_label"$>
</label><br />
```

Here's another template that will list the options along with the number of votes that have accumulated for them (name this one "Poll Option List"):

```
<li><$MTGetVar name="poll_option_label"$>
  (<$MTGetVar name="poll_option_votes"$>)</li>
```

The Main Index template for this polling weblog can list the latest poll as shown (this is just a portion of the main index template; please refer to the companion website for the complete version that has support for TypeKey authentication):

```
<MTEntries lastn="1">

    <h2>Latest Poll</h2>
    <h3><$MTEntryTitle$></h3>

    <$MTEntryBody$>

<form method="post" action="<$MTCGIPath$><$MTCommentScript$>"
      id="poll_form">
<input type="hidden" name="static" value="1" />
<input type="hidden" name="entry_id" value="<$MTEntryID$>" />

<div id="name_email">
<p><label for="author">Name:</label><br />
<input tabindex="1" name="author" id="author" /></p>

<p><label for="email">Email Address:</label><br />
<input tabindex="2" name="email" id="email" /></p>
</div>

<p><label for="url">URL:</label><br />
<input tabindex="3" name="url" id="url" /></p>
```

```
<p>
<MTPerlScript package="polls">
  polls::list('Poll Radio Option');
</MTPerlScript>
</p>

<div align="center">
<input type="submit" name="post" value="Vote" />
</div>
</form>

<div class="posted">
  posted @ <a href="<$MTEntryPermalink$>"><$MTEntryDate
format="%X"$></a>
</div>

</MTEntries>
```

Note that the usual textarea input field has been replaced with a call to our "polls" PerlScript package, which lists the individual poll options as radio buttons. This is the primary change to the comment form.

Showing the Results

On the individual archive template (you should enable these for the permalinks), you'll want to list the poll results. Here is the portion of the template that produces the poll results along with the votes recorded so far:

```
<div class="blog">
    <h2>Poll</h2>
    <h3><$MTEntryTitle$></h3>

    <$MTEntryBody$>

<MTEntryIfCommentsOpen>
    <h4>Results So Far...</h4>
<MTElse>
    <h4>Results</h4>
</MTElse>
</MTEntryIfCommentsOpen>

    <ul>
    <MTPerlScript package="polls">
      polls::list('Poll Option List');
    </MTPerlScript>
    </ul>
</div>
```

Figure 17-2 illustrates a sample poll results page.

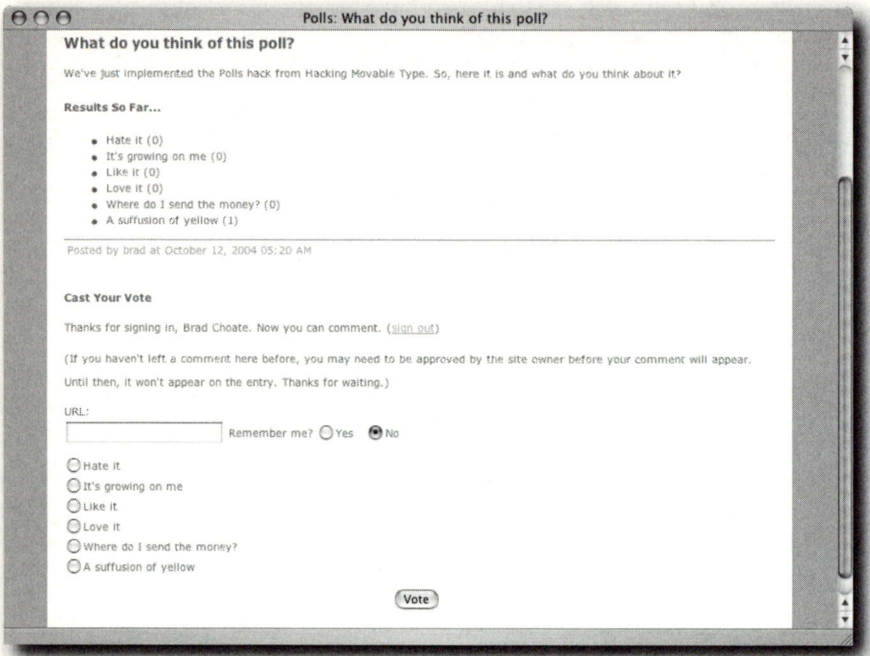

FIGURE 17-2: Sample poll results page

Once you close comments for a poll, the heading for the results changes from "Results So Far. . . " to just "Results." You can include the polling form on the individual archive page as well, but you will want to wrap it in another <MTEntryIfCommentsOpen> block so that the form is not available once the poll has been closed. I would also recommend disabling the comment preview option and even customizing the comment preview template so that it doesn't list any comment history (doing so would reveal the identities and votes of others).

In addition, keep in mind that if you change the order or the content of the poll options after you have received votes, those pre-existing votes will be mismatched because they are based on the order of the polling options at the time the vote was cast.

Knowing Your Audience

Online polls are often used for entertainment. It is difficult to prevent fraud or abuse of the polling system, but fortunately, with Movable Type 3, you can limit abuse by requiring user registration through TypeKey or by moderating comments. This does not prevent fraud altogether, but because it requires some level of identification, it will help to discourage abuse.

Sharing with Other Weblogs

You may want to include the latest poll on the main page of your website or weblog. To do this, you would create another main index template that contains just the portion of the main index template provided in this chapter. Name the output file something like `latestpoll.html`. You could then pull the contents of that file into another web page using server-side includes or a PHP include. See Chapter 2 for more information about these techniques.

Summary

The polling functionality covered in this chapter makes use of the most sophisticated Movable Type hack you can drop into a template: Perl scripting.

The software's template-driven publishing system was already ridiculously capable, with support for dozens of standard template tags and hundreds more by way of plugins.

By employing the PerlScript plugin, you can write Perl directly in a template and produce output that is rendered statically on the pages of a site.

What do you think about that capability? We're taking a poll.

LazyWeb

One interesting use of Movable Type has been the site at www.lazyweb.org. There, an installation of Movable Type has been appropriated to extend the idea that should you ever find yourself yearning for a technological improvement, you need only announce this need publicly and someone will either point out that it already exists or be sufficiently excited to go off and build it themselves.

The LazyWeb site acts as an aggregator of these wishes. People make their wish on their own site and then TrackBack to the LazyWeb site, where a short excerpt of their post is displayed and a link back to them produced. People can visit the LazyWeb site or subscribe to the RSS feed for continual inspiration. Figure 18-1 shows the LazyWeb site.

This sort of site isn't limited to the open Internet. In a corporate setting, you could create multiple LazyWeb sites, using the same functionality to highlight specific subject areas. Because it works by TrackBack, and because you can configure MT to send a TrackBack ping whenever a post is made within a certain category, it is easy to set this up as an automatic subject aggregator. For such a simple application, it has hidden depths.

Having said that, it must be emphasized that this is a very simple application, but it is an application. Movable Type, with only the addition of one, almost trivial, script, can be made into an application with a good deal of social sophistication. It is hoped that it gets you thinking about how your use of MT might be made richer within your own environment, public and intranet both.

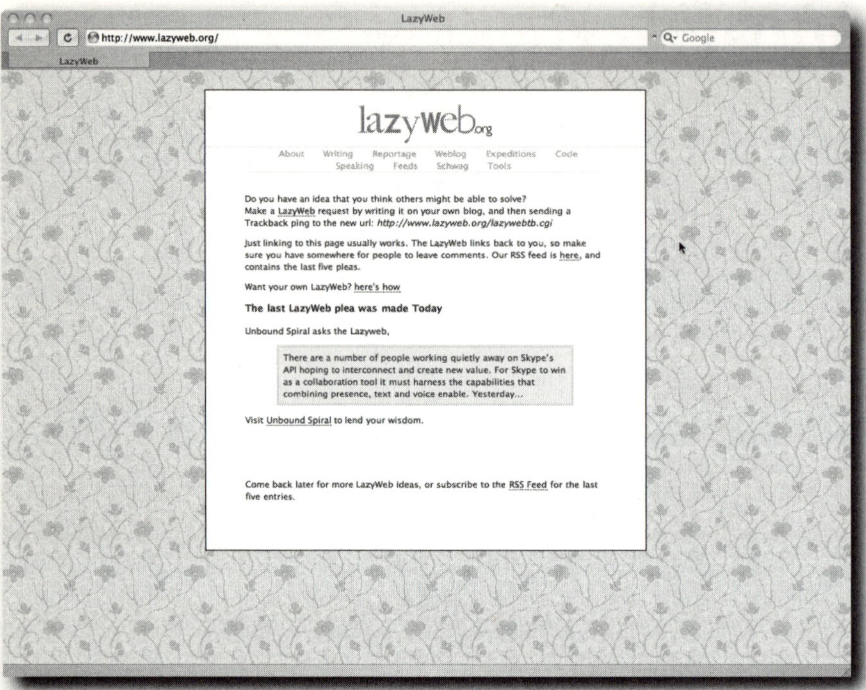

FIGURE 18-1: The LazyWeb site

Using All the Entry Fields

One other thing that differentiates the LazyWeb set up from others is that it uses the existing MT entry fields for its database. It doesn't create any additional tables in the real MT database, or require additional code within the templates to get at it. Instead, we're using the more rarely used fields to hold all the extra data the TrackBack ping gives us.

The ping, remember, gives us the pinger's entry title, its URL, an excerpt, and the real name of the pinging blog. Our code places them like this:

- Ping title = Entry title
- Ping excerpt = Entry Text
- Ping URL = Extended Entry
- Ping blog name = Entry keywords

How the LazyWeb Application Works

To simplify things further, let's look at the steps the application takes.

1. Someone writes a post on his or her own weblog containing a link to the LazyWeb site.

2. Their own installation of MT, with auto-trackback detection turned on, goes out to the LazyWeb site and loads the page looking for the Trackback RDF snippet.

3. It finds the snippet and parses it for the path of the Trackback script.

4. It pings the Trackback script.

5. The LazyWeb site receives the ping and acknowledges it.

6. The LazyWeb site takes the ping data and creates an entry from it.

7. The LazyWeb site rebuilds.

The process requires three main changes to a standard MT weblog: a front page with a modified RDF snippet, a script to listen for TrackBacks and post them as new entries, and a template system for entries that takes the additional data available into account. Let's go through these one by one.

The Front Page Template

Ordinarily, the Trackback RDF snippet would only appear inside individual entry archives. It's placed there with the `<$MTEntryTrackbackData$>` tag. This tag takes no attributes and is basically unhackable, so we need to put in our own hardcoded snippet instead:

```
<!--
<rdf:RDF xmlns:rdf="http://www.w3.org/1999/02/22-rdf-syntax-ns#"

xmlns:trackback="http://madskills.com/public/xml/rss/module/trackback/"
          xmlns:dc="http://purl.org/dc/elements/1.1/">
<rdf:Description
    rdf:about="http://URL.TO.SITE/index.html"
    trackback:ping="http://URL.TO.SITE/lazywebtb.cgi"
    dc:title="Generic LazyWeb Front Page"
    dc:identifier="http://URL.TO.SITE/index.html"
    dc:subject=""
    dc:description="The Front Page of the Generic LazyWeb site."
    dc:creator="Your Name"
    dc:date="2003-01-15T22:19:48+01:00" />
</rdf:RDF>
-->
```

You need to put this into your site's front page, changing the obvious bits to point to your own site.

In the main LazyWeb installation (`www.lazyweb.org`), we display only the last ping. You might want more than that. Remember that we're using the extended fields to hold all of the data that the TrackBack ping gives us. Listing 18-1 holds the complete template.

Listing 18-1: LazyWeb Index Template

```
<!DOCTYPE html PUBLIC "-//W3C//DTD XHTML 1.0 Transitional//EN"
     "http://www.w3.org/TR/xhtml1/DTD/xhtml1-transitional.dtd">
<html xmlns="http://www.w3.org/1999/xhtml" xml:lang="en"
lang="en">
<head>
     <title>Generic LazyWeb</title>
     <link href="style.css" rel="stylesheet" type="text/css"
media="screen" />
     <meta http-equiv="Content-Type" content="text/html;
charset=utf-8" />

</head>
<body>

<h1>Generic Lazyweb</h1>

<!--
<rdf:RDF xmlns:rdf="http://www.w3.org/1999/02/22-rdf-syntax-ns#"

xmlns:trackback="http://madskills.com/public/xml/rss/module/trackb
ack/"
          xmlns:dc="http://purl.org/dc/elements/1.1/">
<rdf:Description
    rdf:about="http://URL.TO.SITE/index.html"
    trackback:ping="http://URL.TO.SITE/lazywebtb.cgi"
    dc:title="Generic LazyWeb Front Page"
    dc:identifier="http://URL.TO.SITE/index.html"
    dc:subject=""
    dc:description="The Front Page of the Generic LazyWeb site."
    dc:creator="Your Name"
    dc:date="2003-01-15T22:19:48+01:00" />
</rdf:RDF>
-->

<p> Do you have an idea that you think others might be able to
solve?<br/>
Make a <a href="http://iawiki.net/LazyWeb">LazyWeb</a> request by
writing it on your own blog, and then sending a Trackback ping to
the new url:
<em>http://URL.TO.SITE/lazywebtb.cgi</em></p>

<MTEntries lastn="1">
<MTDateHeader>
```

```
<h3>The last LazyWeb plea was made <$MTEntryRelativeDate
format="%B %e, %Y"$></h3>
</MTDateHeader>


<p><MTEntryKeywords> asks the Lazyweb,
<blockquote cite="<$MTEntryMore$>">
<$MTEntryBody validable="1" smarty_pants="1"$>
</blockquote>
</p>

<p>Visit <a href="<$MTEntryMore$>" title="A call to the LazyWeb
from <MTEntryKeywords>"><MTEntryKeywords></a> to lend your
wisdom.</p>

<p>Come back later for more LazyWeb ideas, or subscribe to the <a
href="http://URL TO SITE/index.rdf" title="The LazyWeb in RSS">RSS
Feed</a> for the last five entries.</p>
</MTEntries>


</body>
</html>
```

Note The MTEntryBody template tag includes a `smarty_pants` attribute, as do the other templates in this chapter. This attribute is supported by SmartyPants, a Movable Type plugin by John Gruber that makes quotation marks, em dashes, and ellipses use more attractive characters (for example, quote marks curl inward on the outside of the text they mark). This plugin is available from Gruber's website at `http://daringfireball.net/projects/smartypants`.

Listening for TrackBacks — mt-lazyweb.cgi

The heart of the application is the `mt-lazyweb.cgi` script. This listens for TrackBack pings and takes their data payload to save as an entry. It does this via the XML-RPC interface. The workings are more finely detailed in Chapter 6, "XML-RPC API."

Look to Listing 18-2 for the code of this script.

Listing 18-2: The mt-lazyweb.cgi Script

```
#!/usr/bin/perl -w
use strict;
use CGI qw( :standard );
use XMLRPC::Lite;
use Class::Struct;
```

Continued

Listing 18-2 *(continued)*

```perl
# Put your own values in here.
my $username = "Ben Hammersley";
my $password = "XXXXXXX";
my $url="http://www.mediacooperative.com/mt-xmlrpc.cgi";
my $blogid = "5";


#####################################
#####################################

my $struct;

struct( struct => {
                            title => '$',
                            description => '$',
                            dateCreated => '$',
                            mt_text_more => '$',
                            mt_excerpt => '$',
            mt_keywords => '$',
            mt_allow_comments => '$',
            mt_allow_pings => '$',
            mt_convert_breaks => '$',
            mt_tb_ping_urls => '$'
               }
          );

if (param()) {
    my $i = { map { $_ => scalar param($_) } qw(title excerpt url
blog_name) };

    $struct->{'title'} = "$i->{title}";
    $struct->{'description'} = "$i->{excerpt}";
    $struct->{'mt_text_more'} = "$i->{url}";
    $struct->{'mt_keywords'} = "$i->{blog_name}";

    # Post the message to the blog
    my $rpc_call = XMLRPC::Lite->new;
    $rpc_call->proxy($url);

    my $call_result = $rpc_call->call('metaWeblog.newPost' =>
$blogid, $username, $password, $struct, 1);

    print "Content-Type: text/xml\n\n";
    print qq(<?xml version="1.0" encoding="iso-
8859-1"?>\n<response>\n);
    if ($call_result->fault) {
            printf qq(<error>1</error>\n%s\n), xml('message',
$call_result->faultstring);
```

```
    } else {
            print qq(<error>0</error>\n) . ($_[1] ? $_[1] : '');
    }
    print "</response>\n";

} else {

    print header;
    print start_html();
    print h1("Lazyweb Trackback Listener");
    print p("This URL is not for the likes of you. It's for
Trackback enabled weblogs to ping.");
    print p("Write your Lazyweb request on your own weblog, and
then link to this site's frontpage");
    print end_html;

}
```

You should place this in your blog's root directory, having changed the variables at the top to suit your own setup. The script is a little more complex than it need be, as it tests for people loading the script directly from their browser.

In earlier versions of this system, I found that people were loading the script (because I had written the URL on the front page as somewhere to manually TrackBack too), which would then leave an entry with empty values in every field.

That wasn't good, so now it checks for the parameters passed by a usual TrackBack, and if they're not there, it displays a vaguely polite warning instead.

As yet, I haven't heard of this breaking any implementations of TrackBack, as all known implementations follow the TrackBack specification to the letter; but there is always a risk.

Put the script in place, setting its file permissions to 755 to enable it to run. Load it up in a browser at its URL and you should see the warning message, which provides a means of testing whether it was properly installed.

When the script receives an actual TrackBack, it uses the XML-RPC interface to make the entry. The script and Movable Type installation don't even need to be on the same server to communicate with each other over XML-RPC.

Using a Template System

As previously discussed, this little application uses the extended entry fields as its database. Therefore, you will need to change your other templates to use the data. Listing 18-3 contains the Individual Entry Archive template for a LazyWeb site.

Listing 18-3: LazyWeb Individual Entry Template

```
<!DOCTYPE html PUBLIC "-//W3C//DTD XHTML 1.0 Transitional//EN"
"http://www.w3.org/TR/xhtml1/DTD/xhtml1-transitional.dtd">

<html xmlns="http://www.w3.org/1999/xhtml">
<head>
<meta http-equiv="Content-Type" content="text/html;
charset=<$MTPublishCharset$>" />

<title><$MTBlogName$>: <$MTEntryTitle$></title>

<link href="http://www.lazyweb.org/style.css" rel="stylesheet"
type="text/css" media="screen" />
<link rel="alternate" type="application/rss+xml" title="RSS"
href="<$MTBlogURL$>index.rdf" />
<link rel="start" href="<$MTBlogURL$>" title="Home" />
<MTEntryPrevious>
<link rel="prev" href="<$MTEntryPermalink$>" title="<$MTEntryTitle
encode_html="1"$>" />
</MTEntryPrevious>
<MTEntryNext>
<link rel="next" href="<$MTEntryPermalink$>" title="<$MTEntryTitle
encode_html="1"$>" />
</MTEntryNext>

<script type="text/javascript" language="javascript">
<!--

function OpenTrackback (c) {
    window.open(c,
                'trackback',
'width=480,height=480,scrollbars=yes,status=yes');
}

var HOST = '<$MTBlogHost$>';

// Copyright (c) 1996-1997 Athenia Associates.
// http://www.webreference.com/js/
// License is granted if and only if this entire
// copyright notice is included. By Tomer Shiran.

function setCookie (name, value, expires, path, domain, secure) {
    var curCookie = name + "=" + escape(value) + ((expires) ? ";
expires=" + expires.toGMTString() : "") + ((path) ? "; path=" +
path : "") + ((domain) ? "; domain=" + domain : "") + ((secure) ?
"; secure" : "");
    document.cookie = curCookie;
}
```

```
function getCookie (name) {
    var prefix = name + '=';
    var c = document.cookie;
    var nullstring = '';
    var cookieStartIndex = c.indexOf(prefix);
    if (cookieStartIndex == -1)
        return nullstring;
    var cookieEndIndex = c.indexOf(";", cookieStartIndex +
prefix.length);
    if (cookieEndIndex == -1)
        cookieEndIndex = c.length;
    return unescape(c.substring(cookieStartIndex + prefix.length,
cookieEndIndex));
}

function deleteCookie (name, path, domain) {
    if (getCookie(name))
        document.cookie = name + "=" + ((path) ? "; path=" + path
: "") + ((domain) ? "; domain=" + domain : "") + "; expires=Thu,
01-Jan-70 00:00:01 GMT";
}

function fixDate (date) {
    var base = new Date(0);
    var skew = base.getTime();
    if (skew > 0)
        date.setTime(date.getTime() - skew);
}

function rememberMe (f) {
    var now = new Date();
    fixDate(now);
    now.setTime(now.getTime() + 365 * 24 * 60 * 60 * 1000);
    setCookie('mtcmtauth', f.author.value, now, '', HOST, '');
    setCookie('mtcmtmail', f.email.value, now, '', HOST, '');
    setCookie('mtcmthome', f.url.value, now, '', HOST, '');
}

function forgetMe (f) {
    deleteCookie('mtcmtmail', '', HOST);
    deleteCookie('mtcmthome', '', HOST);
    deleteCookie('mtcmtauth', '', HOST);
    f.email.value = '';
    f.author.value = '';
    f.url.value = '';
}

//-->
</script>
```

Continued

Listing 18-3 *(continued)*

```
<$MTEntryTrackbackData$>

</head>

<body>
<div id="box">
<div id="head"><h1><a href="/" title="Back
Home!">LazyWeb</a></h1></div>

<div id="weblog">

<h2><$MTEntryTitle$></h2>

<p>On <$MTEntryDate format="%x"$> <a href="<$MTEntryMore$>"
title="A call to the LazyWeb from
<MTEntryKeywords>"><MTEntryKeywords> is asking the Lazyweb</a>,
<blockquote cite="<$MTEntryMore$>">
<$MTEntryBody validable="1" smarty_pants="1"$>
</blockquote>
</p>


<MTEntryIfAllowComments>

<h2>Comments</h2>


<MTComments>
<$MTCommentBody smarty_pants="1" link_titles="1" acronym="1"
$><br/><br/>
<span class="permalink">Posted at
<$MTCommentDate$></span><br/><br/><br/>
</MTComments>


<MTEntryIfCommentsOpen>
<h2>Post a comment</h2>

<form method="post" action="<$MTCGIPath$><$MTCommentScript$>"
name="comments_form" onsubmit="if (this.bakecookie[0].checked)
rememberMe(this)">
<input type="hidden" name="static" value="1" />
<input type="hidden" name="entry_id" value="<$MTEntryID$>" />


<div style="width:180px; padding-right:15px; margin-right:15px;
float:left; text-align:left; border-right:1px dotted #bbb;">
     <label for="author">Name:</label><br />
     <input tabindex="1" id="author" name="author" /><br /><br />

     <label for="email">Email Address:</label><br />
     <input tabindex="2" id="email" name="email" /><br /><br />
```

```
        <label for="url">URL:</label><br />
        <input tabindex="3" id="url" name="url" /><br /><br />
</div>

Remember personal info?<br />
<input type="radio" id="bakecookie" name="bakecookie" /><label
for="bakecookie">Yes</label><input type="radio" id="forget"
name="bakecookie" onclick="forgetMe(this.form)" value="Forget
Info" style="margin-left: 15px;" /><label
for="forget">No</label><br style="clear: both;" />

<label for="text">Comments:</label><br />
<textarea tabindex="4" id="text" name="text" rows="10"
cols="50"></textarea><br /><br />

<input type="submit" name="preview" value=" Preview " />
<input style="font-weight: bold;" type="submit" name="post"
value=" Post " /><br /><br />

</form>

<script type="text/javascript" language="javascript">
<!--
document.comments_form.email.value = getCookie("mtcmtmail");
document.comments_form.author.value = getCookie("mtcmtauth");
document.comments_form.url.value = getCookie("mtcmthome");
if (getCookie("mtcmtauth")) {
    document.comments_form.bakecookie[0].checked = true;
} else {
    document.comments_form.bakecookie[1].checked = true;
}
//-->
</script>
</MTEntryIfCommentsOpen>
</MTEntryIfAllowComments>

</div>



</div>
</body>
</html>
```

The latest version of these templates and the script are always available at
www.lazyweb.org.

Summary

The LazyWeb project had its humble beginnings in 2002 as a central spot where people could make a plea to the Internet-using world, hoping to get something they'd love to use, such as a program, a simple software component, or another manner of helpful gadget.

The site is premised on two optimistic notions: Someone else has the same need and built it already, or someone else could be persuaded to do so.

Amusingly enough, one of the most common pleas is to set up a LazyWeb for a subject other than web programming and design. With a specially designed weblog and the `mt-lazyweb.cgi` script, even the laziest Movable Type hacker can launch one of these sites.

Creating a Community-Authored Website

As you already know, Movable Type takes the majority of the work out of personal publishing. However, one of the limitations of the platform (which, of course, viewed from another perspective is also one of its strengths) is that outside of comments and TrackBacks, only registered authors can actually do any of the publishing.

The question at hand is would it be possible to create a Movable Type–powered system that accepts entry submissions from anyone? For instance, could MT power a threaded bulletin board, an open-submission recipe database, or even the wildly popular Metafilter (www.metafilter.com)?

The answer is a big resounding yes.

Because of MT's strict user authentication feature, there is no way to create such a system by going through MT's front door, the browser interface, unless you were to create accounts for every single author. Luckily, Movable Type supports several highly powerful APIs that enable you to interact with the system through the back door.

Introducing MT-Filter

The functionality model I have followed for this example is *Metafilter*, my *Hacking Movable Type* co-author Matt Haughey's well-known community blog. Metafilter is a custom application developed using a scripting/database connectivity hybrid language called Cold Fusion, and it runs on a Windows platform. If you are not familiar with Metafilter, you should check it out at www.metafilter.com.

To match Metafilter's feature set using one of the powerful Movable Type APIs while still keeping this example concise and simple, I have settled on the following requirements:

- Accept entry submissions from anonymous users while minimizing security risks.

- Publish entries immediately after submission to a main index, individual archive, and date-based archive.

- Provide comment and TrackBack functionality for each entry.

You will notice that user accounts, a major feature of Metafilter and an important element of its community cohesiveness, has been omitted. This is not because it isn't possible, but because it adds a great deal of complexity and overhead in terms of code to the example. If you understand fully what we do here, you will be able to extend the example using TypeKey or a local authentication system to create the same effect.

The API Choice: Perl versus XML-RPC

In determining which language and API to use for this exercise, there were two main options:

- The Perl API and Perl

- The XML-RPC API and a random scripting language

Because we have devoted a very large portion of this book to Perl and the Perl API, I thought it best to choose the road less traveled. This choice was further strengthened by the fact that a kind soul named Keith Devens (www.keithdevens.com) has created and continues to maintain a fabulous XML-RPC library for PHP for the world to use. This library makes the formation, sending, and receiving of XML-RPC requests and responses as simple as a subroutine call.

I wrote a companion XML-RPC library for Movable Type that specifically aids in the creation of the basic MT function calls (for example, publishing an entry, rebuilding a weblog, setting a category, and so on) in the form of PHP functions.

Using these two libraries, communicating with MT via PHP has never been so easy, and this seemingly monumental and complex task is really quite simple and merely a matter of setup and configuration.

Note You may want to briefly review Chapter 6, "XML-RPC API," to refresh yourself about the basic details of the API. However, because most of the work is done for you in the form of these two libraries, you actually don't need to be an XML-RPC guru to build something really cool. Never let it be said that we don't love our readers.

Overview of the Application

When a user submits the entry from the web form on the site, it is processed by a main data processing script (`submit_inc.php`). Along with the two XML-RPC libraries it calls at runtime, there are two main sections of the program (see Figure 19-1) that we shall concern ourselves with:

1. The droll but dreadfully important data processing

2. The XML-RPC transformation and request

The procedures in the data processing step are really no different from processing any form on the web via PHP. We typically look for three things:

- Completion of required fields

- Validity of the data (for example, e-mail address)

- Security of the data

Again, for the sake of clarity, I've minimized this step in this example because most of it is fairly standard and out of the scope of this text. However, you should always pay careful attention to how data from unknown sources is handled, and modify the `submit_inc.php` library before using this in a production setting. Figure 19-1 provides an overview of the application from the initiation of a request to its delivery to MT.

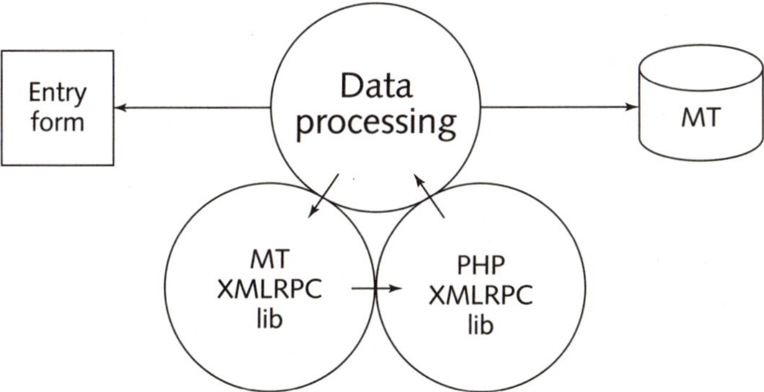

FIGURE 19-1: Overview of the application from the initiation of the request to its delivery to MT

Once the data is verified and ready to be sent to MT, we will use our two XML-RPC libraries to package it as a fully-formed entry and transmit it as an MT-compatible XML-RPC request. MT parses this data and, if everything goes well, sends us back the XML-RPC version of a thumbs-up. After that, our script will use the same method to kick off a rebuild of the pages so that the entry is publicly visible.

Like Metafilter, MT-Filter will feature four major page types:

- A main index page
- Individual archives
- Date-based archives
- An entry submission page

These are completely customizable through the regular MT template editing interface.

Creating MT-Filter

As is often the case with more complex projects, you must first take care of some requirements in order to build a community-authored site. Luckily, most of the requirements are standard in the majority of web-hosting environments, and the ones that aren't are a simple download away.

Following is a list of these requirements as well as the current versions (in parentheses) I used. Other versions may be also work but have not been tested.

- Movable Type (v3.11)
- PHP (v4.3.2)
- Jay Allen's XML-RPC library for MT (v1.0) and submission form handling code (v1.0)
- Keith Devens' XML-RPC library for PHP (v2.5)
- Brad Choate's KeyValues plugin for MT
- Custom template code for the following:
    - Main index template
    - Individual archive template
    - Monthly (date-based) archive template
    - Submission handling script

The general steps we will undertake to create MT-Filter are as follows:

1. Download the code for this chapter.
2. Create a new weblog and user.
3. Upload the plugin, libraries, and scripts.
4. Configure the weblog.
5. Install the templates.
6. Configure the submission script.
7. Publish your blog.

Step 1: Get the Code

All of the required code used for this exercise, except for PHP and Movable Type itself, is available for download in zip and tar/gzip formats at www.hackingmt.com.

You may, however, want to check for the latest versions of Keith Devens' XML-RPC library for PHP and Brad Choate's KeyValues plugin:

- http://keithdevens.com/software/xmlrpc
- www.bradchoate.com/weblog/2002/07/27/keyvalues

Step 2: Create New Weblog and User

Create a new weblog and MT user for the community-authored site. All submissions will be posted to this weblog under this single author's user ID.

For the purposes of this exercise, I called the blog MT-Filter and did not make a special archive directory (meaning site path and archive path are the same, as are site and archive URL).

For the sake of security, the new MT user is essentially a dummy user who has rights only to the MT-Filter weblog, and permission only to post entries. The actual user details (username, password, e-mail, URL) are unimportant because they are only used by the script and never seen in public, although the e-mail address should be a working one in case you want to receive notifications or perform a password recovery.

I created a user called mtfilter_user with a password of secretpass. You should use a different username and password, which you will enter again in Step 6.

Step 3: Upload Plugin, Libraries, and Scripts

In the code archive you downloaded in Step 1, you will find an includes directory that contains the XML-RPC helper libraries and auxiliary submission code. Upload those files together to a publicly accessible place on your web server.

For this exercise, I put them in a directory called includes at the root of my web server. You can put them wherever you like, but you will need to change some minor details later in Step 6 if you deviate from the procedure outlined here.

Brad Choate's KeyValues plugin should be installed as outlined in the README file in the plugin archive.

Step 4: Configure the Weblog

After selecting Config ⇨ Preferences, you must change default text formatting for new entries to "None." In keeping with the Metafilter style, you may also want to configure the following options unless you have a reason not to:

- "Allow Trackback Pings" On by default - checked
- Accept Comments from Unregistered Visitors - checked

- Require Name and Email Address Information - checked

- Uncheck "Enable Unregistered Comment Moderation" - unchecked

- Accept Comments from Registered Visitors - checked

- Automatically Approve Registered Commenters - checked

- "Allow Comments" Default: Open

- Allow HTML in Comments - checked

After selecting Config ➪ Archive Files, ensure that the individual and monthly archiving options are checked and that they have the following Archive File Templates:

- Individual:

```
<$MTArchiveDate format="%Y/%m/"$><$MTEntryID pad="1"$>
```

- Monthly:

```
<$MTArchiveDate format="%Y/%m/index.php"$>
```

Step 5: Install the Template Code

Four main templates are used in this exercise:

- Main index

- Individual archives

- Monthly (that is, date-based) archives

- Submission form

The first three are already included in the default setup, but you will have to create the fourth as a new Index template. You can name the output file whatever you like (I used `submit.php`), but you must name the template itself "Submission form" in order for the `MTLink` tag in the other templates to work correctly. To speed things up, you can uncheck the Rebuild This Template option on this template if you like, but remember to manually rebuild when you make changes.

If you like working with linked template files, you can simply upload the four template files from the `mt_templates` directory found in the code archive you downloaded in Step 1 to your web server and link them on their template editing pages. Otherwise, you will need to copy and paste the code from each file into its respective template.

Step 6: Edit the Submission Configuration

If you have deviated from the default setup in any of the preceding steps, you may need to change one or more of the configuration options at the very top of the submission form template in the sections labeled "USER-DEFINED VARIABLES".

PATH_TO_LIBRARIES is the relative path from the document root of your website to the directory in which the auxiliary submission handling script (submit_inc.php) and the two XML-RPC libraries are located. For example, if you put those files into http://YOURSERVER.COM/misc/lib/, the PATH_TO_LIBRARIES setting should look like so:

```
define('PATH_TO_LIBRARIES', 'misc/lib');
```

Be sure to omit any leading and trailing slashes.

The username and password of the user you created in Step 2 will also need to be entered into XMLRPCREQ_USER and XMLRPCREQ_PASS unless you have chosen the following defaults:

```
define('XMLRPCREQ_USER', 'mtfilter_user');
define('XMLRPCREQ_PASS', 'secretpass');
```

Of course, you absolutely should not use the default password for security reasons, if that wasn't obvious.

Unless you want to alter the actual submission page template code located at the bottom of the template, or you know from experience that you should alter something in the section entitled "MT-DEFINED VARIABLES", you are finished editing this template.

Step 7: Publish Your Blog

Rebuild all of the files in the MT-Filter weblog. Once the rebuild is finished, your pages will be visible, although there won't be any entries. You can click the Post an Entry link on the top right-hand side of the main page to enter your first one.

Once you post your first entry, take a look at it inside of the regular MT interface. You will notice that the title and entry body are entered into their respective fields. You will also see that the extended entry field looks something like this:

```
 
Name=Jay Allen
Email=mtfilter@hackingmt.com
URL=http://www.jayallen.org/
IPAddr=127.0.0.1
```

What you see here is the brilliant creation of the KeyValues plugin. The plugin enables you to overload the MT field(s) of your choice to create an extensible database out of a simple Movable Type entry. With KeyValues, you can stuff as much information in key-value pairs as you like into one single field and pull them out as you need them in the publishing step. This is where the actual submission user information is stored, as opposed to the single MT user profile.

Improving MT-Filter

Once you have the code working, you will see that you have created the essence of Metafilter — a community-authored blog — using Movable Type as a platform for development.

Well, there is a lot more you can do.

First and foremost, everything remains to be done in terms of data verification and sanitizing. With the PHP porting of the MT functions in MT 3 (see the `php/lib` directory in your main MT application directory), you could, for example, tap directly into the `sanitize` function and beef up the security of the application.

Second, I didn't bother to implement categories in this example, but it's not difficult. Furthermore, using parent/child categories provided by MT 3, you could easily create a very interesting Yahoo!-directorylike site driven by the site's own users.

Last, and much more on the exotic side, you could utilize TypeKey (or a local authentication system such as Tim Appnel's Tiny Orwell, `www.timaoutloud.org/archives/000357.html`) to implement user authentication. All you need to do is examine the MT comment form code to understand how to force user authentication before presenting a user with the entry submission form.

Once you have user authentication in place, you can create a profile page and user statistics, which you would store locally in a separate database. User banning, karma, moderation, and administrator rights are not far behind with just a bit more thought.

In fact, I previously created a system for a client, based loosely on this same code, that had a full administrative interface for selective moderation and differential publishing to interconnected intranet or Internet websites depending on the identity of the submitting user or the moderation status of the entry itself. All necessary MT functions were reimplemented in the custom user interface (UI), and there was never a need for the system's administrators to actually use the normal MT interface. The system was immense, powerful, and built entirely in PHP and Movable Type using the XML-RPC API.

The power of the Movable Type APIs is truly limited only by your own imagination.

Summary

By using Movable Type's Perl and XML-RPC APIs, you can power a website that doesn't require MT's normal browser interface.

Movable Type still stores, retrieves, and publishes data for you, but it does so on *your* terms. When you use the APIs, you select the few functions you wish MT to perform, and create an infrastructure of your own to do the rest. Likewise, when you are creating backdoor access to a system, the responsibility for the security and integrity of the system falls solely on your shoulders.

The browser interface serves as a means for you to peer under the hood and see how well the engine is running. No one else need see it.

The MT-Filter project, perhaps more than any other in this book, shows the flexibility and power of Movable Type as a platform on which an inspired hacker can develop full-fledged web applications.

So get hacking!

Index

Symbols

D

E